BO, JENNY, AND I

— HUGUETTE HERRMANN —

BO, JENNY, AND I

HUGUETTE HERRMANN

Boston
2013

Library of Congress Cataloging-in-Publication Data:
A catalog record for this title is available from the Library of Congress.

Copyright © 2013
Huguette Herrmann
Schwabstr. 87
D-71672 Marbach a.N.
Germany

ISBN 978-1-936235-73-5 (hardback)

ISBN 978-1-61811-298-9 (paperback)

Book design by Olga Grabovsky

Published by Academic Studies Press in 2012, paperback edition 2013.
28 Montfern Avenue
Brighton, MA 02135, USA
press@academicstudiespress.com
www.academicstudiespress.com

I dedicate this book to

*Miriam
Rainer
Hans-Wolfgang
Simone*

and to the memory of Jean-Michel.

I wish to thank Dr. [Dorothee] "Dodo" Richter, John McKenzie, and Judith Ann Schulze, who gave me valuable encouragement; last, but definitely not least, I thank Sabine Metzger, who unstintingly gave of her time and energy to help me find a publisher.

CONTENTS

INTRODUCTION
Jim Wald ix

PART I
A Childhood in Antwerp

   1. The Family 3
   2. The Invisible Man 16
   3. The Children's Home 27
   4. The Preventorium 36
   5. Elementary School 49
   6. Isy 60
   7. Silvie 73
   8. Flight from Antwerp 84

PART II
Adolescence in England

   9. The Blitz 99
  10. Bedford Central School 111
  11. King's Warren School (1) 121
  12. King's Warren School (2) 131
  13. Jenny 141
  14. The Summer Camp 157
  15. Abe 168

AFTERWORD
John McKenzie 179

INTRODUCTION

I.

Huguette Herrmann's superbly evocative memoir of a Jewish girlhood in pre-World War II Belgium and wartime England offers both an invitation and a challenge to the reader. It beckons us into a world that seems at once very similar to and very different from our own. On the one hand, it is a world in which new furniture is a rarity, a radio a luxury, and tampons a novelty. On the other hand, many of the experiences and scenes described are entirely familiar, or at least mundane: There are skinned knees, bandages, and a tonsillectomy. We meet a girl who is outgoing and eagerly makes friends, yet is shy or not fully socialized in other ways; who didn't know how to play with a doll, and (to the horror of better-off relatives) still had no table manners at age 10. But what she lacks in etiquette, she makes up for in precocious intellectualism: linguistic aptitude and scholastic achievements earn parental praise and give her the confidence that contrasts with and compensates for her nightmares and fear of abandonment. She loves reading and language play. Even before she herself can read, we learn, books are her great passion. As her memoir comes to a close, we read of romance and career plans. This volume would seem to be a sort of autobiographical *Bildungsroman*.

However, its opening lines make clear not only that we are in the presence of a very unusual voice, but also that this was a very unusual life:

> We all have our private mythologies: for the children of "normal" families, the father and mother are the towering deities. I did not grow

up in a normal family, and the gods that ruled over the first years of my life were oversized goddesses—they were my formidable grandmother... and her youngest daughter, my mother.

As fate would have it, the narrator grows up in "a family composed principally of widows"—moreover, one in which men, even when present, are sources of trial and travail. Grandmother Bo "disliked men intensely" (though she managed to marry three of them), found sex "dirty and disgusting," and "was a mother who had no tenderness in store for anyone and certainly not for her daughters, on whom she cast disapproving glances and poured out lavish scorn and mockery." Huguette's mother, Jenny, by contrast, is a flirtatious free spirit, socialist, and self-described pagan and atheist, as sensual as her own mother is repressed. Bo, whose preferred method of interaction with her daughters consists in "cursing and screaming," is incensed by Jenny's behavior, and regularly denounces her as a whore. Readers may be surprised at Huguette's frankness. From earliest childhood on, she is regularly confronted with her mother's sexuality and sexual activity, and she herself calmly relates several of her own experiences which would nowadays be considered sexual abuse or harassment, one involving an adolescent relative and the others involving middle-aged men. For her they were a matter of detached puzzlement and curiosity rather than outrage. For adults in the family, they were simply best forgotten. Here the distance from our world is palpable.

To be sure, Jenny represents a familiar and distinctly modern type of woman. And yet, it would be too simple to reduce the conflicts between Bo and Jenny to those of generations, or of one between tradition and secular modernity. Both women are strong and resourceful, fiercely protective of family, forced to earn a living, and struggling to balance production and consumption. Each in her own manner finds a way to navigate the new post-war world in which the old gender system is neither fully intact nor abolished.[1] Although irresistibly attached to

---

[1] Lynn Abrams, *The Making of Modern Woman* (London: Pearson Education, 2002), here, in particular, the closing chapter on the Great War, 297-323. The Austrian-Jewish author Stefan Zweig, who committed suicide in exile in 1942, attempted to portray the three lifetimes (as he put it) that he experienced between the end of the nineteenth

men as a species, Jenny has no use for her distant and soon-absent husband, and the child grows up with an image of her father as an "insensitive monster." In one of the book's most memorable scenes, the young Huguette is sitting on the toilet but lacks toilet paper: "Jenny fetched her engagement photograph, tore it down the middle, thus severing her face from Simon's, and then wiped me clean with his likeness." It is an unusual family dynamic, to say the least. Because Jenny spends the days at work and the evenings at night school, "she filled the place of the father in a normal family, while Bo assumed the functions of a mother." Yet it is still more complicated: even while assuming the role of the absent father, Jenny doubly underscores and recapitulates his absence, first by regularly leaving the disconsolate and wailing Huguette alone when going out at night "for the serious business of seducing strange men," and finally by marrying again. For the child, the resultant exclusion from the maternal bed "was the expulsion from the Garden of Eden." And yet it is in this fallen world that the narrative unfolds.

Clearly, this would have been an unusual life under any circumstances, but it proved to be doubly abnormal: how could there be such a thing as a "normal" Jewish life in the Europe of the Second World War? The author closes the book by expressing the hope that her "war experiences... succeed in describing a personal history that is as yet underrepresented in the literature of the era." How are we to read this? Is it a family romance, or a wartime memoir? The text allows for and invites both possibilities. A further question arises: is this the memoir of a Holocaust survivor? The author never uses either word, and indeed refers only obliquely to the catastrophe, though its presence hovers over the entire work. There has always been some debate over the definition and use of the term, "Holocaust survivor." Initially, and for very understandable reasons, the tendency was to restrict it to those

---

century and the Second World War in his now-classic memoir. The second chapter, "Eros Matutinus," unsparingly describes the old sexual morality: *The World of Yesterday* (1943; rpt. Lincoln: University of Nebraska Press, 1964), 67-91. On mores in interwar and wartime years, see, e.g., Richard Vinen, *A History in Fragments: Europe in the Twentieth Century* (Cambridge, MA: Da Capo Press, 2001), 89-127.

who had suffered *in extremis*.² Today, however, the prevailing practice is to take a broader view, letting the term encompass anyone who suffered persecution under Axis rule or who hid or fled in order to avoid such persecution.³ This is eminently sensible and can also help us to approach the present volume. Every memoirist has to decide where to begin and where to end—at what age or phase of life—and how to frame the life-story. Still, regardless of whether the survivor's narrative begins in the pre-war era or *in media res* there is always a caesura, whether explicit or implicit, a division into before and after. We assume an irrevocable loss of a past world, a trying and transformational experience, and the struggle to recreate a "normal" life.

There are patterns with regard to content as well as structure. As in the case of other survivors' memoirs, we do not look for revelations in the sense of new information. The contours of the tragedy are known down to their finest lineaments. Thus, many scenes—the columns of refugees trudging across France with their possessions in carts and baby strollers, the description of the Blitz, bombed houses, and the rush to air raid shelters, and so forth—will be so familiar to the reader from other accounts of word and image as to be virtually interchangeable. It is not for them, as such, that we turn to books of this type. The last work of the great French-Jewish historian Marc Bloch, who fought in the Resistance and died at the hands of the Gestapo, was a meditation on his *métier*. There, among other things, he argues that history is not the study of the "past" (not a meaningful category of analysis), and is rather "the science of men in time":⁴ the infinitely varied manifestations

---

2   Paradigmatically, for example, Terence Des Pres, who included the Soviet Gulag in his acclaimed *The Survivor: An Anatomy of Life in the Death Camps* (New York: Oxford University Press, 1976). On the specific case of the Final Solution and definitions, see Martin S. Bergmann and Milton E. Jucovy, eds., *Generations of the Holocaust* (New York: Basic Books, 1982), 313.

3   "A survivor is anyone who suffered and survived persecution for racial, religious, sexual, physical or political reasons while under Nazi or Axis control between 1933 and May 8, 1945; or who was forced to live clandestinely; or to flee Nazi or Axis onslaught during the war in order to avoid imminent persecution." University of Southern California Libraries LibGuide: Shoah Foundation Institute Visual History Archive FAQs: http://libguides.usc.edu/content.php?pid=58585&sid=548017

4   Marc Bloch, *The Historian's Craft: Reflections on the Nature and Uses of History and the Techniques and Methods of Those Who Write It* (New York: Knopf, 1953), 47.

of human nature in changing circumstances. It is in that sense and for this reason that we turn with such eagerness to a new memoir. Rather than seeking revelations of fact, we look to learn from the accumulation of detail: each piece contributing to the whole and yet retaining its distinctive role, so that we see the catastrophe not as an abstraction but as a composite of individual fates and voices. In the process, we recall those who did not survive to tell their stories.

II.

Huguette explicitly divides her memoir into two parts: "A Childhood in Antwerp" and "Adolescence in England." For all the abnormality of the family structure and family dynamic, her social and cultural environment was fairly typical of Belgian Jewry in the early twentieth century. On the eve of World War II, the approximately 65,000-75,000 Belgian Jews made up less than one percent of the population—roughly the same share as in neighboring Germany. However, only some six percent of them were Belgian citizens. Most were immigrants or the children of immigrants, the vast majority from eastern Europe (85 percent had arrived since the end of World War I), recently joined by several thousand refugees from Nazi Germany. They were also highly urbanized: 53 percent lived in Antwerp, 38 percent in the capital of Brussels, and the remainder primarily in Liège, Charleroi, and Ghent.[5] Huguette and her mother were unusual in that they were Belgian-

---

[5] There has long been uncertainty regarding the size of the twentieth-century Belgian Jewish population. As Lieven Saerens observes, "Belgian laws and regulations did not note racial or religious characteristics." "Antwerp's Attitude Toward the Jews from 1918 to 1940 and Its Implications for the Period of Occupation," in Dan Michman, ed., *Belgium and the Holocaust: Jews, Belgians, Germans* (Jerusalem: Yad Vashem, 1998), 159-94; here 159-60. Raul Hilberg, citing wartime and immediate postwar US and Belgian sources, employs the high figure of 90,000. *The Destruction of the European Jews* (Chicago: Quandrangle Books, 1967), 383. However, most scholars now believe the figure was considerably smaller." Saerens uses an estimate of 70,000-75,000 (p. 160). Rudi van Doorslaer speaks of "65-75,000." "Jewish Immigration and Communism in Belgium, 1925-1939," 63-82; here 63. During the war, as Saerens notes (160 n.4), the population percentages of the Jewish populations in the two chief cities "were reversed": 38 percent in Antwerp and 52 percent in Brussels.

INTRODUCTION

born and citizens, but they otherwise fit the profile: Bo's family came from Odessa, in what was at the time the Russian empire, and Jenny's husbands came from Poland and Lithuania. Socially and culturally, too, they were typical: traditionally Jewish, Yiddish-speaking, and lower middle-class.

Although a Jewish presence in Antwerp is documented in the Middle Ages, the origins of a significant community date from the sixteenth century with the arrival of "New Christians" from Spain, who established themselves in merchant banking and the international trade in sugar and spices.[6] Beginning in the eighteenth century, the community assumed the character of the new Ashkenazi immigrants from central and eastern Europe and, particularly after Belgian independence in 1830, grew rapidly: the Jewish population stood at only 151 in 1829, but it rose to 8,000 at the end of the century. In 1927, the year in which the narrator's parents married, it had reached 25,000.[7] In effect reversing their historical pattern of migration—from west to east and from more to less developed lands—Jews emigrated en masse from eastern Europe seeking economic opportunity and, particularly from 1881 onward, refuge from growing antisemitism in the Russian

---

[6] As is well known, a combination of expulsions and new opportunities propelled the majority of the European Jewish population eastward from the late Middle Ages on. Following the expulsion from Spain, Sephardic Jews (and later, converted Marranos or "New Christians" who still faced persecution), migrated mainly to the Mediterranean region, though some settled in France, the Low Countries, and England. Ashkenazic Jews from western and central Europe migrated to east-central and eastern Europe, in particular to Poland, Ukraine, Russia, and Lithuania. Whereas, in the fifteenth century, approximately one third of the Jews lived in Europe and two thirds in the Near East, by 1880, eastern European Jews alone constituted three-quarters of the global community. See the statistics in Paul Mendes-Flohr and Jehuda Reinharz, eds., *The Jew in the Modern World: A Documentary History*, second ed. (New York: Oxford University Press, 1995), 701-4. On Jewish patterns of migration in the early modern era: Salo W. Baron, Arcadius Kahan and others, ed. Nachum Gross, *Economic History of the Jews* (New York: Schocken Books, 1976), 59-61. For the modern period: David Vital, *A People Apart: A Political History of the Jews in Europe 1789-1939*, Oxford History of Europe, ed. Lord Bullock and Sir William Deakin (Oxford: Oxford University Press, 2001), Chapter 4, on "Movement," 283-345. On the early Jewish presence and economic activity in Antwerp: Baron and Kahan, 57, 187, 189, 216, 276.

[7] The entry, "Antwerp," in the *Encyclopedia Judaica* provides a useful overview and is conveniently available online via the Virtual Jewish Library: http://www.jewishvirtuallibrary.org/jsource/judaica/ejud_0002_0002_0_01172.html

INTRODUCTION

empire.[8] Some settled in far-flung Ottoman Palestine, South Africa, and South America, but the vast majority went to the United States. Still, the number that settled in western Europe more than compensated for out-migration from that region. Antwerp, which was a major port of embarkation, became a particularly attractive destination in its own right, enticing many would-be emigrants to settle there in part because of the booming diamond industry, in which field the city now supplanted Amsterdam. New arrivals peaked in the late 1920s: economic hardship and antisemitism drove ever greater numbers of Jews to leave Poland, and increasing immigration restrictions in North and South America led many of them to put down roots in Antwerp.[9]

Jews dominated the upper echelons of the diamond trade, but also made up a fifth to a quarter of its labor force and played a leading role in creating its union movement at the end of the nineteenth century.[10] On the whole, the Belgian Jews were far less prosperous than their Dutch counterparts.[11] Most were lower-middle class, earning a living as craftsmen or workers in the garment and diamond industries, shopkeepers and owners of small businesses, and peddlers.[12] Bo, for example, is engaged in small retailing, and Jenny works as a secretary.

In the world in which Huguette grew up, Judaism was simply a given. She and her family tended to reside in the "voluntary ghetto": not a place of confinement and discrimination, but rather an almost self-contained cultural community. Most Jews of the poor and middling sort lived here, in the district around the central railway station, whereas the more prosperous ones, especially those involved in the

---

[8] In 1910, Jews left Russia at a rate of 8.4 per thousand, i.e. twice or more the rate of other major immigrant groups in the empire. Vital, 309. Following the rise of pogroms, over half a million Jews arrived in the United States between 1881 and 1900. Between 1900 and 1914, of the more than two million Jews who emigrated, three-quarters chose to go to the US, accounting for some ten percent of the total immigration. The so-called First Aliyah, or wave of immigration, saw 25,000 Jews go to Palestine between 1882 and 1903. In the Second Aliyah, lasting from 1904 to 1914, the number rose to 40,000. Mendes-Flohr and Reinharz, 704-6, 715.
[9] Saerens, 159-60.
[10] On the diamond trade in general, Baron and Kahan, 158-61. On labor radicalism and the diamond trade, Van Doorslaer in Michman, ed., 77-79.
[11] See, e.g. Hilberg, 384-87.
[12] Van Doorslaer, and Saerens in Michman, ed., 64-66, 161-62.

diamond trade, migrated to the "more elegant parts of the town." Although the community in Antwerp was generally much more religious than that of Brussels, it sustained a rich life of secular as well as sacred Jewish culture that reflected the increasing influence and changing profile of the immigrants: first Orthodoxy and liberal Zionism, and then, with the arrival of larger numbers of the poor, the full panoply of increasingly radical political groupings, including left Zionism, the socialism of the Jewish workers' Bund, and communism.[13] Because of the preponderance of recent immigrants, however, many Belgian Jews, whatever their social profiles, were not linguistically acculturated.[14] Bo thus knew enough Hebrew to navigate a prayer book (if not comprehend the content) and spoke Yiddish, but never "managed to acquire even a smattering of the linguae francae of Antwerp." Instead, she communicated with gentile customers through gestures or by jotting down prices. Jenny and Huguette, by contrast, move easily between cultures, speaking with Bo in Yiddish but with one another in French. They are affected by but not participants in the intensifying language war between Flemish- and French-speakers. Significantly, although antisemitism of course existed, it barely appears as such in this account.[15] Nonetheless, Huguette's experience is strongly and

---

[13] On the range of political and social groupings and movements, see van Doorslaer and Saerens, in Michman, ed., as well as Daniel Dratwa's essay on "The Zionist Kaleidoscope in Belgium" 43-62.

[14] Scholars have classified European Jews as di- or heteroglossic and multilingual: That is, they may have used multiple languages within their own community—Hebrew for worship and scholarship, Yiddish for daily conversation and business—and have spoken one or more of the languages of the surrounding population. See, e.g., David Biale, ed., *Cultures of the Jews: A New History* (New York: Schocken Books, 2002), xxi-xxii. On Jewish literacy in general in this era, see Vital, 306-7. Although Antwerp had a strong locus of Dutch-Jewish culture, more than half the Jewish population (as in Brussels) was Polish, and in both cities, as Saerens notes (161), Yiddish-language Jewish magazines accounted for more than half of the total. One might contrast the Belgian situation with that of Bohemia, in which nationalist rivalry also played out on the linguistic plane—in this case, Czech versus German, but the Jewish community was long-established and historically and culturally more identified with the German. In the end, it came to face some hostility from both sides. See Derek Sayer, *The Coasts of Bohemia: A Czech History* (Princeton: Princeton University Press, 1998), 82-118, 168-69.

[15] See, e.g., Saerens, "The attitude of the Belgian Roman Catholic Clergy Toward the Jews Prior to the Occupation," and "Antwerp's Attitude," in Michman, ed., 117-94.

continually marked by a sense of difference, as shown in her realization that the Jews are "set apart" from the wider Catholic world, which she finds at once alluring and threatening. In her frightened mind even "insipid" religious statues "imperiously demanded conformity, and I feared that if I remained Jewish a terrible retribution would one day be wreaked on me."

Antwerp, in the movements of the author's family, performed for them its role as an *entrepôt* for the Jewish community as a whole. Huguette's maternal grandparents emigrate to America, but after failing to establish themselves economically return to settle in their port of embarkation.[16] A future uncle falls in love with the narrator's aunt while awaiting passage to Canada, and refusal of entry allows him to return to Antwerp and marry her (much to the consternation of the grandmother, who had thought herself rid of him). Another aunt and uncle, fleeing the nascent Nazi regime, pass through Antwerp on their way to a new life in England, and finally a third aunt and her husband emigrate to America and become farmers in New England. The extended family also reflects the social and class distinctions of the Jewish community. Some among them begin to assimilate, and a few become well-to-do. When visiting the family of a prosperous aunt and uncle, Huguette can only marvel at and covet the unimagined luxury of a separate world: modern furniture and most of all, a large tiled lavatory, with art on the walls. Yet she and her mother are outraged when the uncle, visiting them with wealthy gentile friends, is embarrassed by Bo's Yiddish and pretends not to understand her. Soon, such cultural distinctions would make no difference.

---

[16] Rates of return to Europe from the United States at the turn of the century were higher than one might imagine, given the importance of immigration in the national consciousness and mythology. Between 1908 and 1910, well over half of Italians, nearly a third of Poles, and one-fifth of German immigrants returned home. The return rate of the Jews was a mere 8 percent (only the Irish were less likely to return to their country of origin, at 7 percent). In 1908, around the time that Huguette's grandparents returned, fully half of arriving immigrants left the United States, in what was a year of particular hardship. Vital, 308.

III.

The outbreak of war is the turning point of the narrative, for it casts the members of the family into the stream of world history and irrevocably changes the course of their lives. The news breaks just after Huguette and Bo return from a seaside vacation at Ostend. The paradoxical recollection of a particularly "glorious" summer in which, "in my mind, the sun shines perpetually," eerily echoes an earlier tragedy: contemporaries and historians agree that the shock of the First World War derived not just from its unexpected length and bloodiness, but also from the ironic contrast with the unprecedented beauty of the summer in which it began.[17] In fact, the Austrian-Jewish author Stefan Zweig, who was in Ostend in 1914 and in exile in England in 1939, explicitly connected the two cataclysms meteorologically as well as psychologically.[18]

By now everyone knew that a fearsome war was approaching, but no one knew exactly what it would bring.[19] During the ten "Days of Awe" between the New Year (Rosh Hashanah) and Day of Atonement (Yom Kippur), Jews ponder their behavior over the past year in preparation for divine judgment. An ancient New Year's prayer speaks of the uncertainty of human existence:

> On Rosh Hashanah will be inscribed, and on Yom Kippur will be sealed, how many will pass from the earth and how many will be created; who will live and who will die; who will die at his predestined time and who before his time; who by water and who by fire, who by sword, who by beast, who by famine, who by thirst, who by upheaval, who by plague,

---

[17] Two modern classics of cultural history make this point: Paul Fussell, *The Great War and Modern Memory* (London: Oxford University Press, 1975), and Modris Eksteins, *Rites of Spring: The Great War and the Birth of the Modern Age* (NY: Doubleday Anchor Books, 1990).

[18] Zweig, 214-22, 432-36.

[19] Contrary to popular opinion, Germans too, recalling the hardships of the Great War, feared the outbreak of a new one. Part of Hitler's success consisted precisely in managing to revise the provisions of the Treaty of Versailles and make territorial gains without recourse to war. Ian Kershaw, *The Hitler Myth: Image and Reality in the Third Reich* (Oxford: Oxford University Press, 1987), e.g. 121-68.

who by strangling, and who by stoning. Who will rest and who will wander; who will live in harmony and who will be harried; who will enjoy tranquility and who will suffer; who will be impoverished and who will be enriched; who will be degraded and who will be exalted. But Repentance, Prayer, and Charity avert the severe Decree![20]

One can only imagine how the Jews of Europe, including the author's family, experienced the recitation of that prayer in 1939. The New Year fell on September 14, midway between the start of the war on September 1 and the capitulation of Poland, as it was partitioned between Nazi Germany and the Soviet Union, on September 28. No one knew when or whether the invasion in the west would come.

To be sure, there had been warning signs, beginning with the arrival of relatives fleeing Germany in 1933. And in June of 1939, the narrator witnessed the ordeal of the passengers of the steamship *St. Louis*, refugees from Nazism, who were denied entry to both the US and Cuba and forced to return to Germany. Belgium accepted 214 passengers, who disembarked at Antwerp.[21] Still, as Huguette explains, even eyewitness testimony of former concentration camp inmates failed to shatter the complacency of many Belgian Jews, who thought the refugees' tales exaggerated or self-serving.[22] The precocious child herself had no such doubts, for the steady string of bloodless Nazi conquests during the era of appeasement (in Churchill's memorable image, feeding the crocodile in the hope that he will eat you last) and the fascist victory in the Spanish Civil War filled her life with "a feeling of impending doom." In fact, after the tense waiting period of the "Phony War" comes to an end with the German attack in May 1940, it is she who has to force her

---

[20] The Wikipedia entry, "Unetanneh Tokef," provides a thorough explanation of the text and its origins. http://en.wikipedia.org/wiki/Unetanneh_Tokef.

[21] The United States Holocaust Memorial Museum provides a convenient overview of the *St. Louis* episode and even commissioned the first detailed study of the fate of the passengers: "Voyage of the St. Louis." *Online Exhibitions.*
http://www.ushmm.org/museum/exhibit/online/stlouis/ and "Voyage of the St. Louis." *Holocaust Encyclopedia.*
http://www.ushmm.org/wlc/en/article.php?ModuleId=10005267. Eighty-four of those who landed in Antwerp perished during the war.

[22] See, e.g., Jean-Philippe Schreiber, "Belgian Jewry Reacts to the Nazi Regime Prior to the Occupation: The Case of the Economic Boycott, 1933-1939," in Michman, ed., 83-114.

indecisive family to join the rapidly growing exodus into neighboring France, which may in the end have involved anywhere from one to 1.5 million Belgians.[23] As the German advance continues, they decide to attempt to flee France, as well, thanks to Bo's possession (via a third marriage) of a coveted British passport, which means that they—or perhaps only she? or perhaps none of them?—will be able to board a ship and cross the channel. After many travails, the family succeeds in making the crossing. Whereas Stefan Zweig recalled that in the years before World War I people traveled freely and he had never even seen a passport, now having the correct papers could mean the difference between life and death.[24]

Bo, Jenny and Bernard, and Huguette were unusual and fortunate in escaping. If, up to this point, it had been difficult for Jews fleeing Nazism to reach safety abroad, it now became virtually impossible.[25] Some of the Belgian Jews found refuge in the southern, "unoccupied" portion of France until deportations to the death camps began there in 1942. Aunt Golda and the Disenhaus family were relatively lucky: after a series of harrowing experiences, they were able to escape from Vichy France to Switzerland, even though they were interned there

---

[23] Michael R. Marrus and Robert O. Paxton estimate the number at one million: *Vichy France and the Jews* (New York: Basic Books, 1981), 65. Lucien Lazare uses the higher number: "Belgian Jews in France," in Michman, ed., 445-55; here 447.

[24] Zweig, 410.

[25] Among the standard works are: David S. Wyman, *Paper Walls: America and the Refugee Crisis 1938-1941* (Amherst: University of Massachusetts Press, 1968), and *The Abandonment of the Jews: America and the Holocaust 1941-1945* (New York: Pantheon Books, 1984); and Bernard Wasserstein, *Britain and the Jews of Europe, 1939-45* (London: Institute of Jewish Affairs; New York: Oxford University Press, 1979). Just how lucky Huguette, Bo, Jenny, and Bernard were may be seen from the fates of other Antwerp Jews who also reached the border town of De Panne/La Panne but ended up spending the war years on the continent. Israel J. Rosengarten's family likewise passed through the crossing but was unable to escape and returned to Belgium and deportation to the death camps, a story he tells in *Survival: The Story of a Sixteen-Year-Old Dutch Boy*, (Syracuse: Syracuse University Press, 1999). Perhaps even more disturbingly similar is Patricia Herskovic, *Escape to Life: A Journey Through the Holocaust. The Memories of Maria and William Herskovic* (Jerusalem: Yad Vashem, 2002). One member of the family possessed a British passport, but fear that they might not all be allowed to board the rescue ship caused them to hesitate until it was eventually too late.

INTRODUCTION

under harsh conditions.²⁶ However, among the roughly 75,000 Jews eventually deported from France were some 5000 Belgians.²⁷ We are stunned to read that "Uncle Lezer," near the French border, declared that he would rather die than go to England and experience again the antisemitism he encountered there during the Great War. "Little did he imagine" the fate that awaited him, Huguette observes. He seems to have vanished in the smoke of the Holocaust. Yet only his rationale was unusual. Many others (astonishingly, it seems today) elected to return home.²⁸ We must remind ourselves, however, that no one yet knew what was going to happen. Although there had been reports of persecution and atrocities in Poland, even the Nazis had not decided on the "Final Solution to the Jewish Question."²⁹ Moreover, the historical experience

---

26 For a strikingly similar tale of an Antwerp family's suffering and survival, which likewise involves flight to the south, internment in the camp at Gurs, and eventual escape to and internment in Switzerland, see Fred Gross, *One Step Ahead of Hitler: A Jewish Child's Journey through France* (Macon, GA: Mercer University Press, 2009). Even a successful escape did not guarantee entry. As the US Holocaust Memorial Museum observes, "Switzerland took in approximately 30,000 Jews, but turned back about the same number at the border." "Refugees." *Holocaust Encyclopedia.* http://www.ushmm.org/wlc/en/article.php?ModuleId=10005139. On attempts by Belgian Jews in France to reach Switzerland, see Lazare, in Michman, ed., 449-50.
27 Steinberg (203 n. 9) cites a total of 5,043.
28 The issue of the number of Belgian Jews in France is as fraught with controversy as the question of the overall Belgian Jewish population. Hilberg, proceeding from a high starting figure of 90,000, states that "mass flights into France reduced the prewar figures to fractions. One Jew in every three sought sanctuary in the South." (383) Lazare (445), although noting the difficulty of arriving at reliable figures, similarly suggests that anywhere from one-quarter to one-third of the Belgian Jewish population—15,000-23,000 (including 7000 foreign Jews expelled by Belgium and subsequently interned)—ended up in France. Steinberg (203 n. 9), by contrast, doubts whether the total in France after the start of hostilities could have exceeded 10,000. (Hilberg, 383-84, adds that the new German occupation regime also expelled some 8,000 Jews—again, mostly refugees from the Reich—into France.) The number of Jews who returned is likewise unclear. The entry on Antwerp from the *Encyclopedia Judaica*, referring only to that city, states that "most" fled at the outbreak of hostilities but 30,000 returned after the surrender at the end of May. Jewish resistance fighter Jacob Gutfreind claims that 45,000 returned to Belgium as a whole. "The Jewish Resistance Movement in Belgium," in Yuri Suhl, ed. and trans., *They Fought Back: The Story of Jewish Resistance in Nazi Europe* (New York: Crown Publishers, 1967), 304-11; here 304-5. By contrast, Lazare (447) claims that the Jews, unlike other Belgian refugees, did not return home, three-quarters of them remaining abroad.
29 Contrary to the popular view of the Holocaust, this is the scholarly consensus today,

of the Jews was that intense violence flared up and then subsided, and the remaining persecution could be endured until circumstances improved.³⁰ Weighing the certainty of internment or impoverishment in France against reports that the situation in Belgium was stable and manifested none of the open terror seen in the east, returning to home and familiar surroundings quite logically seemed the lesser of two evils, or at least a calculated risk.³¹

As historians and Holocaust survivors alike affirm, survival of any given individual was in large measure a matter of chance. At the same time, we can generalize with considerable precision about the fates of national populations. In the face of strong SS control and high levels of prewar antisemitism, there was almost nothing that the Jews could do to avert their fate. By contrast, where these two factors were less present, Jews stood a better chance of survival. Crucial, it seems, was the extent to which the Nazis were able to speed the process of breaking the bonds of solidarity and isolating the Jews from the surrounding population.³²

---

though there is a broad range of views clustered around the middle between the so-called "intentionalists" at the one extreme end of the spectrum and the "functionalists," at the other. Adam Shatz provides a convenient summary in "Browning's Version: A mild-mannered historian's quest to understand the perpetrators of the Holocaust," *Lingua Franca*, Feb. 1997, 48-57.

30   Hilberg forcefully asserts the thesis that this historically conditioned Jewish response was determinative—and fatal (e.g. 1-30), though many have found it too harsh, particularly in its neglect of Jewish resistance and other responses, a subject that has been much more thoroughly and subtly studied in the meantime.

31   Gutfreind, here 304-5. Regardless of the accuracy of his figure of 45,000 returnees, the logic is compelling. We find corroborating evidence in a report by the Jewish Telegraphic Agency from September 1940, according to which "many have returned to Belgium out of sheer despair" and others seek to do so. Jacques Adler, *The Jews of Paris and the Final Solution: Communal Reponses and Internal Conflicts, 1940-1944*, Studies in Jewish History, ed. Jehuda Reinharz (New York: Oxford University Press, 1987), 244 n. 28. The Nazi rulers were in any case pragmatic and hesitant to highlight the "racial" question lest its premature revelation interfere with their overall goals. See, for example, Hilberg, 383; Steinberg, 199, 211.

32   See the rather dense but important sociological study by Helen Fein, *Accounting for Genocide: National Responses and Jewish Victimization during the Holocaust* (Chicago: University of Chicago Press, 1984). Maxime Steinberg, "The *Judenpolitik* in Belgium Within the West European Context: Comparative Observations," in Michman, ed., 199-221, although more specialized and nuanced, generally supports this conclusion.

In all such regards, Belgium represented a relatively positive case and stands in instructive contrast to neighboring France and the Netherlands. As an ethnically "Aryan" territory, the Netherlands was destined for partnership and an eventual role in the Reich. By contrast, France and Belgium were in effect occupied territories under provisional military administrations, to which the "Jewish Question" was of secondary concern after the maintenance of security and stability. The crucial difference was that in France the local authorities became active partners in the Final Solution. In Belgium, by contrast, the threat to the Jews eventually aroused in the wider population a sense of collective danger and responsibility.[33] As the Nazis complained, the Belgians had no understanding of the "Jewish Question."[34]

Antisemitic policies unfolded similarly to and more or less simultaneously with those in the Netherlands, but with different results. In October 1940, the Nazis instituted a series of discriminatory measures, defining Jews, purging the judiciary and civil service and other public domains, and registering population and property. Although the Belgian Jews were far less prosperous than the Dutch, "Aryanization" of Jewish assets proceeded apace between the spring of 1941 and the end of 1942.[35] In late 1941, the Nazis created the obligatory Jewish intermediary body.[36] In the spring of 1942, Jews were ordered to wear the star, and deportations soon commenced, at first to forced labor in Belgium and northern France, but eventually, via the camp at Mechelen (Malines), to Auschwitz. Few Jews volunteered for deportation in either country. However, thanks to the combination of national solidarity and

---

See, further, Saerens, "Antwerp's Pre-War Attitude," which cites the model of Dutch historian Dik van Arkel regarding "stigmatization, separateness, and terrorization" as prerequisites for the development of antisemitism and racism (188-94).

[33] Fein (143-64, 152-58) classifies France among the regions with the lowest SS control ("colonial zone") and the Netherlands and Belgium as in the "command zone," where there was some SS control, in contrast to the territories of the Reich and east, which constitute the full-fledged "SS zone."

[34] Hilberg, 382-89; here 387. See further Steinberg, "*Judenpolitik*."

[35] The Nazis aryanized or liquidated nearly 8,000 enterprises. See Hilberg, 384-87, and Steinberg "*Judenpolitik*," 200-2.

[36] Scholars of the Belgian case emphasize that this body, the Association des Juifs en Belgique (AJB) should not simply be equated with the "Jewish Councils" that the Nazis set up in eastern Europe to do their bidding. See, e.g., Michman's introduction, 33-37.

INTRODUCTION

the existence of an independent Jewish leadership, fewer than half of the Jews in Belgium were shipped off to almost certain death (out of approximately 25,000 who were deported, 96 percent perished). By contrast, 80 percent of Dutch Jews were deported.[37]

Although Huguette criticizes the vain attempt to maintain Belgian neutrality until the eleventh hour, observing that the press seemed more hostile to communism than Nazism, the organized collaborationist element was small, confined to the ultranationalist Flemish separatists and the fascist "Rexist" party, whose fortunes had plummeted on the eve of the war.[38] The highest Belgian civil authorities, backed strongly by the government-in-exile (which also threatened future punishment for collaborators), refused to promulgate Nazi anti-Jewish measures including registration and distribution of the star.[39] The Crown and Church intervened on occasion, particularly on behalf of native Jews

---

[37] In Steinberg's words (347): "In the history of the 'Final Solution,' at least in Western Europe, the 'Belgian case' is perhaps the most significant illustration of the importance of the Jews' behavior—determinative in the end—in the face of racial persecution and deportation." Depending on the figures used, the percentages vary, but the conclusion is the same. Fein, 153, 322; Steinberg, "Judenpolitik," 202-3, 219. He notes that, of 25,257 persons deported (including 351 gypsies), 63.7 percent were gassed immediately upon arrival at Auschwitz; only 1,205 survived to the end of the war. In his introduction to his *Belgium and the Holocaust*, Dan Michman questions and problematizes the tendency to distinguish between "Belgian" and specifically "Jewish" resistance. "Research on the Holocaust in Belgium and in General: History and Context," 3-38; here 31-33.

[38] Jean Stengers, "Belgium," in Hans Rogger and Eugen Weber, eds., *The European Right: A Historical Profile* (Berkeley: University of California Press, 1966), 128-67. See further, e.g., the two excerpts by Léon Degrelle and José Streel, and sources cited in Roger Griffin, ed., *Fascism*, Oxford Readers (Oxford: Oxford University Press, 1995), 204-7. See further Fein, 167; Steinberg, "*Judenpolitik*," 211-12. On occupation and collaboration in general: Jacques Willequet, *La Belgique sous la botte: résistances et collaborations 1940-1945* (Paris: éditions universitaires, 1986).

[39] See Véronique Laureys, "The Attitude of the Belgian Government-in-Exile in London Toward the Jews and the Jewish Question During World War II," in Michman, ed., 287-306. Local government in Antwerp, however, constituted an eager exception: Fein, 154; Saerens, "Antwerp's Pre-War Attitude," 188-94; Steinberg, "*Judenpolitik*," 205-10; and Mordecai Paldiel, "The Rescue of Jewish Children in Belgium During World War II," in Michman, ed., 307-25; here 307-8. As Saerens further observes (194): "the Jews of Antwerp were less protected and more vulnerable than Jews in the rest of Belgium": whereas the death tolls for "registered" Jews in other cities were in the range of 35-42 percent, fully 67 percent of Antwerp's Jews perished.

and the elderly. The Belgian leftist resistance in particular made saving Jews a priority and, working in collaboration with Jewish resistance groups, sabotaged Nazi policies and alerted and sheltered potential victims.[40] Some 25,000-30,000 Jews—including 3,000-4,000 children—were thus able to go into hiding.[41] It was a striking accomplishment and manifestation of solidarity, given that over 90 percent of the Jews were non-citizens, and most of them did not even speak the languages of the country.[42] In the end, the death toll among the probable wartime population of some 67,000 Belgian Jews stood at

---

[40] Fein, for example 322. See further José Gotovitch, "Resistance Movements and the 'Jewish Question'," Paldiel, and Maxime Steinberg, "The Jews in the Years 1940-1944: Three Strategies for Coping with a Tragedy," and Dan Michman, "The Belgian Zionist Youth Movements During the Nazi Occupation," in Michman, ed., 273-85, 307-25, 347-95, and the following monographs: Betty Garfinkels, *Les Belges face à la persecution raciale 1940-1944* (Brussels: Editions de l'Institut de Sociologie de l'Université Libre de Bruxelles, 1965); on the major Jewish resistance group: Lucien Steinberg, *Le Comité de defense des Juifs en Belgique 1942-1944* (Brussels: Editions de l'Unversité de Bruxelles, 1973), both published under the auspices of the Centre national des hautes études juives).

[41] Statistics: Michman, 30; Fein, 157-58; Paldiel, 307; and Sylvain Brachfeld, "Jewish Orphanages in Belgium Under the German Occupation," in Michman, ed., 419-31; here 419. Brachfeld's essay deals with the "official" Jewish orphanages subject to German authority. On the complex attitudes and policies of the Catholic church, see Mark van Wijngaert, "The Belgian Catholics and the Jews During the German Occupation, 1940-1944," Luc Dequeker, "Baptism and Conversion of Jews in Belgium, 1939-1945," in Michman, ed., 225-71. Beatrice Muchman tells the story of her concealment with a Catholic family in *Never to Be Forgotten: A Young Girl's Holocaust Memoir* (Hoboken: KTAV, 1997). See further Suzanne Vromen, *Hidden Children of the Holocaust: Belgian Nuns and Their Daring Rescue of Young Jews from the Nazis* (New York: Oxford University Press, 2010). See also Sylvain Brachfeld, "Jewish Orphanages in Belgium Under the German Occupation," in Michman, ed., 419-31.

[42] Fein, 153, 322. The literature in English is surprisingly sparse. The tight summary in Hilberg's pioneering work (382-9) remains an important account, but the literature (some cited above) has grown considerably in recent years. The authoritative overview is Michman, ed., *Belgium and the Holocaust*, which offers essays on the whole spectrum of topics, from Nazi policy to Jewish life and Jewish and Belgian response. He surveys the historiography and the reasons for its comparatively slow evolution in the first chapter, "Research on the Holocaust in Belgium and in General: History and Context," 3-38. The authoritative work on Belgian Jewry during the war is the magnum opus by Maxime Steinberg, *L'Étoile et le Fusil: Les Cent Jours de la Déportation des Juifs de Belgique*, 3 vols., Collection "Condition humaine" (Brussels: Vie Ouvrière, 1983-86). The three volumes are: *La question juive 1940-1942* (1983), *Les Cent Jours de la Déportation des Juifs de Belgique* (1984) and *La Traque des Juifs 1942-1944* (1986)

approximately 29,000. Just how lucky Huguette was can be appreciated from the fact that, of the 5,093 children deported, only 55 survived.[43]

From our vantage point, the Allied victory seems inevitable, but this was not necessarily the way things looked when the destroyer bearing the narrator and her family crossed the Channel. From the early 1930s until the middle of the war, liberal democracy itself in many ways appeared to be losing the struggle against the vital new movements of fascism and communism.[44] And even those who did not share the defeatist sentiments that Huguette encounters from one genteel middle-aged English couple could have been forgiven for wondering how long England could stand alone after the string of relatively easy Nazi conquests of 1939-40. Newly settled in London, she recalls, "We refugees felt that we were only enjoying a respite." Poring over reports on German military power in magazines, she says, "brought a chill to my heart, for I could not help feeling that this formidable enemy could not be defeated." Even though military historians now agree that a

---

[43] Estimates for the death toll of Belgian Jews typically range from about 44 to 53 percent, depending on the starting assumptions. Most sources, as noted, now place the population at the beginning of the occupation around 66,000-67,000 (e.g. Steinberg, 203 n. 9; Fein, 155). When only 42,652 Jews complied with the requirement to register in late 1940, the Nazi authorities estimated the actual total (including those below the required reporting age) at 52,182. (Fein, 154; Hllberg 384; Lazare, 445 n. 2). Steinberg (203 n. 10) is able to document 55,670 eventual names in the German card registry. Serge Klarsfeld reproduced the names of all the identifiable French deportees in his *Le Mémorial des Juifs de France* (Paris: Beate et Serge Klarsfeld, 1978). Working with Maxime Steinberg, he repeated the task for Belgium in the *Mémorial de la Déportation des Juifs de Belgique* (Bruxelles : Union des déportés juifs en Belgique et filles et fils de la déportation; New York, NY : Beate Klarsfeld Foundation, 1982), which lists 25,475 "racial" deportees (among them 351 gypsies and 516 Jews from northern France under Belgian administration). Yad Vashem, the Holocaust Remembrance Authority in Israel, now puts the total Belgian Jewish death toll at a very precise 28,902 (www1.yadvashem.org/odot.../microsoft%20word%20-%205944.pdf). For further discussion of Belgian and comparative statistics for France and the Netherlands, see Steinberg, "Judenpolitik," 202-3, 219. Statistics on children are from Brachfeld, 419.

[44] Mark Mazower makes this point powerfully in the opening of his *Dark Continent: Europe's Twentieth Century* (New York: Vintage Books, 2000), ix-40. As late as 1942, Belgian fascist ideologue José Streel looked to an Axis victory as paving the way for "what historians will call the century of fascism or national socialism." See the excerpt in Griffin, 206-7. Ian Kershaw describes how the early wave of Nazi military victories in 1939-40 overcame the initial fear of a new war and fed the "Hitler Myth," 151-68.

German invasion would have faced long odds, Hitler's boast that "by August 1940 he would make a speech from the balcony of Buckingham Palace" seems to her "a real possibility." The prerequisite for that invasion was command of the air, which the Germans sought but failed to attain in the Battle of Britain from 12 August to 30 September. By early September, they shifted their focus from the bases of the Fighter Command to the capital and other major cities. The "London Blitz" began with bombing raids on 7 September and continued for over two and a half months. Massive night raids on London and other English cities lasted from October until the following May.[45]

No one, we should remind ourselves, knew what the air war would bring. Writers in the first decades of the century speculated on the future: some thought that aircraft would make warfare unthinkable; others, that it would make it unimaginably horrible.[46] The Nazi attack on Guernica during the Spanish Civil War, and then the subsequent raids on Warsaw and Rotterdam in 1939 and 1940, suggested what was to come. The British government was deeply concerned: secret estimates anticipated a massive German assault dropping 3500 tons of bombs on the first day and 700 per day thereafter, leading to some two million casualties in two months. In the event, the estimates proved to be wildly exaggerated. But the circa 60,000 dead, 86,000 seriously wounded, and 149,000 injured over the course of the war—half of them in London alone—were bad enough.[47]

British evacuation plans were thus similarly exaggerated, but in the event, some four million people initially relocated from high-risk target areas to other communities (approximately 1.75 million by the government and another 2 million of their own volition). Among

---

[45] See Peter Calvocoressi, Guy Wint, and John Pritchard, *Total War: Causes and Courses of the Second World War*, second revised ed. (New York: Pantheon Books, 1989), here vol. 1, by Calvocoressi: *The Western Hemisphere*: 146-63 (on "The Battle of Britain"), and 512-32 (on "Mass Bombing"). Further, and more generally: R. J. Overy, *The Air War 1939-1945* (New York: Stein and Day, 1981).

[46] Stephen Kern, *The Culture of Time and Space 1880-1918* (Cambridge, MA: Harvard University Press, 1983), 242-47.

[47] Calvocoressi, 150. And of course they pale alongside the 19 million Soviet civilian dead (Vinen, 185). As Calvocoressi notes (432), "the tonnage of bombs dropped on London in the whole war was less than what had been expected in the first two weeks."

those relocated by the government are Bo, Jenny, and Huguette.[48] The government's projection of widespread panic and three to four million cases of mental breakdown in the first six months of the air war proved no more accurate, but the raids did cause social dislocation and individual trauma.[49] They certainly take their toll on Huguette, who recalls being "quite hysterical as a result of the incessant alarms," for which reason the three generations of women relocate to Bedford, (leaving Jenny's husband Bernard behind). There they are generally free of the threat of air raids. Still, they feel the terror of a near miss when they again take to the shelters on a night "full of tense fear," only to learn the next day that the bombers had passed directly overhead en route to the devastating raid on Coventry.[50]

On that evening, she recalls, "I was filled with sheer terror owing to my inexplicable innate awareness of profound guilt, so that I was convinced that every single bomb dropped was seeking me out personally." Descriptions of air raids, like much else here, serve less to describe the historical events themselves than to portray the way that they reflected and influenced the development of a young girl. We are meant to look both backward and forward. To endure bombing raids would be a terrible experience for anyone, but how much more terrifying to "a very fearful child" haunted by premonitions, phobias, and forebodings. Huguette recollects nightmares of pursuit by beasts or sinister men, fears of abandonment, premature burial, disappearing down the toilet, and choking to death on the cotton swab being used to treat her tonsils, and even fear of the end of the world through a collision with an asteroid. Such thoughts paralyzed her at times. And yet collectively, episodes such as these lead to self-insight: "Whenever I have been in actual danger of dying, I have not felt any fear; this is not bravery, to which I am, unfortunately, not inclined, but derives from an abrupt cessation of the production of imaginative fantasies and from an inability to recognize the reality of what is happening." Powers of intellect and introspection are thus a mixed blessing, and

---

[48] Calvocoressi, 431-32.
[49] Calvocoressi, 431-33.
[50] On the Coventry raid, see Calvocoressi, 432-33, 516-17

INTRODUCTION

yet paradoxically they are precisely what enable her to realize this. Ultimately, they are moreover what gives the memoir its power and distinctiveness.

Eventually, as she says, things settled down, and "we were on the whole living a life of uneventful normality." As the tide of war turns in 1942 and 1943, she can at last believe that an Allied victory is only a matter of time, and she takes a sort of quiet and grim satisfaction in the knowledge that German cities, too, are now being bombed. For those of us who know the war only as an epochal event experienced vicariously through books and film, it is valuable to be reminded that there was such a thing as "normality," that daily life crept along at its quotidian pace with its mundane chores and worries. And every experience or phenomenon is grist for her mill. Thus, the warm reception upon landing in England occasions not the predictable effusive outpourings of emotion, but rather the observation that the British rather than the Germans are "the best organizers in the world." A moment later, comparing the spare British identity card with the much more extensive documentation that Belgians are required to carry, she adjudges the former efficient rather than primitive, and thus further proof for her thesis.[51] After Jenny's death, Aunt Sophie's careful ritual rending of Huguette's dress, so that it can be easily repaired, illustrates both the persistence of traditional Jewish mourning practices and the effects of wartime rationing. In any case, the war, as such, is here not so much the subject as the framework within which the earlier themes are elaborated upon. Above all is personal development in the context of the family dynamic and education, but now it is mediated by relocation, housing with strangers, and new schooling in a new language. The main challenge to acculturation is not that she is a foreigner but that she takes learning so much more seriously than the other girls. And ironically, because the "goddesses" of this unusual household are all

---

[51] Calvocoressi's chapter on "Great Britain at War" (426-55) finds that the country was not in fact fully prepared or able to convert to a wartime economy, though it notes that other factors were an advantage: "Although socially stratified to an extraordinary degree, this society was ideologically more coherent than most in Europe" (427). He also points to the rationing system as one of the greatest and most effective successes, while noting that housing proved to be a more difficult problem.

INTRODUCTION

female, it perhaps suffers less from the dislocations of the war than did the typical family, for whom the absence of the father could be traumatic.⁵² Jenny's ne'er-do-well and abusive husband is, if anything, more execrable to Huguette by his presence than his absence, and she is in any case used to fending for herself, in this case, living with Bo in Bedford while her mother works in London. Still, separation from her mother proves as painful as ever: first, in the literal or spatial sense, and increasingly also in individuated personality development, complicated by a growing awareness of sexuality, which also later causes tensions with her grandmother.

The bombings, evacuations, mobilizations, rationing—all these things placed strains on civilian life. Although the mythology would have us believe that the struggle against the German enemy seamlessly brought people of all stripes together, the war in fact exacerbated social tensions as well as strengthened national unity in England, as it did elsewhere.⁵³ We read about clashes of culture and class between city and country, for the local schools regarded the native London evacuees as "a lower species of humanity." Antisemitism, by contrast, is notable by its absence, even though George Orwell provocatively argued that the war had caused it to increase at home.⁵⁴ At the most, we get the sense that Jews were something of a curiosity. We do, however, witness a growing (or at least evolving) Jewish consciousness, in particular when Huguette, after her mother's death, attends a socialist-Zionist summer camp intended to instill ethnic pride and train future pioneers for the kibbutzim of Palestine.⁵⁵ Only then, more than a year after the

---

52   On the disruption of family life, see Calvocoressi, 433-37.
53   Calvocoressi, 430-33.
54   George Orwell, "Anti-Semitism in Britain," *Contemporary Jewish Record* VIII no. 2 (April 1945): 162-71. Looking back from the perspective of the historian, Wasserstein concurs, though noting that "the most important manifestations of wartime anti-Semitism" arose from bigotry in the Polish Army in Exile, which became so intense that it prompted desertions by Jewish troops. See pp. 81-133, here, especially 114-30.
55   On the left-Zionist youth movements, see, e.g., Walter Laqueur, *A History of Zionism* (New York: Schocken Books, 1976), e.g. 270-377. "Habonim," the movement behind the camp that the narrator attended, arose in the Jewish East End of London in the 1930s. See pp. 487-89.
     The heady idealistic atmosphere in which the young people sang "Hebrew songs and Negro spirituals," sought redemption through labor, and cultivated left-

fact, does she learn about the Warsaw Ghetto Uprising, noting with satisfaction "that Jews were able to fight to defend themselves."⁵⁶ She would no doubt have been equally proud to learn that, on the day the revolt began, Belgian-Jewish resistance fighters—in the only such incident of the war—attacked a deportation train destined for Auschwitz and succeeded in liberating some of the prisoners.⁵⁷

The emotional climax of the book is the death of Jenny, which is all the more striking because it is told exclusively through heartbroken and heartbreaking diary entries. For Huguette, this loss of the center of her world *becomes* the center of her world. How does one measure and convey the death of an individual loved one in the midst of mass death? (One wonders whether she recalled at the time the story of her grandfather's funeral on the day of the Armistice in 1918, when, "On their way to the cemetery, the widow and orphans were surrounded by people rejoicing and dancing in the streets.") At several points, the bewildered diarist describes herself feeling "as if I were living a book" or experiencing things hitherto known only from books and movies. In most cases, we would dismiss this as a trite analogy from an adolescent lacking in imagination and literary tools. Not so in this case.⁵⁸

---

wing politics, calls to mind Zionist leader Chaim Weizmann's description of "poor Galician immigrants who arrive in Palestine with no clothes but one hand holding Marx's 'Capital' and in the other, Freud's 'Interpretation of Dreams.'" Eran J. Rolnik, "Psychoanalysis in Israel: Past and Present," 5-6. http://tiny.cc/ryvs8.

56 Ironically, then, she was also unaware of the fate of Szmul Zygielbojm, a Jewish member of the Polish National Council in Britain, who committed suicide to protest the failure of the world to help the Jews in Poland. On the coverage of the Warsaw Ghetto Uprising in Britain, see Wasserstein who notes that "although Zygielbojm's death was widely reported in the press, the motive behind it received little notice." (303-5; here 305).

57 Of the 231 prisoners who escaped from the transport of over 1,600 persons, 115 managed to avoid death or recapture. See Marion Schreiber, *Silent Rebels: The True Story of the Raid on the Twentieth Train to Auschwitz*, trans. Shaun Whiteside (London: Atlantic Books, 2003).

58 In some ways, the trauma that a child experiences upon the death of a parent is not unlike that of the soldier, suddenly thrust into unprecedented circumstances. Paul Fussell argues, "The problem for the writer trying to describe elements of the Great War was its utter incredibility, and thus its incommunicability in its own terms." He thus explains the tendency to resort to literary tropes and allusions when recounting the combat experience. *The Great War*, 139, and further, in particular, Chapters 5 and 6 ("Oh What a Literary War" and "Theater of War"), 155-230.

INTRODUCTION

The narrator was born into the epoch of the "universalization of the media," in which the technologized word, already ubiquitous thanks to the print culture of books and the mass periodical press, was now also reproduced in picture and sound recording, its impact magnified by the context of national and global conflict.[59] Texts and images delighted and assaulted the senses everywhere, more than ever before. Stefan Zweig spoke of "our new organization of 'simultaneity,' in which media truncated time and space as never before.[60] Literature and film thus serve not just as props in the drama of narrator's life, but also as central elements of personal development, as well as one of the many bridges between schooling and adulthood.

Huguette speaks of "ravenous reading" as an addiction, even confessing "with shame" that, bored at Bo's slow gait, she used to hold her grandmother's arm in one hand while reading from a book clutched in the other. Coming from straitened circumstances, she haunts the English public libraries and is terrified that the loss of a book might lead to revocation of borrowing privileges. Discovering that most of the other pupils are more interested in boys than their studies, she forms bonds with rare kindred spirits through shared tastes in reading. She is almost as enthusiastic about movies. She recalls "weekly visits to the cinema" in early childhood as "the highlights of my life," speaks of "my film-blurred mind," and describes herself as "film-crazy" during the war. It is almost impossible to avoid an invidious comparison with Anne Frank, born a year later. Although Huguette admits to spending hours poring over news of stars in glossy Hollywood magazines while in England, her interest was ultimately always a deeper one. She precociously compared Central European and Hollywood styles or comments on various genres, and later rendered elaborate judgments of books versus their film adaptations.

---

[59] James Wald, "Periodicals and Periodicity"; Jonathan Rose, "Modernity and Print I: Britain 1890-1970"; and Adriaan Van der Weel, "Modernity and Print II: Europe 1890-1970," in *A Companion to the History of the Book*, ed. Simon Eliot and Jonathan Rose (Malden, MA: Blackwell Publishing, 2007), 341-67, 421-33. On the universalization of the media: 422-23.

[60] Zweig, xxi.

―――――――――――――――― INTRODUCTION ――――――――――――――――

Culture, in the form of books, music, theater, and films, moreover functions as a crucial element in intergenerational bonding. Film is the "only leisure interest and activity" that mother and grandmother share, so Jenny translates the subtitles of foreign films into Yiddish for Bo, which also enables Huguette, as yet too young to read, to follow along. Above all, books link mother and daughter. For the as-yet unlettered Huguette, turning the pages of her mother's book in the shared paradisiacal bed assumes the quality of a sacred nocturnal ritual. When she at last learns to read on her own, she finds equal pleasure in reading aloud to her mother. And the magnetism that her mother exercised on gentleman callers and daughter alike, she makes clear, was connected to her being an intellectual as well as a beauty. When Jenny came from London to visit Huguette on weekends, the joy was compounded because she invariably "arrived laden with books." Finally, as if to complete a circle, Huguette's reading aloud to Bo from newspapers and books becomes their shared means of staving off the grief of Jenny's death. To relate lived experience to the world of books and film, then, was not an affectation but second nature.

We are thus not surprised when an air raid conjures up thoughts of the siege of Atlanta in *Gone With the Wind*. But several extended passages make masterful connections, seamlessly weaving together art and life. In one, the film of "The Invisible Man" terrifies her and comes to haunt her childhood dreams. After detailing these multifarious fears, she concludes, "*The Invisible Man* had such a hold over me because he stood for the missing element in our exclusively female household. Men were absent and yet present at the same time." The absent is the father. The present are the lovers whom her mother regularly brings home, and "dark and dreadful things took place." Under such circumstances, one almost wonders what the young Huguette thought of "normal" families. For that, too, there is an answer.

The mature narrator is both proud of her youthful intellectual achievements and suitably embarrassed at her former cockiness. In retrospect, she candidly admits to having been "a real little pest" and, however innocently, a show-off who managed to annoy fellow pupils and instructors alike: "an obnoxious swot who not only did the required homework but also, out of a devouring desire to excel, voluntarily added further exercises no teacher had asked for." She confesses to having been "a budding cultural snob," to boot. Although excelling in most academic subjects, she at last comes to grief with sewing:

> Here I learned something very important—what it is to feel dim and utterly stupid. I understood nothing of what I was told and shown and was not even able to produce a simple straight seam. I reluctantly realized what ungifted classmates in Belgium and England must have suffered during the lessons of composition, history, geography, etc., at which I shone and which I enjoyed so much.

Soon thereafter, she and Jenny visit the house of a friend and come upon her, along with her mother and sisters, baking a cake, "all of them with floury arms and pastry sticking to their hands." She likens it to "a picture from *Little Women*," which she knows intimately, having seen the film four times as a child, read the book in French, and at last enjoyed it in the English original. In the hands of a less sensitive and subtle observer, the scene might have been churlishly disparaged as irredeemably bourgeois or longingly sentimentalized as an emblem of the traditional family she never knew. Instead, she simply and admiringly accepts it for what it is, "and to my surprise, Jenny found this housewifely idyll absolutely charming."

Two final incidents, in which the girl ran up against the limits of language and decided to throw caution to the winds and improvise, may serve to convey both her character and the combination of shrewd observation and self-deprecating humor of which the adult narrator is capable. Among the books that Huguette read aloud in spontaneous translation to Bo was the massive *Gone With the Wind*, but because her Yiddish vocabulary was that of household conversation rather than literature, it was not always equal to the task: "I accordingly condensed descriptive passages into a nutshell, and the details of landscape, in particular, were summarily waved aside by my saying, for instance, 'The garden is in bloom and smells good.'" Some time before that, Huguette finally became fed up with harassment from fellow school girls: "I lost my self-control and, half in tears, half in anger, blurted out, 'You're, all of you, very mean to me! Stop bullying me!' adding that I wasn't sure that I had pronounced the word 'bullying' correctly and didn't care, either." In that peculiar and wonderful gesture, simultaneously reflecting punctiliousness and the nascent ability to transcend it in the cause of a greater good, we glimpse both the essential personality of the protagonist and the beginnings of her journey over the threshold into adulthood.

IV.

Given the author's intimate familiarity with world literature, one is tempted to wonder why she did not turn to two literary quotations that immediately suggest themselves. (Perhaps because they are too obvious?) In the opening line of *Anna Karenina*, Tolstoy famously observes, "Happy families are all alike; every unhappy family is unhappy in its own way." Was this, then, an "unhappy family"? It certainly was unusual, and wracked by conflict. Still, the author would presumaby reject the Tolstoyan classification. In another famous opening line, David Copperfield wonders, "whether I shall turn out to be the hero of my own life, or whether that station will be held by anybody else." The title of the present work reminds us that this is a memoir of a life, but a life lived in and defined by family relationships. It is not so much the story of a wartime life as that of a life lived under the shadow of the war, in a family that at times seemed to be at war with itself but, on the deepest level, was bound together by a common love as well as the common struggle for survival.

As the two preceding vignettes demonstrate, we welcome the invitation into the world of this autobiography because it is spoken by and introduces us to an eloquent and distinctive voice: part memoirist, part psychologist, part ethnographer. The smallest event or detail becomes the object of precise description: a sober, at times loving, and as often as not gently ironic reflection. Among the author's most distinctive skills is her ability to employ the tools of the adult to capture the voice as well as the experiences of the child. To be sure, this is a voice filtered and edited through memory and art, and yet it has a striking freshness, authenticity, and immediacy. The descriptions ring true.

One gets a perfect sense of the personality struggling to emerge and then unfolding before us. One can envision the scenes so meticulously described.

We need not allow ourselves to become embroiled in the debate concerning the gendered nature of the Holocaust experience[61] in order to affirm that the story of survivors has mainly been told in the male voice, and that a powerful and original woman's account such as that of Huguette Herrmann is a very welcome addition to the literature. Two of the greatest women's autobiographies involving the interplay of family and the era of the Holocaust are Ruth Klüger's unsparing account of a childhood in Auschwitz and Eva Hoffman's memoir of growing up as a Polish-Jewish immigrant in postwar North America.[62] To say that the present memoir can profitably be read alongside them is to say a great deal.

Introducing the account of Jenny's final days, the author expresses the desire that she might one day write a proper biography of her colorful mother. And, at the close, she notes that her postwar life "can fill a book of its own." One may hope that she will make good these intentions, for they whet the reader's appetite. In the meantime, though, there is plenty to savor in the volume before us.

Jim Wald
Associate professor of history, Hampshire College

---

[61] See the contrasting views: Sybil Milton, "Women's Survival Skills," and Lawrence L. Langer, "Gendered Suffering?" in Donald L. Niewyk, ed., *The Holocaust*, third ed., Problems in European Civilization (Boston: Houghton Mifflin, 2003), 119-36.

[62] Ruth Klüger, *Still Alive: A Holocaust Girlhood Remembered*, The Helen Rose Scheuer Jeiwsh Women's Series (New York: The Feminist Press at the City University of New York, 2003); Eva Hoffman, *Lost in Translation: A Life in a New Language* (New York: Penguin Books, 1990).

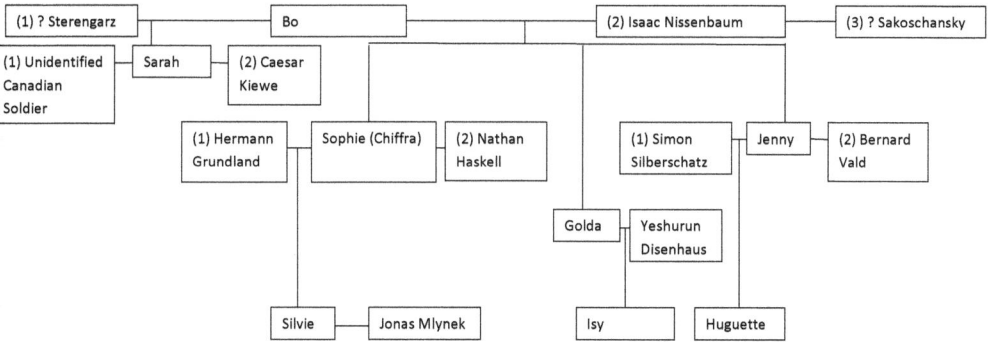

PART I
A CHILDHOOD IN ANTWERP

1. THE FAMILY

We all have our private mythologies: for the children of "normal" families, the father and mother are the towering deities. I did not grow up in a normal family, and the gods that ruled over the first years of my life were oversized goddesses — they were my formidable grandmother, whom I and her other grandchildren called either "Bomama" or just "Bo" (which I always looked upon as an abbreviation of the French "bonne-maman," but more likely refers to the Yiddish "Bobbe"), and her youngest daughter, my mother.

This part of the family hailed from Odessa, whereas my father's came from the Polish town of Lodz, where he was born; my mother Jenny came into the world in Antwerp, the reason being the pogroms that broke out in Odessa in 1904. They had caused my grandmother and grandfather to emigrate.

My maternal grandfather Isaac Nissenbaum was a pious Jew and Bo's second husband. Earlier, she had been briefly married to a young man, who died of tuberculosis a couple of years after the wedding, leaving her with a daughter called Sarah. I can't remember her saying much, or indeed anything, about him; but then she wasn't the reminiscing type. Once, however, I gathered that he had wooed her with ardent kisses, which she had not considered importunate — it was hinted that she might even have enjoyed them, information that was surprising because normally her outlook on sex was that this unfortunate activity had to be tolerated by married women, as the price to be paid for material security and respectability. Intrinsically, however, it was dirty and disgusting and, outside the bonds of wedlock, a foul habit best ignored or scowled at. To tell the truth, she disliked men intensely and thought that their sole function in life was to earn

Part I. A CHILDHOOD IN ANTWERP

a good living and provide their wives with comfort and luxury. This mitigating circumstance might redeem them and make an acceptable creature out of a man. Those who failed to reach that standard were no good; they were invariably regarded as blackguards and villains.

When they left Odessa, my grandparents had, besides Sarah, two daughters of their own: Chiffra, also called Sophie, then four and a half years old, and Golda, aged three. Each pregnancy had brought the hope of a son; food and wine had been stored in expectation of a Brith, the ritual circumcision that is performed on the eighth day of a baby boy's life, an occasion for great celebration. But apparently, Bo's aversion to men caused her body to rebel even against bearing a male baby. In all, she had five daughters, one of whom died at birth.

They had decided to emigrate to the United States, and waited for their passage in Antwerp before embarking for the New World. But their stay in New York turned out to be a failure — they could not find their footing economically and lost the greater part of their savings, so that after a short interval they decided to return to Antwerp, where they had found a Jewish community in which they thought they might feel at home. Their short residence in the States did have one positive result (or a negative one, depending on one's vantage point): like most pious Jewish wives, Bo used to wear a wig, but when the urchins in the streets of New York mocked her, she threw it away in a great unconscious act of emancipation. This could scarcely have met with the approval of my grandfather, but then theirs was not a harmonious marriage. Embittered battles and quarrels were the daily background to the childhood of their little girls.

Back in Antwerp, they began a small retail trade in tablecloths, lace tablemats, and handkerchiefs with elaborate lace borders, antimacassars, and fripperies of that kind. In 1909, my mother Jenny was born, once again disappointing all expectations of a male heir; Bo thereupon decided that she had tried long enough to have a son. She did not want to conceive again and, above all, she did not want to suffer the embraces of her bearded husband, whom she despised and daily berated for not being a prosperous businessman. Yet, although she took an active part in the business herself and worked in the shop, she was not as successful as one might suppose from the overriding importance

1. THE FAMILY

she attached to money. Nonetheless, my grandparents do seem to have achieved a modest subsistence, which is all the more surprising as neither of them managed to acquire even a smattering of the linguae francae of Antwerp, Flemish, and in those days French. True, a large section of the customers were, like themselves, Yiddish-speaking Eastern European Jews; but Belgians also frequented the shop, and the wholesalers from whom the goods were ordered spoke Flemish. They managed by means of gesturing and by writing down figures, by nodding and shaking their heads, those classic helps to which the illiterate all over the world resort. (They were not really illiterate, for both of them could read and write Hebrew and Yiddish — and possibly were familiar with the Cyrillic alphabet from their time in Russia.)

Of this grandfather I know little, except that he suffered from the venomous verbal attacks of his wife — but it usually takes two to quarrel, and he was certainly prone to religious fanaticism. I have been told that if he saw a Jewish man smoking in the street on the Sabbath, he felt no compunction at crossing the road and buffeting him in public. This does not seem to denote a particularly gentle, tolerant, or forgiving disposition, and so it's fair to assume that he probably gave as good as he got from his belligerent wife.

The four daughters differed vastly, not only in appearance but also in disposition and intellectual capacity. Sarah, the oldest, had the same broad, not unattractive Russian type of face as her mother; she was passionately fond of animals (an anomaly in our family), as she discovered in the course of a prolonged stay on a farm belonging to her father's family in the Ukraine. Later she would say that she had never been so happy again. A willful, wayward, disobedient child, scorning rules and prescriptions, she swept aside all conventions as if they were negligible rubbish. One year, she ran away to join — oh horror! — a convent. The next year, she disappeared again; the police were alerted and discovered her — oh horror of horrors! — in a brothel. She knew neither shame nor fear.

Chiffra was neither particularly good-looking nor really ugly — just ordinary. A born conformist, she absorbed the home atmosphere so thoroughly that as an adult her competence in vituperation equaled that of her mother. She was of moderate intelligence, and as a result of her meager scholarly aptitude, she had to repeat a year in school so that Golda caught up with her and they were in the same form.

Golda found the constant scenes and embittered verbal contests between her parents even more repulsive than did her sisters, who resignedly accepted them as a normal part of family life; she was passionately eager to achieve happiness and harmony in her life. Possibly the following incident provided her with a tenuous belief that this might actually be achieved. My grandfather had invited a famous rabbi from Eastern Europe who was passing through Antwerp to honor his home by paying him a visit. As in the case of the anticipated, but never realized "Briths," stores of food and wine were laid up for this august guest; and the hope was secretly harbored that as a result of his sheer presence a son would shortly break the line of female births. After partaking of the Sabbath meal and leading the others in the prescribed prayers and chants, the "Rew" rose to depart. In the corridor leading to the door, the members of the family were lined up in pious expectation; the great man stopped in front of Golda, put his hands on her head, and spoke the momentous words: "This one shall be blessed."

At all events, she was blessed with a greater capacity for learning, an avid hunger for books, and, at a later date, a love for culture and beautiful objects, which distinguished her from her two older sisters, who remained ever indifferent to such matters. At this time, she was a reasonably pretty child who was doing well at the Flemish elementary school and was secretly convinced that she was really a foundling, a kind of cuckoo growing up among totally alien creatures; this did not prevent her from spending her time playing and squabbling with Chiffra, who was only eighteen months older. She felt especially estranged since she was the unloved one of her parents' trio — Chiffra being her father's favorite, while Bo cherished a fondness for Jenny.

On the whole, Bo was a mother who had no tenderness in store for anyone and certainly not for her daughters, on whom she cast disapproving glances and poured out lavish scorn and mockery. Her principal approach was scolding, but they were not neglected. She saw to it that they were decently, even prettily, clothed and properly fed, and she nursed them through the usual childhood illnesses as best she could. Nonetheless, her most striking contribution to their welfare was to create an atmosphere compounded of screaming and cursing.

Jenny, the last born, was an extremely pretty girl with black hair, almond-shaped eyes, and sensuous lips. When the First World War broke out, she was five years old, and it looked as if she was going to be very intelligent. For some reason or other, which I have never quite understood, the outbreak of the war seems to have thrown the Antwerp Jews into a panic. Our family fled first to Holland, which was neutral, and then to England — with what kinds of passports and visas heaven only knows. To start with, my grandfather was interned; as a pious Jew, he refused to partake of most of the food offered him, since it was not kosher. He staunchly resisted all attempts to persuade him that these were exceptional circumstances justifying a departure from strict adherence to the letter of the law in order to safeguard his health. It was later assumed that it was during those months spent in damp cells with inadequate nourishment that he contracted the tuberculosis that was to cost him his life. When he was released, he joined his family, who had been eking out a living in Holland selling lace articles on markets, with Chiffra and Golda both helping their mother as best they could.

Once in England, the family tried to continue trading in tablecloths and Bo, whose command of English was on a par with her knowledge of Flemish and French, nonetheless contrived to travel along the length and breadth of the British Isles on business. The filth and poverty of Glasgow, where she saw children playing barefoot in slum streets in the winter, made a profound impression on her. They lived in London, where Golda rapidly picked up English and, after she had taken a Pitman course, was able at the age of fifteen or sixteen to contribute to the family's income by working as a shorthand typist. Chiffra had no such abilities, and I do not know what she did — possibly she worked in a shop. Jenny learned English as quickly and effortlessly as might be expected of a bright child of her age, and she did well at school.

Sarah, who at the beginning of the war supposedly dabbled in spying activities, was married in 1917 to a Canadian soldier, who died on the battlefield soon afterward. She was pregnant and in due course gave birth to a daughter, and — to complete this story — upon her return to Belgium after the war, she farmed out the baby to foster parents in the country, where at the age of eighteen months the poor infant died of a children's disease — or was it neglect?

My grandfather's health declined rapidly — food was scarce during the First World War, and this hastened the progress of the tuberculosis he had contracted during internment. This man who was so fanatic in religious matters craved ardently for the war to come to an end and for peace to return; ironically, he died in November 1918 and was buried on the eleventh, Armistice Day. On their way to the cemetery, the widow and orphans were surrounded by people rejoicing and dancing in the streets.

Bo went back to Antwerp soon afterward and opened another shop. Golda went out to work, additionally qualified by her proficiency in English, and Chiffra found a husband. She married a pleasant Jewish businessman, who fulfilled Bo's requirements inasmuch as he was able to offer her daughter reasonable prosperity; moreover, apart from being quite handsome in a broad-shouldered, fair-haired way, he was very good-natured. In 1921, my cousin Silvie was born and Chiffra happily settled down to being a good housewife and mother.

It was at the beginning of the twenties that a young man named Yeshurun Disenhaus made his appearance on the family scene and directed his attentions to Golda. He was a Polish Jew from an Orthodox family and had a slight stoop from the many years spent poring over the Talmud in a "yeshiva," one of the traditional Jewish schools devoted to the study of rabbinic literature. During adolescence, he had discarded his religious beliefs as a result of being won over to the brand of pantheism developed by Spinoza, whose works he had illicitly read, and he had, therefore, come into conflict with his father. Now he had decided to try his luck by emigrating to Canada and, like the Nissenbaums nearly twenty years earlier, was in Antwerp waiting for a passage. He had revolutionary notions about the prevailing social conventions — marriage was firmly rejected as a bourgeois institution. Need it be mentioned that Bo viewed him with uneasy suspicion? Golda, who readily adopted his unorthodox opinions, was exposed to the full flow of her mother's maledictions, which were only tempered by the prospect of Yeshurun's imminent departure, for which Bo waited with barely suppressed impatience.

———————————————— 1. THE FAMILY ————————————————

Golda

The lovers tore themselves apart, and Yeshurun set out to cross the Atlantic, leaving a forlorn and desolate Golda behind. Not for long, however. For passport reasons (he was the holder of what was known as a "Nanssen" travel document), he was refused entry and shipped back to Antwerp, where, to her mother's chagrin and increasing wrath, the liaison with Golda was promptly resumed. Hours of ecstatic physical and intellectual communion were subsequently dearly paid for by the most degrading kind of scenes: Bo was so distraught that she resorted alternately to locking her daughter in and to refusing her admittance when she came home late at night.

Love brought about the collapse of Yeshurun's revolutionary convictions — he capitulated to the rules of bourgeois society and called to make a formal offer of marriage. Mollified, Bo realistically considered the nonexistent material foundation for this projected union. Yeshurun

Trick photo of Jenny

was cultured (he had spent hours dozing in opera houses in Berlin, trying to acquire a taste for Wagner — a futile undertaking, incidentally) and highly intelligent; a good-looking man of slight build, he was thoroughly versed in the subtle convolutions of Talmudic argumentation and addicted to reading philosophical treatises. But he had no profession or trade. At the end of her forties, Bo felt that she was getting old and was not averse to giving up her commercial activities. An arrangement was reached to the effect that the young couple would take over the shop and pay Bo a modest annuity for the rest of her life. (She was firmly convinced that she was being exceptionally generous in handing over her business, but Yeshurun soon discovered, after disentangling the chaotic details of her rudimentary bookkeeping, that the firm's liabilities exceeded its assets to an alarming degree.)

And so another wedding was celebrated, and the Nissenbaum family was astounded to find the erstwhile firebrand taking out his phylacteries and prayer mantle in order to duly recite his morning prayers in deference to his parents, who had come from Lemberg to participate in the festivities. After their return from a brief honeymoon in the Black Forest, the young couple moved into a flat of their own

1. THE FAMILY

Jenny and Sarah:
"On the occasion of Sarah's visit to
Antwerp 30th January 1919"

and proceeded to run the business. The shop was situated in a main road that ran under the railway line near the main station — a well-frequented and advantageous location. They settled down to establish what was to become a lifelong pattern: business during the daytime, culture and sports — an unheard-of innovation in our family — in the evenings and on weekends.

The long uninterrupted line of female births was at last broken by the advent of their son, Isy, whom Golda proceeded to bring up in accordance with all the tenets of modern and enlightened motherhood.

Thus, two daughters were now well married; but alas, Chiffra's happiness was short-lived. In 1926, her husband, after suffering from repeated infections of the throat, decided to put an end to this troublesome affliction by having his tonsils removed. The remedy proved worse than the disease — unexpectedly, he died as a result of the operation, leaving Chiffra a widow with a six-year-old daughter and no breadwinner, although for the time being she was quite well provided for.

Bo now only had Jenny at home. She was a gifted pupil, spoiled by one and all; as she grew older, she unfolded into an exotic beauty. With a thick crop of straight black hair, bobbed in the fashion of the twenties, almond-shaped eyes, high cheekbones, pouting lips, and a slim figure, she could not fail to arouse attention. She relished this admiration so much that all else faded into insignificance. The attraction she exerted on men gave her a feeling of pleasurable power, and she developed a remarkable talent for the art of flirting. She was prone to sentimentality and was always falling in love with the young men who came her way. Bo watched these developments with mounting alarm; dire memories of Sarah's amorous escapades haunted her. She had fantasies of Jenny becoming pregnant, the ultimate insult to her self-esteem as a respectable and prudish mother. Finally, she hit upon the solution: in spite of Jenny's extreme youth (she was seventeen), she would arrange a marriage and provide the bulk of her meager savings as a dowry. This meant having recourse to a "Shadchan," a traditional Jewish matchmaker, of whom there was no shortage in Antwerp's Jewish community, where many of the features of life in Eastern European "shtetls" were successfully duplicated.

One of these Shadchans came up with a candidate from Brussels — the oldest son of the Silberschatz family, which had left Lodz when my father, Simon, was two years old, at about the same time as the Nissenbaums left Odessa. They had five children: the oldest was my father, then came three daughters, followed by another son. They were honorable but poor. My paternal grandfather had tried to establish a small commercial enterprise, trading cheap cloth between Poland and Belgium. "Shmattes" (the Yiddish word for rags), which provided the raw material from which new cloth or paper could be manufactured, were an important part of this business, which resolutely refused to flourish.

1. THE FAMILY

Engagement photo of Jenny and Simon

Simon had been a brilliant pupil at school, always effortlessly achieving the best marks of his class, in which two other gifted boys grew up to become a lawyer and a doctor, respectively, at a time when to rise in these professions still required unusual ability. Simon, however, was a dreamer, a gentle young man of twenty-five, characterized by a striking lack of willpower. Besides being a distinguished chess player, he boasted a melodious bass voice, it being reported that if the window was open when he sang, people would gather in the street below to listen enraptured, in the best style of those hackneyed scenes popular in musical films of the thirties.

In view of the unromantic circumstances of their introduction, the two young people seemed to like each other better than might be expected. Simon had light brown hair, a forehead denoting unusual intelligence, eyes that seemed to hover about some distant mirage, and a sensitive mouth. He fell in love with the seventeen-year-old girl who, in spite of her slender build, seemed to hold out the prospect of luscious sensual pleasures; in this he proved to be mistaken, for her passions were a figment of her fantasy and not fixed in reality. At all events, his courtship was a passionate one, and he wrote her love poems that filled a small booklet. One day, I was to find them relegated to an old suitcase in the attic. I remember neat handwriting filling page after page with verses. If there is something I regret above other losses, it is that they were no longer available to me at an age when the character of the handwriting and the wording and style of the poems might have conveyed and revealed more than they did to the child of eight or nine years who discovered them and looked at them for a brief moment before closing the suitcase again, having registered no more than a fleeting impression.

One of Simon's sisters ventured to ask whether the fact that he would be marrying into a family composed principally of widows (Bo, Sarah, and Chiffra) did not deter him, but he did not heed this warning. He was very much in love and acquiesced to respect a wish brought forward by his young bride — she asked him not to consummate the marriage on their wedding night. In spite of her numerous flirtations, she was a virgin and, in this the daughter of her mother, was afraid of the act of sexual intercourse.

The wedding celebrations were held in Antwerp in March 1927 and were marred by an incident that seemed to bode no good; while dancing with my father, Jenny, who was a light-footed and expert dancer, fell. Worse was to follow: confronted with the beautiful girl in the bedroom allocated to them in Bo's apartment, Simon could not restrain himself and broke his word. Jenny was heard screaming in the middle of the night and calling her mother for help.

They moved to Brussels where the money provided by Bo as a dowry served to set them up in a millinery shop; my father was supposed to earn a livelihood by running it. A more unsuitable candidate for this kind of activity can scarcely be imagined. He was on the one hand a dreamer lost in a world of fantasy, on the other a highly gifted abstract thinker; totally divorced from reality, he had none of the down-to-earth-qualities required of a competent businessman or shopkeeper. Within record time, he managed to ruin the small firm and to squander the meager funds at his disposal.

Three months after the wedding, Jenny became pregnant and now spent her time cooped up in a gloomy flat in which the cheap furniture matched the background of vulgar flowered wallpaper, of the type that is found in innumerable apartments rented by the poor. The couple did not develop any real intimacy — moreover, she was indolent, and, as Bo had lacked the patience to show any of her daughters how to run a household, she had no inkling of how to cope with cleaning or washing. She couldn't cook and made no effort to learn. As for Simon, he took to gambling at cards and to playing chess instead of coming home. Her sole comfort was an eccentric domestic pet, a cat prone to taking great leaps of several yards from one vantage point in the living room or kitchen to another. Yeshurun, eager to expand his business, had begun to travel all over Belgium to collect orders for his goods and found a heavily pregnant Jenny alone one evening , obviously very lonely but proudly refusing to complain. As for Bo in Antwerp, she exercised rare self-control during the first months of Jenny's marriage and refrained from interfering in the affairs of the young couple.

My birth was expected in February 1928, but I was overdue. Jenny felt desolate, forlorn, and humiliated. Nine months had passed; and February, including the memorable date of the twenty-ninth, came to an end. At the beginning of March, labor at last set in. It was inordinately protracted, exhausting the mother and presumably causing the child corresponding anguish as it felt blocked in the contracted birth canal. Finally, after Jenny had gone through interminable hours of screaming, sweat, and desperation, I was born at five o'clock in the morning on Saturday, March 3.

2. THE INVISIBLE MAN

In those days, few women went into hospital for a confinement, and the prolonged and painful birth took place in my parents' bedroom. As a result of the less than sterile surroundings, my mother contracted puerperal fever and became mortally ill. The milk that I suckled must have been addled, for I could not keep it down; on the other hand, it was thought that I should be put to the breast in order to draw out the poison that was festering there. Jenny's condition was so serious that the prayers to avert imminent death were recited in the synagogue on her behalf.

During those dramatic weeks, when my mother's life hung by a tenuous thread, my father was asked to fetch bandaging material from a nearby chemist's one night. He did not turn up again that evening, as he lost the money gambling at cards. This story, repeatedly related to me in later years, served to demonstrate the kind of insensitive monster he reputedly was.

Finally, friends of the Silberschatz family alerted a famous gynecologist, who managed to check the infection — a pailful of pus was drawn out of Jenny's exhausted body — and she slowly began to recover, at least physically. But she had suffered a shock, and the long lonely months of pregnancy, the collapse of the couple's modest financial hopes, the traumatic birth, and its aftermath left her brimming with bitterness. As soon as she felt up to it, she decided to turn her back on a thoroughly failed marriage and return to Bo. This step must have been taken very soon after her recovery, since my inoculation certificate for smallpox, issued when I was six weeks old, already bears an Antwerp stamp.

Jenny immediately began to look for work and landed a job as a shorthand typist. Bo was there to look after the baby, and Jenny not

2. THE INVISIBLE MAN

only worked her weekly forty-eight hours but also went to evening classes to acquire additional qualifications. As a result of the years she spent in London during the First World War, her English was fluent, and she proceeded to learn bookkeeping and Spanish and German commercial correspondence as well.

In accordance with the Jewish tradition of perpetuating the memory of departed relatives by bestowing their names on newborns, I was named after my paternal grandmother, who had died during Jenny's pregnancy. She was called Hudes, and it was generally agreed that this was not a suitable name for a child that would grow up in Belgium. They hit upon Huberte, and this is the name that was entered on my birth certificate. Fortunately, one of my father's sisters turned up a few days later and suggested that Huguette was much to be preferred, and from that moment, Huguette I was.

As a baby, I sensed that I was not accepted and a burden to both mother and grandmother — I can well understand that my mother felt little love for a child fathered by a man who she thought had let her down in every respect. She had just turned nineteen, had the responsibility for an unwanted child, and was forced to live with her mother, with whom she quarreled incessantly. This was mainly because she very soon reverted to flirting with men; she took to going regularly to weekend dances, usually held in popular halls, and there she easily struck up acquaintanceships with her partners. This worried and infuriated Bo, and scenes flared up at the slightest provocation.

Neither of them thought it right to pick up the baby who so often cried desperately for hours on end (this attitude was in accordance with the accepted tenets of proper child rearing in the twenties), and eventually it somehow grasped that this appeal was unavailing. Resignation set in. Protest against this rejection found expression in a dogged refusal to eat. An enormous baby at birth, weighing an unbelievable eleven pounds, I rapidly lost weight, became inordinately thin, and was perpetually ailing. On the other hand, I soon discovered that to fulfill certain expectations was to earn fulsome praise, and I was able to perform on the potty before I was a year old, a preternaturally early age. I also learned to walk and to talk well ahead of the usual age, and all these achievements brought me admiration in lieu of love.

Not only did I talk at an early age — I may mention that I have always been puzzled by the fact that the first word uttered by a child notoriously unwilling to eat should have been "encore" (more), possibly denoting a strong will to live — but I developed a talent for using grown-up language, conveying my meaning in long well-formulated sentences and not, as small children normally do, resorting to the shorthand of a single noun or verb. I was also bilingual, talking Yiddish with Bo and French with Jenny and never mixing up the two. My memory was good, and at the age of eighteen months, I had stored the addresses of Bo's numerous relatives in Antwerp and could reel them off like a horrible little parrot. She apparently found it useful to consult me when she had forgotten exactly where one of her numerous nephews, nieces, or cousins lived. This was also a welcome means of showing me off, a bad habit in which both Bo and Jenny indulged. Jenny went to some pains to teach me to recite La Fontaine's fable of "Le Renard et le Corbeau," and I diligently performed on demand, although I had only the vaguest idea of what such turns of phrase as "vous êtes le phénix des hôtes de ces bois" might mean.

We lived in dingy, cheap flats, and for some reason or other were constantly moving. Once — I must have been between eighteen months and two years old — we rented rooms above an *estaminet* (a kind of pub) frequented by workers and sailors, the noise of whose carousing floated upward every evening. My first memories are situated there: the earliest one is of being straddled across my mother's knees, screaming and struggling because she was trying to give me an enema, and of strongly resenting this painful invasion of my private parts (it was an age that accorded inordinate attention to regular activity of the bowels) and of her mercifully desisting in the middle of the act because the doorbell was rung. Bo looked out of the window and announced that "Chiffra the Bell" was at the front door. This was not Chiffra my aunt, but one of Bo's many nieces, thus nicknamed because of her incessant babbling.

Aunt Chiffra, incidentally, had departed from the family scene in Belgium in 1929. She had felt the status of a widow to be so intolerable that she had invited the Shadchans to present suitable candidates to her. Among them was an English Jew, a widower with three children, called Nathan Haskell. He was in the fur business, and she broke up her home in Antwerp to join him in Leipzig, then the European center of the fur trade.

Another early memory of the flat above the pub is of lying in a cot in the bedroom Bo and Jenny shared, and of having a series of nightmares that caused me to regularly wake up screaming in panic. One was of a big dog or wolf chasing me; another was of a man coming up the cellar steps. His face was smeared with coal dust, and I was mortally afraid that he would catch me. I wanted to run away from him, but my legs unfailingly turned to water and I became a mass of anguish. My screams sometimes brought Bo into the dark room, dimly lighted by the lamp-posts in the street below. Finally, they hit upon the solution of letting me sleep in Jenny's bed.

From there, we moved to the Kiewitstraat or Rue du Vanneau (Plover Street), a street right in the center of the ghetto the Eastern European Jews had of their own accord established in Antwerp. This too was a dark, gloomy flat, in which I spent mealtimes ensconced in a high-chair, and where in a rare gesture of rebellion I once hurled a dummy my mother brought home from a window onto the pavement below. I remember winter evenings with the lamp casting a dim light over the table and leaving the corners in darkness. When Jenny left to attend her evening classes soon after she came home from work, my heart regularly contracted and a feeling of absolute desertion gripped me. I was acutely frightened of being abandoned — it must have been about a year later that I was confirmed in these fears by an incident that occurred as I was walking in the street with Jenny. I had a tantrum, typical of a child aged three. My mother took no notice and walked resolutely on; when she turned the corner of the road and vanished from my view, I knew that I had been left alone forever. An indescribable panic seized me and I ran after Jenny, unconditionally ready for abject submission in the future.

We moved once again, this time to a quieter road on the edge of the ghetto district; there we had rooms on the second floor that were lighter and pleasanter. I took to playing hopscotch in the street, and this meant approaching other children. An attempt to send me to kindergarten failed after only two weeks, most of which I spent sitting helplessly at a little table because I had no idea of how to go about coping with the play material, which required manual skills. The reason why they stopped sending me there was not, however, because I felt so unhappy, but because I promptly caught some childhood disease that led Bo and Jenny to decide that continued attendance would only expose me to unnecessary risks. Even so, I was perpetually ill and at the slightest provocation prone to running high temperatures. On one occasion, I caught diphtheria and nearly died, and as I lay in the cot to which they had transferred me again, I was well aware of that fact and strangely indifferent to the prospect of dying, possibly because even at this lowered level of consciousness I relished the hushed and enhanced attention with which the aura of death surrounded me.

When I was not ill, the days were punctuated by battles with Bo about meals. I steadfastly refused to eat "properly," while she thought it her duty to prod or wheedle me into doing so. She would stand guard over me while I chewed a mouthful of bread for an unconscionably long time: I could not bring myself to swallow it, so that I managed to spend half an hour eating half a small slice, after which she usually capitulated. She was no great cook, and I left her concoctions untouched. I remember the disgust that I felt when I smelled her "borscht," which in those days she still cooked and ate with relish. I did make some exceptions, however; there was a dish of semolina boiled in water, to which she applied a pat of butter and of which I deigned to eat a small plateful. When she made dumplings from grated raw potatoes (called "latkes" in Yiddish) or fried chips, I even positively enjoyed eating them; unexpectedly, in view of her otherwise mediocre cooking skills, she was very good at preparing both these dishes.

We were poor and lived on a combination of the allowance that Yeshurun irregularly paid Bo and my mother's wages. During the Depression years at the beginning of the thirties, Jenny was continually in and out of work. She worked for a series of small firms that went bankrupt between one day and the next, and she then came home in the middle of the day, discouraged and downcast. But she would indomitably start looking for another job on the next day, and after a while she always managed to find a new set of employers. Once she was at home for a longer spell, because she dislocated her collarbone, when she failed to switch the light on when going to the lavatory in the middle of the night and fell down a flight of stairs. This was a minor tragedy, as she received less money or none at all during this enforced stay at home.

She was still very young, twenty-three or twenty-four years old, and, understandably, wanted to enjoy herself, so on weekends she went out dancing in the evenings. She took inordinately long for her preparations — she would wash with extreme care, and after dressing there followed an elaborate cosmetic ritual, which involved plucking her eyebrows (it was the fashion to only hint at their existence by leaving a very thin outline), applying mascara to her eyelashes, powdering her nose, and putting on lipstick in earnest concentration. All the while I hovered about her, observing how she made herself ready for the serious business of seducing strange men, and painfully conscious of the fact that she would at some point consider her work of art to be completed, after which she would sally forth, often leaving me alone, if Bo had also gone out to visit relatives. I then lay in her deserted bed and in my anguish would wail and cry so desperately that the neighbors repeatedly complained about the disturbance.

It was possibly this circumstance that induced Jenny and Bo to take me with them at an extremely early age when they went to the pictures regularly once a week, this being the only leisure activity and interest that they shared. I was three years old on my first visit to a cinema just round the corner of the railway station, next to the entrance to Antwerp's zoo. The film shown was the German movie, *The Congress Dances*, and I remember walking into the dark cinema, holding my mother's hand and becoming aware of people seated in rows, all looking up enraptured at a screen showing Lilian Harvey being whisked along in an open coach, where she reclined singing some tra-la-la ditty. I promptly fell in love with this slender girl, who had such a pretty face and wonderful blond curls. This vision fed my fantasies for many months. Indeed, the weekly visits to the cinema came to be the highlights of my life; the memories of scenes I had seen both haunted and enchanted me so that I looked forward with a mixture of impatience and trepidation to the next cinema visit.

During the early thirties, we saw a lot of German and Austrian films — these were either highly artificial comedies in a remote world peopled by aristocrats, in which young men clicked their heels and bowed ceremoniously, young girls curtsied and giggled, and love was a healthy and absolutely unerotic activity, or they were extremely gloomy stories that claimed to be realistic and psychologically subtle. Thus, I remember a film with a little girl whose wicked father pursues her in her nightmares and fantasies — she wanders at night in a forest, where the trunk of every tree turns into the grimace of her father's distorted face. The more frantically she runs to and fro trying to escape, the closer those dreadful trunks close in on her so that she finally collapses in a feverish faint. In the end, she dies — whether she is really ill or succumbs to her paranoid fears, I do not know, but in afterlife she ascends a vast staircase to heaven where she is welcomed by a host of angels. Another film begins with a woman throwing herself from a bridge and being rescued by a rich couple; the woman attempts to commit suicide because she is pregnant and her husband unemployed. As the rich couple is childless, they offer to buy the penniless unemployed pair a farm, in return for which it is agreed that they will let them adopt their child as soon as it is weaned. After the birth of the child, the mother's love for her baby becomes so overpowering that she cannot bear the thought of being parted from it. As the days pass (symbolically illustrated by the tearing of one calendar leaf after another), she grows so desperate that on the scheduled day, she wraps a shawl around the baby and, holding it in her arms, walks into the sea as the tide comes in. I cannot remember whether the film ends on this tragic note or whether her husband rescues her and the rich couple is so moved that they relinquish their claim without demanding repayment of their money, but I definitely know that this story, in which the maternal instinct has such irresistible force, made a strong impact on me.

Hollywood films were of course in a completely different category. Very early on, we saw the first Tarzan film with Johnny Weissmüller. The world of the jungle, full of exotic dangers, was one with which I was to grow familiar over the coming years when I saw all the sequels to this initial film plus endless variations on the theme, among them Dorothy Lamour as the "Jungle Princess"; but this does not mean that I grew less scared of the manifold dangers lurking in these exotic forests. As soon as a snake was shown uncoiling its sinister body as it glided toward its victim (usually the heroine), or a crocodile or cayman shot out of the shady corner of a stagnant pool to snap at a native, a fearful fascination petrified me. On the other hand, Tarzan's characteristic ululating cry was strangely thrilling and struck a primeval chord, evoking the virility of primitive man.

Another genre was the gangster film; in particular, I remember one in which the hero escapes from prison and a manhunt is initiated to recapture him. Silvie Sidney, with her slightly Chinese cast of features, is his partner, and the film ends tragically with the death of the hero.

Then there were the Cecil B. DeMille movies with their giant casts and spectacular pageantry. One of them is situated in ancient Rome and Egypt. In one episode, slaves are tortured in dark cellars in which fires are kept raging to heat the instruments. This sequence aroused a fearful dread in my soul that was to haunt me in my lonely hours when I lay awake in the evenings. The film has an impressively solemn ending: Cleopatra, played by Claudette Colbert, seated on a throne, opens a casket from which she lifts vipers that she lays to her bosom.

We went to popular cinemas where the prices were cheaper than in the splendid buildings where films had their first showings in Antwerp. These cheap cinemas nonetheless aspired to be palaces of entertainment; oversized photos of film stars lined the entrance hall and the corridors and stairs leading to the auditorium, creating an aura of extraordinary anticipation, so that one felt as if one were entering a temple. The film copies were old. It frequently "rained" copiously on the screen, and every now and then the film tore. This was immediately greeted by loud hoots and whistles on the part of the audience, as if the cacophony would expedite the mending of the reel. When Pathé's newsreels were shown and we saw first Mussolini and later Hitler, the public reacted even more violently. They hissed and stamped in a manner that left one in no doubt as to where their sympathies lay. Jenny thought Mussolini funny and enjoyed his appearances as a kind of comic interlude provided by a gifted clown.

Bo liked undubbed German and Austrian films best, because she could follow their plots unaided, Yiddish being a close relative of their language. When American or French films were shown, Jenny acted as interpreter, explaining *sotto voce* what was going on, and since she preferred to see films that were not dubbed, I likewise benefited from this running commentary, so that I really got the gist of the action at this early age, before I was able to read subtitles.

Belgian laws of censorship were very strict, and as soon as there was the slightest hint of immorality or indecency, children were refused entrance. However, the definition of a child was that it must be six years old; under that age, children were regarded as imbeciles incapable of understanding what was going on, and thus incorruptible. As I was small, and age was gauged on the basis of physical size, I managed to get into films that were forbidden for children until I was eight or nine years old. I am, incidentally, a living example of how misguided this theory was. I soon grasped the import of illicit love, and although I had no notion of the sexual act, every time the man's mouth moved slowly, to the accompaniment of appropriate music, toward the woman's willing lips, I was keenly aware of the pleasure these passionate embraces must afford. Bo found such scenes revolting and would indignantly comment, "Shoyn wieder kischen sie sech!" (They're kissing again!)

One film that she approved of wholeheartedly was *Little Women*. She liked it so much that she went to see it whenever it was shown, so that over a period of a few years, I saw it four times. Katharine Hepburn as Jo was as irresistible as the character in Louisa Alcott's book, and I developed a strong liking and respect for this actress.

Another film had a totally nefarious effect on my fantasies; this was *The Invisible Man*, the plot of which imprinted itself deeply on my childish mind. A sinister traveler, muffled in a greatcoat, voluminous shawl, and hat drawn deeply over his eyes, which one does not see through his dark glasses, arrives in a small country hotel. He is heavily bandaged; one sees nothing of the features of his face or any other part of his body: no hands, no feet, only clothes. At one point, the bandages unwrap to reveal nothing, while the invisible man's voice mocks the horrified onlookers. He proceeds to terrify the populations of entire regions and towns, killing and maiming as he tries to establish his evil power. At long last, a policeman manages to kill him, and the last shot shows him slowly materializing physically. Well do I remember Jenny's astonished remark: "But he's handsome!" We had all naively imagined that his looks must have matched his loathsome deeds.

2. THE INVISIBLE MAN

The Invisible Man proceeded to haunt me regularly over the coming years. When I lay awake in bed, afraid to fall asleep because I felt sleep to be akin to death and extinction, I felt sure that he was in the room with me, and I knew that it was no use to get up and look whether he was hiding under the bed I shared with my mother, since, after all, I would not see him even if he were there. I perversely heightened my fear by throwing off the eiderdown and the pile of pillows onto the floor, only to put them back in place precipitously and then hide, huddling under the cover.

The Invisible Man had such a hold over me because he stood for the missing element in our exclusively female household. Men were absent and yet present at the same time. Jenny not only went out dancing in pursuit of the male; she brought lovers home late in the evening, and they lay down on the sofa in the living room and switched off the light, and then dark and dreadful things took place. Bo was always making terrible scenes on this account. She called Jenny a whore, a term for which she had many synonyms at her disposal, and went on to curse her daughter with a seemingly inexhaustible repertoire of dire imprecations. The Yiddish idiom boasts an extraordinarily rich vocabulary in this domain. I was witness to these poisonous altercations, and I felt that the walls of our flat were shaking and the world was coming to an end.

And what was the cause of all this tumult? A man. No wonder men loomed in the shadows, and there too lurked my father. Jenny nursed a profound hatred for him; she could not forgive him for having let her down during her pregnancy and the long days when she was on the brink of dying after my birth.

I was three years old when the following incident occurred: I was sitting on the toilet (another place where I felt that I was in great danger, as I believed I might fall into the bowl and be flushed away), and there was no paper available with which to wipe my bottom. Jenny fetched her engagement photograph, tore it down the middle, thus severing her face from Simon's, and then wiped me clean with his likeness.

Yet somewhere inside me I also harbored a kinder image of the man who was my father. Many years later, I found out that he had warmly taken me into his arms at my birth, accepting me more wholeheartedly than Jenny had. Even during my childhood, I cherished the memory of two or three experiences that had a very gentle quality about them and were linked to two visits he paid me, the first of which took place when I was two and a half years old. During that summer, Aunt Sarah was running a boarding house at the seaside, and, to add to her complications (or perhaps at her own suggestion?), Bo and Jenny sent me there — no doubt to have me out of the way for a few weeks and also perhaps in the vague hope that the sea air would fortify the puny and ailing child I was. The boarding house was quite a distance from the sea, and I vaguely remember that I found the way to the beach long and arduous. One day, my father came to see me, no doubt taking advantage of the opportunity not to have to meet Jenny at the same time. I do not recall anything about the hours that we spent together except that he bought me ice cream, for which like all children I was always begging. He did not buy me a normal child's portion but, to show how fond he was of me, an enormous plateful. On the next day, I was plagued by acute stomach pains and lay, well covered with blankets, on a deck chair on the balcony, while the guests came one after another to commiserate with me. But while they extended sympathy for the sick child, they could not help laughing at the foolishness of the departed father — "typical of a man" was the general verdict.

He also came to see me once in Antwerp, and I once found a snapshot commemorating the occasion — a dreamy, good-looking young man holding a thin little girl in his arms in the park on the outskirts of the town to which he had taken me. I remember he took his watch out of his waistcoat pocket and held it to my ear so that I could hear it ticking — tick-tock, tick-tock.

How little this is with which to form a real attachment! How could I develop anything remotely resembling a normal daughter's relationship to her father? Then, one day, he was suddenly dead. Jenny discovered this by reading a three-line notice in the newspaper stating that Belgium's chess champion, Simon Silberschatz, had died. He was barely thirty-three years old, and I had just turned five — we were both Pisces, a sign doomed to be unlucky in love and with no great capacity for fighting. Bo, in an attempt to express sympathy with my grandfather's bereavement, took me to Brussels to visit him.

That was my last contact with my father's family.

3. THE CHILDREN'S HOME

I think it was from this point of time that I was beset by yet another fear. I was afraid of being the victim of a sham death and being put in a coffin. I imagined waking up after the burial, lying stifled, unable to scream, unable to move — interred alive, doomed to remain in a dark abyss of helplessness, darkness, and aloneness, until real death set in.

Thus it was that my aunt's prediction came true. Jenny did not need to get a divorce anymore — at the age of twenty-four, she too was a widow.

I loved her, I adored her, and I believed her to be the most beautiful woman in the world. Not only did I worship her physical presence, but her temperament and imaginativeness also fascinated me. She invented rituals that were the essence of delight. As a very small child, I had a bath once a week in a tin tub filled with warm water, on which occasion my hair was also washed. She then wrapped me in a large towel, folding it round and round my thin wet body and, after she had converted me into a bundle, deposited me under the table, whereupon she switched off the light and went out of the room to return a few seconds later and pretend to look for me. I cannot explain why this filled me with such deep, exquisite pleasure, but I do not think that I have had many experiences since then that have afforded me anything like the pure joy I felt lying in the dark, waiting for her to come in, pretending not to know where I was and then pouncing upon me and claiming me as her own.

When I accompanied her on her shopping sprees, usually on a Saturday when she had the day or at least the afternoon off, she played various games with me. One was to give marks for elegance to all the women we met. She looked at them with piercingly critical eyes, and I learned to adopt her standards and to anticipate her judgments. One year, fox furs were all the rage (Jenny got one herself, and I remember how uncomfortable the glass eyes of the dead animal made me feel); women wrapped them round their neck and shoulders over the jackets of the rather masculine costumes they wore. We took to counting them to see how soon we could run up a score of a hundred.

At a very early stage, I became her confidante, whom she regaled with stories of her numerous infatuations, for she was perpetually falling in love with her dancing partners. She pledged me to absolute secrecy — which I faithfully kept, I never betrayed her — in particular, toward Bo, who probably never suspected that I was the repository of such unlikely confessions. But all these affairs were short-lived and superficial; she had what I can only call a kind of perverse genius in finding men who were out to have an ephemeral spot of fun. They soon tired of her charms and failed to turn up at the appointed times and places. She took these desertions tragically and spent hours in bed crying her heart out. But after a couple of days, she would recover and sally forth, ready for fresh conquests.

Her taste in clothes was a mixture of fashionable and individual elements. In those days, ready-made dresses in big stores were shoddy. Most women bought a length of cloth and went to a dressmaker. After Jenny had purchased such material, whether in a big department store, a small shop, or from a market stand, she would start on her journey to whatever dressmaker she happened to be patronizing at the time. She discovered a great many over the course of my childhood years, but they all seem to have met one common requirement: they lived very far away from where we happened to reside. She dragged me on interminable journeys on foot (for we never took a tram), invariably believing that she had hit upon a short cut to our destination. This, however, always turned out to be the most roundabout way of reaching our goal. I trailed alongside of her, staunchly keeping up because of my adoration of her sheer presence, while she stopped at regular intervals to take off her cheap, high-heeled and therefore ill-fitting, shoes to give momentary relief to her aching feet. When we finally found the desired address, she would sit with the dressmaker — I remember them as young women — in an unheated dining room, which was obviously only used on Sundays or when visitors came, for at least half an hour,

3. THE CHILDREN'S HOME

before she made it clear exactly what it was that she wanted. The dressmaker had one or two of the latest fashion magazines — Jenny looked at various designs, but never once did she choose to copy one as it was depicted. No, the top part of one drawing was combined with the skirt of another, and for the sleeves she had recourse to yet a third pattern. The result was never simple; she was fond of frills and *ruches*, presumably because she thought they enhanced her femininity. She also aimed at originality, which she undoubtedly achieved, but real elegance, which shuns superfluous trimmings, eluded her.

Even though the loss of a lover would cause her to cry for hours on end, plunging her into the depths of apparent blackest despair, she was fundamentally cheerful, and this in spite of the fact that her life was really rather dreary. She managed to enjoy the small pleasures it afforded, and while in retrospect I can see that she was an efficient secretary who never lost a job on account of inadequate performance, but solely because the firm for which she happened to work went bankrupt in the Depression years, what impressed me — no doubt because this was what I actually saw — was her capacity for laziness on her days off. Mornings were spent luxuriating in bed, sleeping in a kind of absolute abandon, her body relaxed and exuding a wonderful animal warmth. I was then unable to understand the attraction of this kind of sleep, for I was afraid of falling asleep and becoming a prey to nightmares, out of whose clutches I had yet found no escape. A particularly harrowing recurring experience was to dream that I was paralyzed, my mouth unable to voice any sounds. Somehow in my sleep, I realized that I was dreaming and wanted to wake up; yet in spite of desperate efforts to do so, I did not succeed. Feeling bound and gagged, I finally managed by dint of an excruciating exertion to tear myself from the bonds of that terrible realm and to return to the normal everyday world where I was able to speak and move at will.

I still shared Jenny's bed and lay alone awake for long hours in the evenings, waiting for her to join me, which she did at about half past ten. She always read before switching off the light, and I claimed the right to turn the pages for her. Captivated by her English novels, she usually forgot to tell me when she reached the bottom of the page, and when she turned the leaf, I became very cross and insisted that she go back so that I could do it for her. Before falling asleep, I always climbed over her to fall down on the other side of her body. This was a compulsion, a ritual that had come about I know not how.

But there was a second powerful deity who determined the course of my childhood — Bo — and possibly her influence went deeper. After all, Jenny spent the greater part of her days at work, and evenings were allotted to courses providing her with additional qualifications. I suppose that she filled the place of the father in a normal family, while Bo assumed the functions of a mother. She was a fat, hefty woman with thinning gray hair and a broad face. There is a snapshot taken when I was four years old at some popular seaside resort, probably Blankenberghe. We are walking toward one of those professional street photographers who sell their snapshots at cheap prices. Her hair is blowing in the wind; she wears sensible white linen shoes, a long skirt, and a cardigan, and looks enormous beside the thin, puny child, with its peaked little face, who trustfully holds her hand.

She dominated our daily life, which was punctuated by loud, dramatic scenes that filled me with terror. Jenny's amorous escapades regularly provided the pretext for Bo's explosive, venomous attacks, always richly larded with dreadful curses and imprecations. I do not think that Jenny was frightened of her, but I was a trembling witness who never got inured to the furious torrents of ill-wishing that flowed from Bo's mouth. Because it instilled in me a great fear of being bad myself and of the consequent terrible punishments that must be meted out, the faint promptings to rebel against authority that any child may reasonably be expected to entertain were stifled so thoroughly that I was not even aware of having suppressed them.

During those early years, Bo fell ill repeatedly, and she exploited the dramatic potentialities this afforded to the full. I do not know what ailed her, but I think she had heart trouble, and her varicose veins were so inflamed that she had to take to her bed. When members of the family came to visit her, she would cry hysterically, "I'm dying! I'm dying!" I usually lurked behind the door, one part of me scared stiff and

3. THE CHILDREN'S HOME

Bo and Huguette 1932

another beset with faint doubts as to whether the whole performance was not really a superb melodramatic masquerade.

Bo was not unkind to me. She never slapped or really punished me, in spite of the daily tussles we had as she tried to get me to swallow some food in her vain attempt to get some flesh onto my skinny frame. When I was ill, she looked after me well enough for me to relish the comforts of being nursed. On the one hand, she was inordinately proud of my intelligence, and when I demonstrated this by some precocious remark, she commented approvingly; "a welt auf dei keppele," which literally means "A world on your little head," and implies that a universe of learning and wisdom is contained in the child's small skull. On the other hand, when she called me "Rebb' Iget" (Rabbi Huguette), she was being ironic. Another derogatory appellation was "oisgedarrte hering" (desiccated herring), with which she alluded to my unprepossessing appearance.

I accompanied her when she went shopping or visited relatives. She liked to drink tea and eat cake in the cafés of big department stores. I was then let loose to roam the various departments, and I made a beeline for the toy section, where I stared in wonder at hundreds of dolls of all sizes, all of them with those glassy eyes and that vacuous expression in their supposedly pretty faces which gives them such a lifeless look. I coveted them, well aware that we had no money to buy one, but actually

I had no use for them, as I discovered when by chance some relative gave me one. I had no idea what to do with it, and, although I had no other toys to speak of, the doll was left neglected in a corner. I spent hours playing with Jenny's cheap jewelry and trinkets, arranging the necklaces, rings, and bracelets on the table as if they were displayed for sale in a shop window. Another pastime involved my washing two or three handkerchiefs, soaping and rinsing them enthusiastically, thus satisfying a deep urge to cleanse myself of innate dirt.

For my fourth birthday, Aunt Sarah, who lived nearby, organized a big celebration. In the afternoon, children were invited for a party, and in the evening I was put to bed (which I felt to be grossly unfair, since after all it was in my honor that all this was being organized), while adults trooped in for the social junketing. A big laundry basket had been placed near the entrance, and there people dropped their gifts. This must have brought me the doll. There was also a book teaching one how to read the time; it showed a little boy going through various routines at the appointed hours, and on the back cover it displayed a clock with dials that you could move. But a large proportion of the presents consisted of useful articles of clothing, including underwear, and while these were undoubtedly sensible contributions to a poor household periodically beset by unemployment, I did not appreciate them and felt personally cheated.

At an early age I learned to play a card game called "Totsch" with Bo and developed a passion for it. Although it involved some luck, it required concentration rather than intelligence, as the flagging of attention benefited the other player, so my chances of winning were normally very good. Jenny, assailed by dire memories of Simon's addiction to card games, looked upon this askance, but as she was usually away at work, she did not have much opportunity to intervene.

I played a lot with other children in the street or wherever else I found an opportunity to strike up an acquaintance. At that stage of my life, shyness was a phenomenon I observed with astonishment in other children — I was not familiar with it and boldly went up to little girls I saw to ask whether they would play with me. Mysteriously, Bo had acquired an entrance ticket for the zoo, allowing her to enter free of charge for several years. When the weather was fine, she

3. THE CHILDREN'S HOME

regularly went there and usually sat on the outer edge of the benches or rows of chairs surrounding a kiosk where bands occasionally gave free concerts, consisting of *potpourris* of Strauss waltzes, Schubert marches, and airs from French operettas, as well as melodies from popular films. These were rarely given on weekdays, and it was a peaceful place for her to sit and knit. As soon as she was installed, I went in search of a companion, and when I had sighted a little girl of my age, I unhesitatingly approached her.

Together with such a playmate, but also when I was alone, I explored the zoo. I watched the apes and gorillas, the lions and tigers, and occasionally even ventured into the reptiles' domain, where the air was humid and hot. The serpents that were coiled around the branches of trees, their discarded whitish skins often hanging beside them, and the scaly crocodiles floating in stagnant pools fascinated me into a state of hypnotic dread, so that after a few minutes I fled from this building with something approaching terror. Once outside, I frequently watched children whose parents had the money to spend on such luxuries ride on elephants or donkeys. Although I liked the elephants, I preferred to keep at a respectful distance from them, so that when I was once offered the treat of riding myself, I was too cowardly to agree to let myself be lifted on one, though I was content to be hoisted upon the back of a donkey.

Despite these frequent visits to the zoo, I developed no real relationship with animals. They remained a type of being totally alien and separate from me, at best harmless, at worst threatening and dangerous. In the house where we then lived, I occasionally played with a little boy whose family lived on the ground floor. They must have been fairly well off, and he had a lot of toys. Among these, there was, in particular, a metal construction set that I secretly coveted. One afternoon we were playing in the garden when we discovered a worm inching toward the house. The prospect of it surmounting the minuscule step separating the garden from the forecourt and of it then getting into the house seemed intolerable. Shortly before it reached this small elevation, the boy said that he was going to kill the worm and pressed his shoe upon the slimy thing. We were confident that this would do the trick, but when he lifted his foot, the worm resumed its squirming progress, and when it began to scale the step with the front part of its body, a great panic seized us both, and we ran into the house up all the flights of stairs until we stood trembling in the well space in front of the attic doors, and even then we were not sure that this loathsome monster would not catch up with us and perpetrate some unnameable horror upon us helpless children.

Above us — we lived on the second floor — resided a family structured similarly to my own: grandmother, mother, and daughter. The little girl was about my age, but there the similarity ended, for she was fat, very fat indeed. Her mother and grandmother doted inordinately upon her, and they could think of no better way of demonstrating their love than to continually press her to eat prodigally, plying her lavishly with cake and chocolates. The story, sadly, has a moral: she fell ill and died within a few days, the diagnosis being that her heart was so smothered in fat that it could not function anymore. Apparently, overfeeding had more lethal consequences than my refusal to eat.

One summer Jenny had me sent off to a kind of boarding institution in the country, where — it was thought — I might gain weight and become sturdier. I think she really wanted a few weeks' freedom in order to go on holiday with some other young people, and Bo was not averse to be relieved of the responsibility of looking after me for a short while. The home in question was situated in the flatlands of Flanders; I was herded there with other children and looked after by young women who spoke Flemish, of which I only understood a few words. We slept in dormitories and were taken out for long walks in the moor-like countryside. During my stay there, I had a very strong *déjà vu* experience. We came one day to a sandy patch of land with small hillocks from which tufted grass grew in bunches; an eerie feeling of recognizing the place, while knowing that I had never been there before, overcame me and occupied my thoughts for a long time.

At the end of the first week, an announcement was made while we were having our midday meal, which I understood to mean that anyone who wanted to do so could go to the "kirmes" on Sunday. I took this to be an invitation to visit a local fair and raised my arm to be included in the group. To my horror, I found myself shepherded to a church (I had confused the words "kirmes" and "kerk"). We sat down in the front rows. Subjected to the utterly unfamiliar rite of a Catholic mass, I felt like a traitor to my Jewish family. Absolutely at a loss, I had no option but to kneel and rise with the other children, who had some notion of what had to be done. What terrified me most was the sermon of a priest who mounted the pulpit to engage in fulminating imprecations against the sins committed by the members of the congregation. Without understanding the actual words, I nonetheless gathered the underlying import of his rolling sentences — and as he spat profusely while speaking, drops of his saliva landed on my forehead and cheeks, making me inwardly quail.

Wise now to what awaited me, I did not repeat my mistake on the next Sundays but chose to stay in the dreary building where we were housed. Once we were given a treat, and for about an hour, early Charlie Chaplin silent films were projected onto a screen hung in the refectory. But since in those days I could not find them either funny (physical disasters failed to amuse me) or tragic, and was used to more sophisticated Hollywood fare, they failed to divert me. It only served to increase my nostalgia for home and our wonderful weekly visits to the cinema.

At the end of the summer, I returned home; and in the spring of 1933, we were indirectly affected by the upheaval that was taking place in Germany.

4. THE PREVENTORIUM

Chiffra and her second husband were, as may be remembered, living in Leipzig. Soon after the Nazis had seized power, my cousin Silvie stood on the steps of their house and a procession of SS men was seen approaching. Fearing that she might be molested, her stepfather Nathan was about to hurry her inside when the group of men, seeing that they had a Jew before them, fell upon him and beat him up. Bruised and insulted, he went to see the British consul on the next day to ask for redress. The latter told him in no uncertain terms that while he was, indeed, able to arrange for the group of SS men to be summoned so that he could identify the culprits, he could not guarantee that Nathan would not a few days later be found murdered in some dark alley. He advised him in fact to break up his household and return to England. This presented no problems for Nathan, or for Chiffra, who had become British as a result of her marriage, or for his own three children from his former marriage. But Silvie had retained her father's nationality and did not hold a British passport. On their way to London, the whole family arrived in Antwerp, staying there for only a couple of days; but when they departed, Silvie remained with us until she would be granted an entrance permit so that she could rejoin her mother and the rest of the family.

Our household was thus temporarily enlarged. Silvie was twelve years old but looked a rising sixteen — she was blond, slim, and very pretty indeed, and during the few months that she stayed with us, I felt that I had an older sister. When the neighbor's boy tried to bully me, she took hold of him and whirled him round and round until he felt so dizzy he was obliged to abjectly give in. This display of strength on my behalf delighted me — I had never had a champion before.

4. THE PREVENTORIUM

I grew very fond of her, although I was faintly puzzled by, and also a little envious of, the praises and compliments she got from one and all. In my opinion, it was quite superfluous to comment continually on the fact that she looked so much older than her real age and was, moreover, so attractive. When her permit arrived and she departed, she left the memory of a lovely young girl in a summery cotton dress, her face shaded by a wide-brimmed straw hat. She had developed a protective affection for me, and for many months she regularly sent me lurid English postcards showing supposedly humorous scenes of children up to the usual scrapes. One of them struck me as particularly apt — it showed a fat little girl lustily thumping away on the piano, an activity in which I also indulged. I was unable to read the undoubtedly witty caption, but I saw the point nonetheless.

During the same fateful year, Aunt Golda, Uncle Yeshurun, and my cousin Isy moved to Brussels. They closed the shop on the Pelikanstraat and left the flat they had occupied in the vicinity of the Place des Nerviens, a square bearing the name of a Belgian tribe that had offered heroic, and I believe partly successful, resistance to the Romans, an event commemorated by a gigantic statue of a group of naked pagan warriors whose muscular bodies were entwined in various contorted postures of warlike acts, which greatly impressed me. The flat itself consisted of a suite of rooms, which I must have seen mostly at night, for I remember them as somber and dim. We did not go there very often, Golda and Yeshurun's interests differing widely from ours so that they led a private life utterly alien to our traditional ghetto existence. My cousin Isy, five years older than I, was a member of the Boy Scouts, and Bo and Jenny admiringly told everybody that he could prepare himself a meal of scrambled eggs all by himself — this was regarded as an accomplishment that bordered on the miraculous in a boy of that age.

This part of the family was well on its way to total assimilation, and I felt them to be completely different from our other relatives. Bo was one of the youngest of no less than thirteen siblings, and a whole tribe of nephews and nieces and their progeny had also settled in Antwerp. I never understood the ramifications of this clan that at weddings found no difficulty in assembling four hundred members. I was particularly confused by the fact that she had a niece, the daughter of one of her

Part I. A CHILDHOOD IN ANTWERP

Isy, Golda, Yeshurun, Jenny, Huguette

oldest brothers, who was a year older than she and nonetheless called her "Aunt," which greatly puzzled me. Many of these relatives were Orthodox as my grandfather had been, but others varied greatly in the degree to which they adhered to religious laws. Bo kept a kosher kitchen and went to the synagogue on the traditional feast days, though not on ordinary Sabbaths. She was able to read Hebrew and to follow the service, mumbling the prayers along with the rest of the congregation, but she did not understand the text any more than most Catholics then understood their Latin liturgy. Jenny never went to the synagogue (except for weddings), as she considered herself to be a pagan atheist or an atheist pagan. She maintained that she worshipped the sun.

But I was well aware of the fact that as Jews living in a Christian environment, we were set apart. We then lived on the edge of a distinct Jewish area which was centrally located in Antwerp; there were about a dozen streets forming a kind of voluntary ghetto with an atmosphere reminiscent of an East European "shtetl." The shops — and there were many of them in those days, when the supermarket was unknown even in the United States — sold Jewish food: sauerkraut that was taken, dripping with juice, out of great wooden casks, glistening black olives, for which Jenny had a great predilection; cheesecake; wonderful "halahs," the white Sabbath bread; "beigels," a kind of roll best described as a miniature halah, halva; and, of course, kosher meat and poultry. In these shops, as well as on the busy streets, the language commonly spoken was Yiddish. Most of the inhabitants of this section were poor, the more prosperous Jews, who more often than not engaged in the diamond trade, having moved into modern apartments in more elegant parts of the town.

The main thoroughfares of Antwerp had a slightly cosmopolitan atmosphere. The Pelikanstraat, a busy commercial street, where the Diamond Exchange was situated, was also largely frequented by Jews. More or less at a right angle to it, leading away from the railway station, runs the Keizerlei, Antwerp's main street. It was lined by hotels, cafés, department stores, and smart shops and was the place where Belgians and Jews alike congregated. Sitting at a table outside a café, one could watch the passersby for hours on end, study the women's fashions, note which acquaintances were coming along, and gossip interminably.

But outside these areas, Antwerp was a Catholic town, where Flemish was the official language, and on my peregrinations with Jenny, when she went shopping or on her pilgrimages to whatever cheap dressmaker she happened to be patronizing at that particular moment, we trudged through back streets; these frequently had a niche halfway up a corner wall in which stood a statue of either a sentimental and strangely insipid Madonna holding the infant Jesus in her arms, or an imposing Christ clad in a long white robe and with outspread arms to bring the faithful into the fold— they belonged to a different world from the one in which I was born, and I felt a vague threat emanating from these stone statues. They imperiously demanded conformity, and I feared that if I remained Jewish a terrible retribution would one day be wreaked on me. A longing to belong to these strange people battled with the realization that I was the target of dark proselytizing attacks emanating from these deceptively sweet figures.

In 1934, we moved yet again, twice within a year. In the second flat, we had an invasion of mice. In our first, we had on one occasion been the victims of a massed onslaught of bed-lice — I remember a night in which Bo and Jenny switched the light on at increasingly frequent intervals to try to destroy the conglomerations of black crawling insects by crushing them, an endeavor so ineffectual that they had had to call upon the services of a professional pest controller. In the case of the mouse problem, Bo herself took action. She poured a kettle of boiling water upon a group of baby mice. I was rent by contradictory feelings of gratification over being rid of the disgusting intruders, and a remote awareness of pitiful horror upon hearing their thin squeals.

This action took place in the living room, which was on the ground floor. We slept upstairs, and next to our bedroom lived an English boarder. Lying awake in the long evenings, I could hear his wireless through the partition — he tuned in to English plays, which consisted of interminable dialogues, punctuated by sobbing — it all sounded highly dramatic and very earnest. Were no comedies broadcast in those days?

I played a lot in the neighboring park and was always falling over when taking part in running games. This started the era of bruised knees that was to last for the next five or six years. Jenny believed in the virtues of iodine and mercilessly pressed a cloth soaked with this vile stuff on my knee. An obedient child, I lay in bed suffering and crying, but one evening, even my docile disposition could stand it no longer, and in what was for me a great act of rebellion I threw the wet towel that was inflicting such stinging and burning pain on my wound on the floor. After that, Jenny took to using hydrogen peroxide bandages; these did not hurt so much when initially applied, but had a tendency to dry and then stick to the caking wound, and as Jenny believed in removing the dressing with one abruptly brutal pull, while I wanted her to delicately detach it millimeter by millimeter from the patch of healing skin underneath, she had to chase me round the table so as to get hold of me for her drastic purpose. But I am anticipating — these were operations that were performed later, when we had moved to the Rembrandtstraat.

Before this happened, we lived for the better part of a year in yet another flat, in the vicinity of the one where we had had the mice

4. THE PREVENTORIUM

invasion. Here Jenny came home one day at dinnertime to announce a double tragedy: she had again lost her job, owing to the firm being bankrupt; and Queen Astrid had died in a car accident. This was discussed at great length during the next few weeks. The king had been driving and was bending over to consult a map when he lost control of the car, which hit a tree. Had the chauffeur, who was sitting behind, been driving, he would undoubtedly have had to stand trial. At our next visit to the cinema, we saw a newsreel showing the funeral procession with King Leopold, his injured arm in a sling, following the coffin to the lugubrious sounds of Chopin's *Marche Funèbre*.

During childhood, I frequently suffered from chronic feverish illnesses aggravated by a sore throat. In those days, it was thought that the proper method to treat this was to brush the throat with a wooden spatula covered with cotton wool soaked in a healing tincture. I was in mortal terror that the blob of cotton wool might get unstuck so that I would choke. Only by dint of endless coaxing and cajoling could I be persuaded to open my mouth while I squintingly watched the procedure with wary, fearful eyes.

We consulted a doctor who enjoyed an almost legendary reputation as a model of kindness and medical skill and did not demand a fee from the poor. When he saw my swollen tonsils, he declared that they must be removed, and a date was fixed for this dreadful event. I was convinced that it might well bring about my early death; Jenny and Bo ineffectually tried to console me by telling me that I could have a big portion of ice cream after the operation, since this was supposed to hasten the healing process.

The dreaded morning arrived, and I sat in the kitchen watching the preliminaries for the operation. Whatever other virtues he had, Dr. Baatjes was not a good psychologist, for he proceeded to unpack his arsenal of gleaming surgical instruments in front of the victim huddling before him in her nightdress. I was then told to lie down on the kitchen table and was forcibly held there while Dr. Baatjes's assistant applied a steel contraption holding a cloth soaked with chloroform over my face, while I was ordered to start counting aloud. I got as far as sixteen or seventeen, and then Bo and Jenny, who were crouching on the staircase, heard me scream. I felt myself falling into a black gulf of nothingness. When I woke up, my throat was a vast expanse of soreness. In the afternoon, I was persuaded to gingerly swallow a few spoonfuls of ice cream, which I vomited soon after. The promised reward turned out to be a great swindle, providing none of the delights that had been dangled before me.

After a few weeks, we visited Dr. Baatjes's surgery for a checkup. He had told Jenny and Bo that he had never before removed such enormous tonsils, and presumably they had left correspondingly big gaping wounds. He lived far away from our flat, which was near the center of the town. We got there at about four o'clock and settled down in an extremely crowded waiting room full of dark furniture and plush-covered chairs. I hadn't yet learned to read, and boredom made the passage of time seem interminable. It was close to midnight when our turn at last came. Dr. Baatjes made me say a long-drawn-out "Aaah," while he peered into my throat and stated after thirty seconds that all was well, whereupon he dismissed us so that we could go home. When we left, the waiting room was still half full, and, as we trudged home through the dark and strangely quiet streets of the sleeping town, I began to appreciate the point of an anecdote that was being bandied about in Antwerp with great relish: Dr. Baatjes had recently become the father of twins, but the mystery to be solved was, when had he found the leisure to beget them?

I should have started going to school soon after the removal of my tonsils, but I fell ill again. That is to say, this time, it was apparently only a minor ailment, over the course of which I ran a light temperature every evening, so that the doctor's verdict after a few days was that I was probably prone to such deviations from the normal, and Jenny and Bo should pay no further attention to them. However, soon after that the skin on my hands began — to my great delight — to peel, and the doctor was now able to make a belated diagnosis: he announced that I had scarlet fever, so I was put into quarantine and could not start school punctually.

When I was allowed to mix with children again, Jenny took me to the nearest school, where I joined the first form a month or two after the official beginning of the school year. I was completely at sea, for I was put into a Flemish-speaking class and could not understand what was going on. All that I remember is that other little girls were regularly asked to climb onto the platform where the teacher sat and to point with a long stick at words written on the blackboard or at objects on luridly colored demonstration placards. I felt abjectly stupid and utterly isolated.

Antwerp had initiated a policy aimed at banishing French from public life wherever possible. The Flemish part of the population was asserting itself after a century of what it felt to have been the arrogant domination of the Walloons. This even led to the ludicrous step of removing the French words for "entrance" and "exit" in the hall of the railway station, so that people arriving from abroad were confronted only with Flemish information.

In the elementary schools, the first language in which tuition was given would, as a rule, be Flemish and not French. Seeing that I was unable to learn anything in a language that I did not understand, Jenny moved heaven and earth to arrange for me to repeat my first year in a class in which French was the first language spoken (a few such classes had been retained for privileged families), and she finally succeeded.

Like someone whose limbs had been numbed by frost who is at last able to start reviving in a warm bath, I basked in hearing sentences I was able to follow, and began to take a keen interest in the letters written on the blackboard. How pleased I was when I was able to put them together to form words, and when I finally read, unaided, the first sentence in the primer (which was "RIRI A RI," Riri has laughed, a vacuous statement that seemed to me vaguely witty). From then on, I continually practiced this new skill with growing enthusiasm. I felt immensely proud when I managed to read the difficult title of a film displayed in a perpendicular banner outside a cinema, "La Veuve joyeuse" (The Merry Widow), the sequence of letters "oyeu" constituting a particularly complicated hurdle. Jenny encouraged me to read by regularly bringing me a weekly children's magazine, *Le Journal de Bébé* (*Baby's Paper*) and soon afterward *La Semaine de Suzette* (*Suzette's Week*), both of which engrossed me for many hours, for I was not yet able to read fluently.

At this point, my school career, such as it was, temporarily came to an end. My frequent illnesses had caused Jenny to have recourse to the social services provided by her trade union or some similar association, which sent ailing children for a longer period to the seaside where they were supposed to become healthy and robust, thanks to the invigorating bracing air and wholesome food. Not only my poor health but also my extreme skinniness indubitably qualified me for a spell in such a home, which was called — by analogy with a sanatorium — a preventorium, and was located in Wenduine, a small seaside resort not far from Ostend.

I arrived there on the twentieth of September, 1934, and found myself in an institution that had an unmistakable resemblance to an orphanage. Upon arrival, I was provided with a summer uniform; but on the very next day, I was led together with all the other girls to the cloakroom, where members of the staff issued winter uniforms to us, in accordance with the date, which was the twenty-first of September, officially the first day of autumn.

We led a totally regimented life, sleeping in huge dormitories, eating in a refectory that was even bigger, and walking, whenever we went out, in file. In the mornings, we had school lessons; in the afternoons, we were conducted on long walks in the neighborhood — the landscape consisted of sandy hillocks tufted with bushes and clumps of trees vaguely resembling a sparse wood. There the mistresses organized games, before we reassembled in files of two by two to walk back to the home (what a misnomer!), singing as we went. We were clothed in black capes with hoods, which reinforced the feeling I had of being an orphan.

We had four meals a day, and after a few weeks one knew exactly what would be dished up every Monday, Tuesday, Wednesday, and so on. Some of these meals were a torture for the faddy little girl I was — in particular, I remember potato mash to which boiled leeks had been added so that they were inextricably embedded in the pulp. The mere sight of this revolted me, and my gorge rose at the thought of swallowing the shiny green fibers, and I developed some ingenuity in pulling them out as much as possible. My instruments were fork and spoon, since one only graduated to the use of a knife on one's eighth birthday. Our drinking water, which came from a local spring, had a rusty color and an unpleasant sweetish flavor owing to its high mineral contents; it was supposed to be good for one's health. The passage of time did nothing to make it more acceptable, but I was

4. THE PREVENTORIUM

able to take this in my stride while the rice boiled in milk became increasingly repulsive.

The worst time of day was when I was in bed before falling asleep; I cried my heart out as longing for Jenny and Bo overcame me. Mornings in the dormitory were often marked by dreadful scenes, for a few yards from me slept a little girl who regularly wet her bed. Her mother was the mistress in charge of our group (and I suspect a single mother or, possibly, a divorced or widowed one), and for fear of appearing to treat her daughter as a favorite, she went to the other extreme. But I think that she actually genuinely disliked her — at all events, there was such an outcry, such vituperation and scolding as made the rest of us quail and tremble in unison with the shivering bundle of guilt who had caused the commotion and who, out of sheer terror of her mother, was doomed to repeat her heinous crime the next night.

Our teacher in class was a young woman, and after a few weeks, I became her favorite as a result of the following incident. In the course of telling us the number of days a year has, she explained what a leap year is. The French words for this are "année bissextile," which is rather complicated for six-year-olds to memorize. Each girl was invited the next day to walk up onto the teacher's platform and whisper the words in her ear. Apparently, most of the pupils failed this test, but I passed it with flying colors and was greatly praised for this extraordinary feat of intelligence.

During the following weeks, I basked in the goodwill expended upon me. But alas, this heavenly state of affairs was of short duration. One day, our dinner was spoiled by oversalting, and everybody drank great amounts of mineral water to quench their thirst, which in turn resulted in an irresistible urge to pass water. One after the other, the girls asked to be allowed to go to the lavatories, until the teacher suspected she was up against an organized prank. When I felt that I must go too, she decided to put her foot down and refused to give me permission to leave the schoolroom. Soon afterward I felt my knickers become warmly wet as a stream of water poured downward to form a pool under my desk. What a scene the teacher made! I was ordered to fetch a pail of water and to mop up my mess, tears of hot shame (I had been a very "clean" little girl ever since I was a baby and not a little proud of it) flowing down my cheeks as I knelt to perform this menial task. Nor was I allowed to forget this humiliation, for the teacher reversed her former attitude and now made a great show of being so disgusted by my sheer presence that she kept me at a physical distance, and, when similar word tests were repeated, I was not allowed to come near her. I suffered acutely from being singled out for this ostracism and would have suffered more had there not been another little Jewish girl there, aged ten or eleven, who took to mothering me during breaks, which greatly soothed my bruised feelings. Unfortunately, her stay at the preventorium was soon at an end, and I was left alone again.

On some afternoons, we spent an hour in a bright room where books were handed out to us to read there and then. I was given a French translation of *Alice in Wonderland*, with notes at the bottom of the page to explain the puns and quips of the original text. I found this intolerably dull and took to turning the pages to look at the illustrations. When the mistress-in-charge noticed this, she confiscated the book and gave me another one, more suitable for a child of my age. It detailed the adventures of a Breton maid called "Bécassine" and was abundantly illustrated rather like a comic strip. In the same room, we wrote letters to our parents at home. The text of the letter was written on the blackboard to be copied by us so that it looked as if it had been individually drafted. It conveyed a message of content and happiness and gave no hint of being homesick. The parents' letters were subjected to a similar censorship before they reached us. Jenny sent me postcards that I carried in my apron pocket like a talisman. I once found one on a chair in a corridor, where, prompted by some obscure instinct, I picked it up to discover it was actually addressed to me. She asked whether I was in want of anything, and someone had penciled the words "does not need anything" over the text.

At monthly intervals, the parents were allowed to visit us on a Sunday; they arrived in coaches outside the home, where we gathered to watch them disembark. Jenny and Bo were always in the very last bus to appear, no doubt as a result of Jenny's chronic inability to be punctual. How tensely did I wait for them! And how drearily did we spend the precious day so eagerly awaited! We went to Ostend, which on these bleak autumnal and winter weekends was transformed from a popular resort to a provincial town with closed shops and empty streets, through which we walked endlessly in order to finally sit for long hours in an empty café staring out of the window and eating a cheap meal. To kill time, we went to a cinema that showed only newsreels and documentaries, a genre which in spite of my general addiction to the cinema I found unbearably boring and which I heartily detested. Then, all of a sudden, the day was at an end. At six o'clock, the buses departed for Antwerp, and I was left behind to achingly await the next visit.

At one point, I fell ill and was transferred to the sick bay, a large room subdivided into glass cubicles, each of them enclosing a bed, to ensure that each child was kept in sterile isolation. I must have been quite ill, for, apart from a general awareness of frigid hygiene, I was too prostrate to unduly suffer from this enforced solitude. When I got better, I was removed to a small room in which a younger little girl lay in another bed. Here, vague memories of Oriental tales prompted me one day to perform a greeting, in which, sitting up in bed, I prostrated myself, while uttering some formula like "Hatchi-boom-bay." This provoked an unexpected enthusiasm in my five-year-old companion, so that I was continually entreated to repeat my performance until I was sick and tired of it and deeply regretted my initial impulse to impress her.

When I returned to normal life, I had another experience that taught me that it is not always expedient to provide for the future like the virtuous ant in La Fontaine's fable, this great insight coming about because of the following incident. It was possible for parents to buy a box of sweets for their children, and, after dinner, the names of the privileged girls were called out in the refectory. They stepped out one after the other and chose a sweet from their private box in full view of the envious multitude. Naturally, I did not belong to this select group, but one day I was summoned to the teachers' room and shown a parcel that Jenny and Bo had sent me. Laid out on the table were bars of chocolate, biscuits, oranges, and a few bananas. I was told to help myself to whatever I wished to have, provided it was restricted to a single item. Carefully, I considered my course of action: I really fancied a bar of chocolate but reflected that the bananas would soon ripen and turn brown. I did not like them in any form but found them particularly repellent when they were ripe and soft. So I took one, and looked forward to postponed pleasures. How was I to know that I was never to see any part of the parcel again?

Normally, one was supposed to spend three months in the preventorium, but after this period of time had elapsed, it was found that I had not gained enough weight and the powers that be decreed that I should stay for another month. At last the day arrived when I was allowed to go home. Bo and Jenny had moved once more. We now lived in the Rembrandtstraat, in a "better" part of Antwerp than hitherto — Jenny had become the secretary of a Jewish refugee from Germany, a Mr. Strauss, who had set up a small firm dealing with scrap metal. This job at long last provided my mother with stable employment. The Strauss family, which included six children, lived about a quarter of an hour away in a very big house. They were much more religious than we were, and Jenny now came home early on Friday afternoons and did not work on Saturdays. On the other hand, on Sunday morning, she went to work and, if there was a lot of correspondence to deal with, often only came home at five in the afternoon.

Our new flat was on the first floor and consisted of three large rooms, with high ceilings — a large living room, a smaller bedroom for Bo with windows looking out onto the street, and a bigger bedroom at the back for Jenny and me. The kitchen, which was small, was located a few steps below, off a small landing next to the lavatory. On the same floor there was another tiny room, which we sublet to a young man called Schlam Goldschläger. On the ground floor lived Russian relatives of Bo, Aunt Lea and her (fairly) rich husband, who was a diamond merchant. We were to stay in this apartment for the next five years.

5. ELEMENTARY SCHOOL

This move involved a change of school. As I arrived in the middle of the school year, I felt utterly lost at first and in the winter examinations, which were held very soon after I came, I was ranked thirty-eighth out of forty pupils. However, the elderly teacher treated me kindly, and her benign encouragement soon helped me find my bearings. We wrote a composition one day on the subject "My mother." As I naively described Jenny, relating how she put on lipstick and mascara, how she loved buying jewelry at market stalls, how she regularly went out to dance, it was clear that the mistress was hugely amused. At all events, when the next exams were held in the summer, four months later, I moved up to the sixteenth place in the class rating.

It was then that I discovered the pleasures of reading, not only of plain reading but also of reading aloud, which I did with great gusto and for which I was quite gifted. Most of the books at my disposal were those written by the Comtesse de Ségur née Rostopchine, an aristocratic Russian lady who had married a Frenchman and who must have had a great many children, all of whom also proceeded to procreate in profusion, as can be deduced from the fact that she wrote a book for each grandchild, her production adding up to about forty to fifty titles. They were mostly nineteenth-century Victorian (if one may use that term for French books) stories of children, who were either very naughty ("Un Amour d'enfant," "Les Malheurs de Sophie") or preternaturally good ("Les Petites Filles Modèles"). I read and reread them innumerable times, and on Saturday morning, when Jenny was engaged in her elaborate toilet, I took to reading them aloud to her, following her with my book wherever she went and impatiently waiting outside the lavatory for her to come out so that I could continue. She dutifully listened and often seemed amused by the dialogues I rendered with great vivacity.

Soon after we had moved to the Rembrandtstraat, one of her old flames, the captain of a small merchant ship, about whom she had repeatedly enthused during the long years of his absence, turned up again. He was now a slightly tired yet friendly man, but there was nothing exceptional about him — indeed, he was rather pedestrian — and once more, Jenny buried illusions built upon the memories of the dashing man she had danced with years ago. If she was sentimental, she was also prepared to let reality correct her. But in doing so, she did not allow any other personality facets than those that had originally impressed her to come into play. The fact that the man was not as romantic as she had remembered could not be redeemed by any other more sterling qualities, such as kindness or honesty.

Moreover, her grasp of reality failed her absolutely whenever money was involved. It was at about this time when, no doubt sick and tired of the recurrent reproaches and scenes Bo indulged in on account of her dissolute ways, she made an effort to extricate herself from her dependence upon her mother. She thought of living on her own, and I followed her on many an expedition when we inspected empty flats in order to find alternative accommodation. She also considered sending me to a boarding school, a prospect about which I was anything but enthusiastic. One day, she took me for an interview with a very intimidating lady, the director of one such school. Before we arrived, she turned one of the cheap rings on one of her fingers around to make it look like a wedding ring, in order that she might appear as a respectable woman. (What had she done with her own wedding ring? Had she thrown it away or sold it to buy a pair of trashy shoes?) Fortunately for me, improvident as she was, she would never have been able either to pay the rent of a separate flat or the fees for any boarding school, and finally, to my immense relief, she dropped the whole idea.

I started my third school year, in the course of which I made a great leap forward and suddenly found myself coping easily and painlessly with school tasks. Whereas I had felt helpless and lost before, I now effortlessly understood whatever was required and grasped the problems involved. I became one of the four best pupils in the class and

5. ELEMENTARY SCHOOL

developed a huge relish for the competition and skills involved. I was perpetually raising my arm when the mistress put questions, calling out "Mademoiselle! Mademoiselle!" to draw her attention to me so that I might give the right answer before one and all. There can be no doubt about the fact that I was a real little pest. One day, the teacher made me come and stand beside her desk on the platform where she sat. After about five minutes, she asked a very simple question and nearly all forty pupils stretched their arms, pleading aloud to answer it. She then turned to me and said, "See! This is what *you* do all the time. This is what it looks like from here!" But although I felt abashed and even a bit ashamed, the beneficial effect of this demonstration did not last, and I soon reverted to my importunate ways.

I was now so happy as a pupil that during holidays I was homesick for school and looked forward to going back. Other children counted the days until holidays began. I counted the days until school started again. This sudden new confidence, the feeling that I was finding my way quite capably in my world, marked my ninth year so strongly that I have always since regarded my eighth birthday as a great landmark representing a fresh start in life.

I also made my first friends, all of them Jewish (well over a third of my classmates were Jewish). We went home early on Friday afternoons because of the Sabbath and were excused from attending school on Saturday morning. One of my friends was a girl called Jenny like my mother, a gentle girl with brown eyes. The other, Betty, was very strong-willed, and for a while, she turned into an enemy — we led two opposing gangs during break and waged war against each other. But she was much cleverer than I at this power game, and I suffered many a defeat at her hands. One day, her mother, a pleasant, homely woman, caught us as we came out of school — she had watched with alarm that what had started as a game was degenerating into a mean struggle — and she spoke to Betty and me, urging us to make it up. I was immediately ready to do so — small wonder since I was clearly on the losing side — but Betty held out for a remarkably long time while I stretched out my hand to her. Finally, under the pressure exerted by her mother, she burst into tears of rage and capitulated. I must say to her credit that she never retracted her promise and became a staunch and loyal friend.

We had school from eight to twelve in the morning and from two to four in the afternoon, and when we were released at noon, it became my habit to accompany Jenny and Betty, both of whom lived much farther from school than I did, so as to enjoy their company. One day, I discovered that I had a talent for inventing stories, which I told them on the way, and, to prolong this pleasure, we took to walking to and fro, accompanying and reaccompanying each other, so that I was rarely home before twenty to one, although I lived at a distance of only five minutes from school.

When my ninth birthday came round, my mother decided that she would give me a party. I invited about ten or twelve girls, and Jenny bought sweets and cake and what was then considered a special treat, canned pineapple. She presided at the long table in the living room and organized games with great charm and skill. She did it so well that my birthday parties — for from then on I had one every year — were very successful, much more so than those that I attended elsewhere, where we were frequently left to our own devices, which invariably meant that the afternoon ended in disorder and chaos. When this pattern was not followed, things conformed too much to a fixed pattern, which was dull. The only exceptions were the birthday parties for Miriam Strauss, a daughter of Jenny's employer, who was also in my class.

Miriam was a thin, pale girl who concentrated all her energy on getting good marks. She was what the English call a "swot," and a prig, to boot. I was also ambitious, but I felt it to be a different kind of ambition, for I nonetheless enjoyed playing "catch" or hopscotch at break time, and I cherished a keen interest in films and film stars, which I regarded as part of the "real" world. I felt very sophisticated when I compared myself with most of my contemporaries. I did not like tense, thin-lipped Miriam. I even despised her. Nonetheless, the birthday parties her mother gave were practically as good as Jenny's. As her birthday was in the summer, they were usually held in the very pleasant garden of their house. Mrs. Strauss was a plump and friendly woman. Miriam was one of six children, neatly divided between three girls and three boys. The other children were much more relaxed and likeable than Miriam, and the family led a very harmonious, happy life.

5. ELEMENTARY SCHOOL

As I grew older, I wrote sketches that Betty, Jenny, and I performed at my birthday parties, for the entertainment of the others. At one of these parties, my cousin Isy, who happened to be visiting, improvised a piano accompaniment, stressing dramatic moments in the action by striking impressive chords — this seemed to me incredibly clever and confirmed my conviction that he was nothing short of a budding genius.

In Belgium, school involved hard work, but, to make up for this, the holidays were long, the summer ones lasting for eight to nine weeks. I spent the greater part of them in the central park of Antwerp, where I sped along on a scooter and struck up acquaintances with other children — for I was very sociable and did not suffer from shyness. The rest of the time, I read and reread my books. One summer, Jenny arranged that I should spend three to four weeks with relatives from Bo's large family, who had rented a flat in a village in Flanders. On the whole, I felt lost in the countryside, which was mostly flat moorland punctuated by heather bushes. The days were long and tedious. I had not yet adopted the provident habit of always taking ample reading material with me when leaving home, and so my relatives kindly brought me to the local library. There, I was handed a book full of somber Catholic legends about saints who mortified their flesh by lashing themselves in the solitude of their cells or by eating only monstrous dishes of baked insects and spiders.

One weekend, a man called Bernard, who earned his living by giving private Hebrew lessons, came up from Antwerp to visit my relatives. He was in his mid-thirties and took quite an interest in my precocious prattle. In the evening, when the whole family went out for a stroll, I walked holding his hand in the dark and had a strong premonition that he would become my father. And when he left and asked for my address at home, I replied, "Will you be coming to see me or my mother?" I was a disingenuous child, and well aware of the false naivety of this question put by an apparently innocent eight-year-old.

The following year, Jenny took me to the seaside for a fortnight. We had a tiny hotel room in Coxide or Koksijde, where, at night I heard the regular surge of the sea, the waves breaking tumultuously or very softly on the shore, depending on the strength of the wind. We had a few cold and stormy days when we went for walks and felt cold and miserable, but then the sun came back, and it became warm enough to sunbathe and go into the water. Koksijde was a small but quite lively resort, with the usual shops brightly catering for tourists, and I enjoyed the bustle and noise of the main shopping street. There was even a cinema, but, unfortunately, the film it was showing, Jean Renoir's *La Grande Illusion*, was out of bounds for children, so Jenny left me lying in bed and went on her own. I think she also went out dancing, but, although she was as slim and lovely as ever, she did not strike up any acquaintances on this occasion. In the daytime, she shunned — to my regret — the crowded beach and marched on for fifteen minutes until we reached a deserted spot in the dunes. She then found herself a nook under a hillock, and, having applied olive oil to the exposed parts of her body as a protection against sunburn, she lay down and slumbered for the better part of the day, turning over at intervals to make sure she would get a tan all over. I was thus left to my own devices. Armed with pail and cake forms, spade, and sieve, I roamed the immediate surroundings, collecting shells, digging little trenches and tunnels, fascinated by crabs and mollusks. Although all these pastimes did not prevent me from feeling faintly bored, I was happy to be together with Jenny, despite the fact that she slept for so many hours on end. When she finally woke up, she played games with me — mostly, we threw rubber rings or balls at each other.

One day, she decided we should walk to the nearest French resort, just over the border. Although this was probably not further away than six kilometers, it seemed an endless tramp to me. As we started late, as usual, we were ravenous by the time we finally got there at two o'clock. Quite desperate for food, we went into an expensive and awesome restaurant where I ate hors d'oeuvres for the first time in my life.

In the evenings, lying in bed after supper, Jenny read a scandalous novel called *La Garçonne*, and when I picked it up out of curiosity, she snatched it away from me so that I sensed that this was a very wicked book. I was such a cowardly child that I resisted the temptation to look at it again. Had I been Eve, I would not have accepted Satan's invitation and mankind would still be in paradise. But had I given in to the urge to look at it in Jenny's brief absences, I would not even have recognized what was supposedly perverse in it.

5. ELEMENTARY SCHOOL

Everything Jenny did was charged with fascination, and I absorbed her views and attitudes as a matter of course. I looked at the books that she borrowed from the city library, to which we went about once a month. The system this institution used for borrowing books was singularly uninviting. No books were to be seen anywhere. Catalogues were available, from which Jenny made lists indicating the numbers of the books she wished to read and passed them over a counter to a librarian. After a long period of waiting, some of the books appeared. At home, many of these turned out to be far less interesting than she had hoped. Had she been able to take them from a shelf and cursorily look at them, this carting back and forth of books that were not read would have been unnecessary.

Two streets away from where we lived were the showrooms of the German car firm Mercedes-Benz, and whenever I came past it, I stopped to look at the glossy photographs in the windows showing Hitler, Goering, Goebbels, and other prominent Nazis at various functions in which the fabulous Mercedes cars played a central role. This publicity was still comparatively harmless, but on the way to where my friends Jenny and Betty lived, I came past a newsstand where the *Völkischer Beobachter* and other Nazi periodicals were sold, and I often stood still, petrified by the half-understood anti-Semitic German headlines and vicious cartoons, showing Jews with preternaturally pronounced noses and greedy eyes. Although growing up among Jews (even Jenny, who liked to regard herself as a pagan who worshipped the sun, seemed to consort only with Jews), I knew no one who looked like this, and yet I understood the message. I could not but help feeling that I myself was the target of these caricatures.

With me, Jenny spoke only French, and I switched quite unthinkingly from French to Yiddish and back. All things considered, I spent more time with Bo, since Jenny was at work. Bo took me with her on her excursions to Antwerp's zoo or to the cafés where she liked to spend her afternoons. When I came back from the preventorium, the doctor recommended that I eat ham, which is of course not kosher. I can see her even now ordering a ham sandwich for me in the café. When it came, she turned her head so as not to have to actually *see* me eating the forbidden food.

Part I. A CHILDHOOD IN ANTWERP

On Friday evenings, she often went to Uncle Lezer, one of her numerous nephews from Russia. As he was Orthodox, he wore a beard and dressed in the traditional Jewish garb. He was intelligent and irascible. On Friday evenings, the family sat round a long table laden with nuts, fruit, and raisins and, after the prescribed prayers had been said and the psalms sung, engaged in lively conversation. One evening, Uncle Lezer put various questions to me and found that I was familiar with the principal biblical stories (thanks to two volumes of the prolific Comtesse de Ségur!), after which he held me in high esteem; apparently, I compared favorably with his sons, whose knowledge was scantier, in spite of their having attended "Cheder," the Jewish school for boys. Although this household was a very religious one, it did not lack an element of gaiety. They had a cat who had kittens at least twice a year, and this meant that three or four of these were always frolicking about, running after balls, chasing their own tails, or trying to crawl up the curtains. On one occasion, a family festivity of some sort was celebrated, and a corpulent niece of Bo's sat down at the piano, struck a few chords, and all at once the staid women and men stood up and began to my intense surprise to dance a quadrille or minuet to Russian tunes, advancing, retiring, and turning round with the gracefulness characteristic of certain fat people.

My cousin Isy used to visit us once or twice a year, and was spoiled by one and all. He had grown quite tall and was, I thought, exceedingly handsome. Moreover, he was knowledgeable and would give me introductions to various subjects of which I had no inkling. He told me, for instance, about an artist called Rembrandt, whose paintings exhibited great contrasts between light and dark, this having been a revolutionary innovation at the time when he lived. Spellbound, I listened avidly to these impromptu lectures. He slept in my bedroom, and one evening before falling asleep, he discoursed on astronomy — explaining what a light-year is, how the universe is full of stars and comets — a survey that culminated with the casual mention that one day, in a very distant future, the earth would collide with some other celestial body, bringing about the termination of life and civilization as we know it. I got into a panic, for I did not believe his statement about the "distant future." On the contrary, I was convinced that my end was imminent and scrambled out of my bed to climb into his. Lying beside me, he took it into his head to guide my hand toward a peculiarly long, smooth, warm, hard, and thick part of his body. I had no idea of the existence of any such fleshy organ and thought his wish that I hold it rather odd, indeed incomprehensible, but, since I idolized him, I was willing to oblige. I may mention that this had unexpected consequences, for I was incubating one of my many illnesses at the time. This erupted a few days later, but, whereas I suffered from only a mild version of it, my cousin who, as a result of this incident, had caught my infection, had to lie in bed with a high temperature for several weeks. Was this the retribution of heaven for having seduced an innocent little girl? But seduction implies pleasure on the part of the seduced one, and the episode only left me slightly puzzled. I was much more roused by kissing scenes in films, and so no great harm was done.

At about this time, a fat, podgy old man called Sakoschansky made his appearance in our family. Lord knows how they had met, but there was soon no doubt about the fact that he was courting Bo, to the great amusement of Jenny, who caught a glimpse of his feet playing with Bo's under the table. After a remarkably short interval, he proposed to her, and she accepted him with equal alacrity. It was understood that he was rich, and he thus fulfilled the major qualification for a husband in her eyes. He seemed to answer her fondest hopes in this respect, as was evidenced by his buying her a pair of shoes that were so expensive that it had not remotely entered our heads that prices for footwear could reach such astronomic heights.

Sakoschansky came originally from Romania but had lived for many years in England, where he had been naturalized. For the wedding, they went to London for a fortnight, and when they returned, Bo was not only a married woman for the third time in her life — no mean achievement for one who disliked men in general — but had also acquired a British passport, a fact that was to have far-reaching implications, although we did not realize this at the time.

During Bo's absence, which coincided with the Easter school holidays, I went to stay with Aunt Sarah, since Jenny was not up to cooking for me or generally to tending to my needs, as a result of her full-time employment. At that time, Sarah owned a fairly large shop, a kind of haberdashery, where she sold underwear, pullovers, needles, ribbons, socks and stockings, etc., all the clothes being extraordinarily dowdy and unattractive. Behind the shop was a small windowless room, and again behind this were a tiny kitchen and a lavatory. Upstairs she had a couple of spacious rooms that served as bedroom and living room. She was on very friendly terms with her Flemish, non-Jewish, neighbors, who were constantly dropping in. I had some difficulty understanding them since my Flemish was still rudimentary. I was rather awed by one neighbor, a hairdresser, who peppered every sentence with the word "Gottverdamm" uttered with great emphasis.

Sarah owned a dog, a basset hound, that had been run over some months earlier so that he waddled even more than others of his species. He really had the gait of a duck. I was terrified of him, and he knew it, which he showed by always barking furiously at me, especially when I was alone. I was so scared of him that I would stand on a chair while he circled it below as quickly as his lame legs allowed, all the while barking with great gusto. This could go on for as long as ten minutes, until Aunt Sarah at last came into the room, when she would hold him in her arms so that I could safely climb down.

I spent the greater part of the day on the street outside the shop; there I struck up an acquaintance with a girl a year or two older than I. We were soon inseparable, and she introduced me to the charms of a small baker's shop a few yards down the road, where various cheap cakes, which we thought delicious, could be bought. One day, however, she turned up with a grave countenance and announced that she would not have any truck with me anymore, for I was Jewish (how did she know? They always do, somehow), and the Jews had crucified Jesus. It was Easter, and she had undoubtedly attended catechism classes. I was flabbergasted. Until then, I had had no idea that I could be held responsible for something that had happened almost two thousand years earlier, and the more I pondered this, the less I understood it.

Finally, the newlywed couple returned, and I went back to the Rembrandtstraat. For a while, we were now a household of four. Jenny nicknamed Bo's husband the "mammoth" because of his ponderous appearance and slow movements; we always knew when he came home in the evenings by the creaking of the steps in protest as he made his way upstairs. As for Bo, disillusion came swiftly: the rich man turned out to be a miser, the expensive pair of shoes a ploy designed to deceive her as to the true state of affairs. Moreover, she complained that he was molesting her. "What does he want of me?" she asked. In those days, it was thought thoroughly indecent for older people to have sexual urges or intercourse, and she was a convinced adherent of these views. Soon they were quarreling with all the acrimonious venom she had at her command and which inspired corresponding reactions in her partners. After less than six months, Sakoschansky moved out, never to be seen again. Bo, who had spent hours practicing her new signature by diligently copying it on one page after another like a pupil condemned to deliver two hundred "lines," did not mourn his departure. One day came a letter from Romania, in which he urged her to join him and praised the country in the highest terms, in particular mentioning that potatoes were much cheaper there than in Belgium. She regarded this invitation with the utmost contempt; never for a moment did she even remotely consider accepting it.

6. ISY

Every now and then, I was invited to stay for a week or so with Golda, Yeshurun, and Isy in their new house in Brussels, which meant entering a completely different new world. The house had modern furniture, which filled me with awe: the dining room was equipped with a massive mahogany table and matching chairs, some seating two, all of them square — an extremely simple design in which the right angle was the dominant feature. Upstairs, on one of the walls of Golda's and Yeshurun's bedroom, were wooden bars so that they could perform gymnastic exercises. Isy had what seemed to me a fabulous room of his own, big and sunny and with a huge desk in the middle. I slept in the smallest room of the house — it was no more than a cubbyhole. Over the bed hung two modern paintings. One showed something reminiscent of Seurat's picture of people walking down a lane in their Sunday best, with children playing on lawns. The people were stylized and had a faintly geometrical look about them. This hung on the side wall. Over my head was a picture of a man's head near a birdcage — these pictures were like nothing that I was familiar with and intimidated me with their intimations of a culture from which I was excluded.

On the ground floor was the office, and next to it a long storeroom full of shelves on which bales of material and boxes full of lace handkerchiefs, tablemats, and centerpieces were stacked. On the first floor were the kitchen and the dining room with its somber, ultramodern furniture. It opened onto a terrace full of potted plants overlooking a long and narrow garden. On the other side, it led to the drawing room, in which stood a grand piano and old Louis XV chairs — although I didn't know then that this was what they were. There were lots of rugs, and a couch with a tartan rug neatly folded on

6. ISY

it. Beneath the window with its simple tulle curtains, which ran — in the fashion of most Belgian houses — along the entire narrow facade of the house, was a broad marble sill, on which was spread an assemblage of huge, delicately colored seashells. When I held them to my ear, I could hear a faint roaring, rich and strange, like the distant swell of waves. Underneath were built-in recesses, full of books. Bookshelves also filled the wall on the left behind the piano. Some of the books were old, with leather bindings; some were tall volumes — one of them a magnificently illustrated edition of the *Arabian Nights* and another the *Talmud*. These were flanked by recently published paperback first editions of writers such as André Gide, Valéry, Claudel, and Montherlant.

What impressed me perhaps the most was the lavatory, which was tiled and much larger than the ones I was accustomed to. On its walls were eighteenth-century drawings illustrating the various stages in the education of a young prince, all of them narrowly framed in dark varnished wood. I had never seen pictures in a toilet before, and this seemed to me the very epitome of culture.

I spent my time reading and playing in Isy's room, with boxes full of samples of lace that I arranged in elaborate patterns on his desk as if to tempt prospective customers, a game I had invented at home when I amused myself with Jenny's tawdry jewelry. Golda often bought me clothes when I accompanied her on shopping expeditions, and I realized that in this family money was not the overriding problem that it was in ours.

I was sent to bed soon after supper, and lay awake for long hours while the dimmed strains of Bach played by Golda and Isy on the piano downstairs wafted upward toward my minuscule room.

Once I fell ill — it would have been surprising if I had not done so at some time or another, since I rarely enjoyed reasonable health for more than three or four weeks running — and had to stay in bed for a couple of days. Golda went out and bought me a book — it was the French translation of Pearl Buck's *The Good Earth*, which had recently won the Nobel prize and was a best seller. It was, I think, the first grown-up book I read, and I was so fascinated by the strange worlds of both Chinese civilization and adult problems that no sooner had I finished it than I proceeded to reread it, not just once but three or four times. Jenny, who was a liberal mother, was rather scandalized when I brought it home — the book had allusions to sexuality, which I read with what I can only describe as a superficial understanding, skating lightly over those passages with a very dim awareness that here were mysteries of a dangerous nature, into which it was wisest for the time being not to delve.

Isy came to visit us in Antwerp once or twice a year, and to my surprise, he seemed to enjoy his stay with us. Bo doted on him, in spite of his maleness, and did her best to spoil him as far as her limited financial resources permitted. Above us lived a family with an attractive, dark-haired girl of his age called Mireille, and they soon struck up an acquaintance. Either he went to visit her upstairs or she came down to our flat with great alacrity as soon as she realized he was in the house.

Since I adored him, I steadfastly refused to leave him alone with her, savoring every minute of his presence, thus unawarely playing the role of a no doubt highly obnoxious chaperone. I watched their flirtatious interplays with puzzled wonder at their silliness. Still, I reluctantly realized that Mireille, who was not particularly intelligent and whose charm was of a rather vulgar variety, exercised a potent attraction on my cousin. Some time after, we were both invited to his birthday party, and a friend of her family took us to Brussels in his car. It was my first trip in an automobile, and as it was crammed full, I spent the journey crouching between the legs of the other passengers on the floor at the back of the car, in a state of acute discomfort. Moreover, since my head was well below the level of the small windows, I was quite undistracted by any sight of the landscape or houses we might be passing, so that the hours that elapsed until we reached our destination seemed interminable.

A great many youngsters, all of them between fifteen and eighteen years old, had been invited to the birthday party, and, as they played games that gave an opportunity for much flirting, I realized that I was only a nuisance in their company. For instance, in one of the games, the boys stood behind chairs on which the girls sat, and when a young man who had an empty chair before him winked at a particular girl, she was off like a shot before her guardian could hold her back. Needless

6. ISY

to say, the boy saddled with me had a dead weight on his chair. I sat all agog, ready to fly to whoever beckoned, but it took a very long time indeed until some young man, impelled with pity either for me or, more probably, for my unfortunate backstander, gave the longed-for signal. I did not unduly resent this state of affairs, however, for I was aware of the fact that this discrimination was due to my age, not to my personality or possible lack of beauty. Nonetheless, I was awed by the looks of the girls, in particular by those of an athletic, sunburned blonde called Claude, who exuded a kind of animal beauty to which I succumbed with ungrudging admiration so that I felt it absolutely right that she should be Isy's special friend.

The Disenhauses had been nudists in the past, but for some reason or other, the club to which they belonged had been compelled to abandon the pure practice of their philosophy, I believe because nudism had been legally forbidden. As the next best thing, the club bought a property of quite substantial size in the country, and to this place they frequently repaired on Saturdays and Sundays. The nudist rules had been modified, and they now prescribed that on the club's grounds members should not wear clothes which might be considered even remotely elegant, but only, as a kind of uniform, baggy trousers and a loose zipped jacket, both of them navy-colored, a kind of jogging suit that in those days was also the regular skiing outfit. In hot weather, they wore the simplest kind of bathing wear. We picnicked on the grass and the adults played games, mostly basketball. As there was a playground for children, I could amuse myself there too, but I also spent hours reading or watching my cousin, half-nude and looking quite athletic, displaying his prowess in various sporting activities. Everything was tremendously virtuous and overwhelmingly healthy. Before going home, the members withdrew, separated by sexes, to large cabins where they showered, and in these precincts at least walked about unashamedly naked, before putting on their normal (mostly very elegant) clothes. Although I was used to seeing Jenny naked, I had a shock upon being confronted with this unabashed and totally unconcerned nudity — one woman in particular struck me with the beauty of her very firm body, her plump upright breasts, her rounded thighs. (Jenny's comments at home on the issue of nudity were that it would be a fine thing if all men and women were Adonises and Venuses. As this, regrettably, wasn't the case, she opposed the whole idea, because it offended her sense of beauty.)

I experienced another shock of this kind one day when Yeshurun called out in anger to Golda because he couldn't find something; I opened the door of my cubicle room to find him standing in the open bathroom door, on the opposite side of the landing, stark naked with a sponge in his hand and wet all over: I caught a terrible glimpse of a bush of black hair about his dangling penis as I hastily closed the door, scared out of my wits, my heart pounding like that of Bluebeard's wife after she had opened the forbidden closet.

When the weather did not permit the trip to the club's grounds — during the winter or in summer if it poured with rain — we stayed at home, which was much more to my liking, as I thought the countryside boring. We then played the "dictionary game." The Petit Larousse was taken from its shelf and opened at random. One turned to the beginning of the particular letter of the alphabet involved; here one found a mass of small illustrations of words commencing with this letter. One was allowed five or ten minutes to jot down as many words as possible, and one's score was based on the number written down with an extra bonus for those terms nobody else had managed to discover. I was always at the bottom of the list but had a great triumph when the letter H came up. Among the crowded illustrations was the picture of a man in uniform, a "hussard," a word I had never heard. I wrote down the much simpler word for man "homme" and was universally applauded for this feat, the others all commenting that they had not thought of such an obvious thing.

Sometimes visitors came in the evening. Very close and intimate friends were Georges and Denise, who were to marry at a later date, but were at that time living in sin, each of them trying to get divorced from their respective spouses. They were representatives of Belgium's cultured class, people a world removed from our Jewish milieu in Antwerp. Georges earned his living as a sales representative for his brother's tailoring firm, which specialized in men's suits, but his real vocation was poetry and for this he later gained recognition and some degree of fame, at least in his home country. He was full of gusto and immediately filled the room with vibrant vitality, and I liked him because he took friendly notice of me, little girl though I was, and amused me by making jokes and telling entertaining stories. Denise had recently taken up painting, but this meant nothing to me at the time. What impressed me was her radiant beauty. She was slim, blond, very elegant, and distinguished, exuding a French kind of sensual attraction — reluctantly, yet ungrudgingly, I decided that Jenny was *not* the most beautiful woman in the world.

Back in Antwerp, I returned to my familiar routine. I got up early in the morning and heated my breakfast cup of cocoa, assiduously stirring the milk in the pan so as to prevent any skin from forming on its surface, as this thin film revolted me and I could not have swallowed the drink even if I had gingerly removed it with a spoon, with my gorge rising in disgust.

School was from eight to twelve, and afterward, I escorted my friends Jenny and Betty home for half an hour, entertaining them with made-up stories. I then went home for dinner and at two returned to school until four o'clock. Quite unnecessarily, I dragged all my schoolbooks, regardless of whether they were needed, in my bulging schoolbag, on all my trips to and fro, thus pulling my right shoulder down with the weight so that as time wore on, it always hung somewhat lower than the left one. On reaching home in the late afternoon, I did my homework and avidly read one of my numerous Comtesse de Ségur books. In the summer, I found time to play in Antwerp's central park, which was at the end of our street. Aunt Sarah had given me a scooter with real rubber wheels as a present, and I spent hours speeding all around the park and even recklessly flying down a fairly steep slope, a feat that astounds me in retrospect, for I was a very fearful child, not inclined to take risks as a general rule.

At about this time, Jenny found herself being courted by two very different men, both of whom proposed to her. One of them, called Naftali, lived in Holland. I never met him. He was an engineer and a couple of years younger than Jenny, which, strangely enough, she seemed to feel was a strong handicap. He had sent me a silver necklace with a "mezuzah," made in Palestine and finely worked in Yemenite fashion. To this day, I cannot understand why in this serious predicament as to whom to accept, Jenny never arranged for us to meet each other. The other suitor was the Lithuanian teacher of Hebrew, Bernard, whose acquaintance I had made during the summer I had spent in the countryside with relatives. He was ten years older than Jenny, and this fact, together with the knowledge that I liked him, tilted the scales in his favor. Jenny, who was as much in love with Naftali as she ever was with anyone in her life, chose with her singular talent for acting perversely and against her instinct to make a seemingly sensible decision, and accepted Bernard.

That I should attend their wedding (which was limited to a civil ceremony held at the town hall and was not consecrated by a rabbi) was regarded as somehow indecent, so I spent that day with the family of my school friend Jenny, feeling as if I were suspended in a no-man's-land between two worlds.

When I returned, I had to vacate my place in Jenny's bed and move into the bed next to Bo's, a change I sullenly resented. Forever gone were the nights when I cuddled next to Jenny, secure in the animal warmth of her body — it was the expulsion from the Garden of Eden … and perhaps responsible for the fact that my initial liking for Bernard turned into antipathy. If so, the transformation in my feelings was greatly aided by day-to-day life, which revealed unsuspected — or formerly merely unnoticed — traits in his character. He was a mediocre man, petty and conceited, an uncritical supporter of Russian Communism, glibly swallowing its official propaganda, utterly incapable of forming an original thought. He was, moreover, selfish and old-fashioned. He made an attempt to teach me Hebrew. I sabotaged this to the best of what turned out to be a considerable talent in this direction. I criticized the language continually, saying, "Why is this so? How stupid this is!" raising silly and obnoxious objections, aimed not really at Hebrew but at its teacher, as could be seen from my utterly different attitude to English. Jenny had started teaching it to a group of grown-ups, and there I participated with unabated enthusiasm, regardless of the fact that English is an utterly illogical language, much more so than

Hebrew, as regards both spelling and pronunciation. Admittedly, these seem arbitrary only if one leaves its historical roots out of account, but I didn't know that then. Possibly, the passionate love for English which I later developed was already dormant, but that alone doesn't explain my inordinately hostile attitude to Hebrew, particularly if one bears in mind that I was an eager and ambitious pupil, ever anxious to distinguish herself brilliantly, a feat which I managed with ease in the case of English, where I rapidly outstripped all the adults in the group. Its activities petered out after a few months, and I promptly forgot all I had learned, except for the two words "squirrel" and "yellow," which to French speakers appear odd and exotic and thus permanently impressed themselves on my memory.

Meanwhile, my dislike for Bernard was reinforced by an ugly incident that occurred about a year after he and Jenny got married. During an altercation, he lost control of himself and beat her up. Her face was badly bruised; deeply shocked, she went to a lawyer to discuss the possibilities of a divorce. Whether she feared reverting to the status of a single woman again or for some other obscure reason, a reconciliation took place a few days later — to my great disappointment for I now heartily hated the man — and life went back to what had become normal during the previous year.

The marriage made no difference to our permanently straitened circumstances. Bernard had no regular income, and what he earned from his private lessons was both unreliable and insufficient. As for Jenny, her skill in being insolvent from the third or fourth day of the month remained unimpaired. She occasionally remarked that if her employer were to be aware of this, he would be astonished, for he paid her a generous salary. She was a very efficient secretary, and when I occasionally visited her in her office in the Strauss's villa, I was fascinated by the speed with which her hands sped over the typewriter's keys. She did not do touch-typing — indeed I doubt whether that system had then been invented — and so her fingers jumped up and down the keys in a seemingly chaotic and arbitrary manner.

That summer, we went to a village in the Ardennes for a holiday. We stayed in the home of a farmer who took in guests in the summer. We slept in a dingy room, where mosquitoes plagued us during the night. My love for the countryside was not enhanced by the fact that the lavatory was a plain seat in a hot cabin in the garden, without water flushing. When the wooden lid over the huge hole was lifted, a great stench rose. It was dark inside, and heaven knows what spiders lurked in the corners. Big bluebottles, attracted by the nauseating smell, busily buzzed around one, and I longingly thought of our civilized water closet at home.

We went for long walks, once visiting a beekeeper where I tasted a liquid, strongly aromatic honey, for the first time in my life, but I did not think it worth the risk of being stung by bees, which also swarmed around us at the meals we ate, to my chagrin, in the garden of the farm. During one of our walks, Jenny and Bernard stopped to watch what seemed to me a spectacle void of all interest, in which a bull was straddling a cow in a singularly ridiculous posture. I could not for the life of me understand why this should fascinate them so much.

The holiday lasted a week or ten days and at the end of our stay was overshadowed by the fact that Jenny and Bernard discovered they had not enough money to pay the bill. They were saved at the last minute by the providential fact that a lottery ticket Jenny had bought won the princely sum of 20 Belgian francs, so we were able to depart without fear of prosecution. Jenny had already considered leaving her identity card as a token of her intention to pay. I was ten or eleven years old, but the whole business worried me considerably. How could she be so light-hearted with such prospects of trouble before her? After all, she had been saved only by a highly improbable fluke (I could not remember her having ever won anything in the lottery before).

In many respects, she indeed had a talent for happily ignoring reality. One day, we wanted to go to the pictures to see *The Philadelphia Story*, which had just come out and had been widely praised by the — admittedly never even remotely critical — Belgian newspapers. Bernard was not a cinema-goer, so it was a question of raising enough cash just for the two of us. Jenny demanded that I go and borrow the money from the concierge who lived in the basement. He was a cobbler, a surly, middle-aged man, whom we (rightly) suspected of being anti-Semitic, with a pale daughter of my own age called Maria. They were devout Catholics, and on Ash Wednesday, Maria came from morning mass with a black cross traced in ash on her forehead, which I felt to be a threat aimed at all Jews. And it was from these people that my mother wanted me to borrow money! In an outburst of rare rebellion, I steadfastly refused to do so, whereupon Jenny took to her bed and began to cry. Although I was perfectly aware of the fact that this was blatant blackmail, I could not bear to see her in this state and capitulated. The cobbler, who no doubt earned much less than my mother but was better able to manage his finances, took out his purse and gave me the coveted amount. The irony of the whole affair is that we were bitterly disappointed by the film, whose plot we felt to be contrived and peopled by completely artificial characters, a circumstance that even our beloved stars Katharine Hepburn and Cary Grant were unable to redeem. Thus, I made a sacrifice for something that was not remotely worth the humiliation it cost me.

At about this time, Bo reported that in spite of the removal of my tonsils some years ago, I was snoring in my sleep, and Dr. Baatjes's verdict was that I had to have another small operation to remove my adenoids, which had been taken out with my tonsils and had grown again. Once again, he came to our home and unpacked his gleaming instruments — this time, however, he used ether as an anesthetic. It worked much more efficiently, and I was out before I could count up to three. The aftermath was, moreover, less dramatic. I woke up feeling weak but not sick and spent hours looking at the stucco decoration of the ceiling and at the lamp, which had twelve bulb sockets in the form of candles, a design that I thought very elegant. In the afternoon, I was able to pick up *Marianne*, a weekly political and cultural newspaper that Jenny regularly bought. Politically, it was left-wing, for Jenny was a Socialist, and so were many of her men friends. When the Spanish Civil War broke out, many of them enrolled in the Republican Army, and not all of them came back. At all events, I had recently begun to read some of the articles in *Marianne*. This was where I saw my first caricatures of Hitler, and I remember one that showed him confronted with a hand, each finger of which represented one of his claims — the caption read "GIVE HIM ONE AND HE'LL TAKE THE LOT." In the issue I looked at on this particular day, I came upon the confessions of a kleptomaniac, which I read with fascination and a dim understanding of the overwhelming pull that an irresistible obsession can exert.

The next day I was out of bed and all but recovered, so I did not miss more than two days at school, which was my usual absence rate every fortnight, since I was perpetually ill, afflicted by feverish flus and painful throat infections. Nonetheless, my marks were improving all the time, partly because I was not unintelligent, and partly because I was devoured by ambition and wanted to be better than the others in my class. Thus, I now always ranked among the four best girls of the class. Incidentally, the suspicion was rampant among us Jews that one of the Gentile girls only shared this status because her parents were rumored to be friends of the headmistress. But, leaving my ambition out of consideration, I really enjoyed most lessons. I loved writing compositions and had no difficulty finding the right words to express myself. I was avidly interested in history. As for the other subjects, Flemish, geography, and mathematics, I was willing to learn by heart what I didn't spontaneously remember, my memory being good in those days. In the autumn, at the beginning of the school year, we were given a list of the schoolbooks we would need. A brisk trade was conducted outside the school, where we bought our books from the pupils of the class above us, the prices varying depending on how often these books had already changed hands. A few girls came from families that could afford to buy their books brand-new, but I of course had to look for bargains. At home, we were then busy for several hours wrapping the books in protective sugar paper, which was sold in big sheets. Jenny was skillful at this job, but I was clumsy, and during the space of time I needed to laboriously manage the requisite folds for one book, she disposed of three.

Our classes were huge — and would nowadays be regarded as a disgrace. Mine always numbered forty to forty-five pupils. Yet thanks to strict discipline, tuition was thorough and achieved more than might be reasonably expected. The level of proficiency within our class varied widely — there were about five or six pupils who were really good, then followed the mass of those who were average, either because of ingrained indifference or lack of pronounced intelligence, and finally there were about seven or eight really dumb girls, whose stupidity was such that their most assiduous efforts would have achieved nothing. Nonetheless, I believe that even these pupils were able to read and write, although their spelling might well have been disgraceful, and this was surely no mean achievement for a teacher who had to cope with such numbers. She was a middle-aged woman, dowdily dressed and with a generally unattractive appearance. We were not particularly fond of her; nevertheless, a small group in the class somehow got the idea that we should express our gratitude by bringing her a bouquet as a special surprise. We busily collected the money over several weeks, and a small delegation formed of the most active advocates of this scheme was to hand over the flowers at her home on a day that was a school holiday (it was I think All Souls' Day). We trudged to her home in a remote part of Antwerp, where we found our teacher on her knees, humbly mopping up the floor of the corridor. We certainly succeeded in springing a surprise — she flushed dark red in embarrassment at our seeing her engaged in this menial occupation. We all felt how out of place we were, and on the way back we realized, crestfallen and mute, that what we had fondly imagined to be a delightful idea had turned rather sour.

At around this time, Jenny and Bernard did something unheard-of — they bought a piece of furniture! It was a modern sofa encased in wooden elements, which served as bookshelves, the whole in very light colors that strongly contrasted with Bo's dark and heavy Victorian table and chairs in the living room. They topped this extravagance by purchasing a miniature radio set, and this gave me my first introduction to classical music.

I used to do my homework sitting at the table, and now that we had a radio, I always switched it on. When staying at Aunt Golda's in Brussels, I had of course heard Bach and Mozart played on the piano, but I was not familiar with orchestral music and it was only now that I slowly began to distinguish Haydn from Beethoven. A broadcast to which I regularly listened was a reading of *Wuthering Heights*. I was immediately fascinated by this story and remember especially the episode in which Mr. Earnshaw comes home with a mysterious little boy named Heathcliff, which the French reader pronounced "Isscliff." This captured my imagination so much that I religiously followed the further installments, totally unaware that I was listening to a major work of world literature.

At about this time, Jenny and Bernard ventured into another cultural domain and took out a subscription for the theater. I was taken along and sat in a theater that was half-empty to see Molière's *L'Avare*, which we thought entertaining. A few weeks later, we saw a performance of Racine's *Bérénice*. This is Racine's most uneventful play and is really only a series of elegiac dialogues in elegant alexandrines, the only issue being whether Titus will marry the Jewish queen Bérénice or not. As the company giving this play was composed of third-rate actors and actresses, the few traces of dramatic tension that might be discovered in the text vanished altogether as they pompously and woodenly stood declaiming great poetry as if they themselves were as bored by it as their audience. That I came at a later date to admire the genius of Racine must be regarded as a minor miracle in view of this introduction, although I must confess that *Bérénice* has never ranked as one of my favorites.

7. SILVIE

At about this time, Chiffra and her daughter Silvie came to stay with us in search of a husband for my cousin. Chiffra's second marriage was marred by bitter squabbling with her husband, and in the course of their venomous quarrels, neither of them hesitated to call the children of their partner's former marriage all sorts of insulting names. Chiffra therefore thought it wise for Silvie to get away from this hateful atmosphere, and she proposed to do this by marrying her off as soon as possible. She was seventeen years old and extraordinarily beautiful, blond and slim. No matter what clothes she tried on when she had playfully recourse to Jenny's wardrobe, she was irresistibly attractive, imparting chic to the dowdiest dresses or coats so that we gazed at her, marveling at so much youth and radiance. She really looked like the proverbial English rose.

We put them up in one of our attics, whose windows were not equipped with the netting fitted in the windows downstairs, with the result that they were mercilessly attacked by the mosquitoes that laid their eggs in the stagnant water of the small artificial lake in Antwerp's central park and infested the town during the summer. Despite the protection of the netting, isolated insects managed to slip through even into our downstairs rooms, and I'd had a traumatic experience one night when I was awakened by the hysterical buzzing of a mosquito that had strayed inside my ear. Panic flooded me until it managed to find its way out again, and to this day, if I glimpse any such insects in my bedroom, or am woken up by their obnoxious sing-song, I cannot fall asleep unless I cover my head with a blanket, even if the heat thus generated makes me acutely uncomfortable. At any event, it was alleged that the mosquitoes smelled fresh blood, that is that of persons not normally living in Antwerp, and this was supposed to be a further reason why they fell with such ferocity on my aunt and Silvie.

In true traditional Jewish manner, Chiffra resorted to the services of various Shadchans in her search for a suitable husband, and the days of mother and daughter were mainly spent inspecting various candidates. Finally, the choice fell upon a man of Polish origin called Jonas Mlynek, who was fifteen years older than Silvie and a successful diamond cleaver (a craft that requires greater skill than that of ordinary diamond cutters), and who did a bit of trading with the stones as well. The wedding was scheduled to take place on 4 September 1938, and after the date had been fixed, our relatives returned to England, where Silvie continued to work for the time being as a shorthand typist.

Another dramatic change in the family setup occurred that year. Aunt Sarah made the acquaintance of a German Jew incredibly called Caesar. He had been a steward on a German merchant ship and had been warned by a colleague that the Gestapo was waiting to arrest him when the ship next berthed in Hamburg. He took the opportunity to desert, if that is the right word in this context, when the ship cast anchor in Antwerp. He and Sarah agreed to get married and emigrate to the United States where they planned to buy a farm and raise cattle.

Shortly before my birthday, he asked me what I should like to have as a present, and I — in total naivety and unawareness of the reality of his financial circumstances — asked for a writing desk, a wish that originated from my being dazzled by the one in Isy's room in Brussels. When the day came, my sanguine expectations were dashed when I was given a plain wooden pencil box instead. My bitter disappointment was heightened by the dim realization that I had been tactless in voicing such an inordinately extravagant request.

Several months elapsed while they waited for their visas and affidavits, during which Aunt Sarah sold her business. The day of their embarkation arrived soon after, and the whole family, including Isy, who had come in from Brussels, escorted them to the docks, where tearful farewells were made, after which we watched the steamer slowly get under way while we frantically waved our handkerchiefs and the figures on the decks gradually became indistinguishable. After that, we occasionally received letters in which Aunt Sarah described the

7. SILVIE

Aunt Sarah

hardships of her new life, in which she got up at five in the morning to milk twenty-five cows and went to bed at ten at night. Whether she was nonetheless happy, bearing in mind her enthusiasm for animals, I never learned.

The appointed date for Silvie's wedding arrived. It was a grand affair with a dinner for the four hundred members of the bride's and bridegroom's families who were considered to be close relatives, followed by a ball, to which more distant relatives and acquaintances had also been invited. The couple had been married in front of a registrar in London, but this was regarded as a mere formality. The "real" thing was the ceremony in the synagogue, in the course of which I was nonplussed by the sight of my mother crying her eyes out. She was, moreover, not alone in so doing, for all the women around us were busy dabbing their eyes over something that seemed to the ten-year-old I was to be after all a joyful event.

Afterward we repaired to a hired hall, and when everybody had sat down for the banquet, Aunt Sophie, who was paying the bill, gave me the job of unobtrusively walking around and counting the number of guests assembled, a task that proved quite ticklish, since, when I checked my results, I invariably got a different number each time I went round, presumably because of people getting up to greet somebody sitting at another table or having to go to the toilet.

In the early evening, people began to arrive for the ball. Jenny had had an evening gown specially made, which I thought quite ravishing and worthy of a Hollywood film: it was of black taffeta, which was gathered in big flowers round her neck and naked shoulders and which billowed out at the waist into a very wide, almost crinoline-like skirt. Pinned in her black hair and on her left shoulder were two orange-colored flowers, which gave her an exotic Spanish look. True elegance, however, was represented by Aunt Golda, who came in a model gown by a French designer called Grès — it was a simple beige Greek toga falling in a great many small pleats, and it undoubtedly struck a note of exquisite culture unattained by the many flamboyant dresses worn by most women. As for Silvie, she wore a lavishly cut traditional white dress with a train of three or four meters and looked more lovely than ever.

The ball began at eight and went on until the unheard-of hour of four o'clock in the morning. I also hopped around with little boys and girls. Two melodies were played time and again — one was a then-popular Yiddish song, "By mir bist de shayn"; the other was the "Lambeth Walk" and came from England. The proper way to dance it involved folk dance-like steps, which everybody instantly learned. The assembly all lustily joined in singing as they danced, and high spirits prevailed the whole evening.

In true family tradition (my mother, it will be recalled, had had a similar accident at her own wedding), Bo — although not dancing — slipped and fell on the polished parquet floor of the ballroom. And during the coming days, she became very ill indeed, developing phlebitis and being obliged to take to her bed. As she had to have a competent person to nurse her, we had recourse to the services of a convent located at the bottom of our road. They delegated a very young English nun called "Sister Mary" to look after her; she was quiet and had a beautiful, luminous, angelic face so that Jenny immediately assumed she had become a nun because of an unhappy love affair and felt that she herself was in danger of converting to Catholicism on

7. SILVIE

account of Sister Mary's overwhelming beauty. However, after a few days, she was replaced by an old nun, and we suspected that the reason for this was that the convent had discovered that there was a man (my stepfather Bernard) in the household, and it was thought safer to avoid all temptation. I could not understand how Bernard could be considered as even remotely alluring, but no doubt they did not examine his erotic qualities closely — the fact that he was a male sufficed, in the way that when old maps indicated "Here be monsters and dragons," navigators exercised unusual care in the regions thus described.

The old nun (she was eighty years old, hale and hearty with red cheeks and a good-humored smile) proceeded to attempt to convert Bo by talking to her about Jesus, for she trusted that since she was in danger of dying, she might be persuaded to embrace the Catholic faith. Bo could not reply in words, since she spoke only Yiddish, but she understood what was afoot and resolutely pressed her lips together while energetically shaking her head from left to right and back to demonstrate that no doubt could be entertained as to her adhering steadfastly to her own religion. Her life hung on a thread until the doctor decided to have recourse to an old remedy and apply leeches to her legs. I looked with disgusted horror at the glasses in which these slimy black worms swam, but as a matter of fact they brought about a swift improvement, and Bo miraculously recovered.

After their honeymoon, which they had spent on the Riviera and from which they brought back numerous photos of the beautiful, sunburned bride, Silvie and Jonas moved into a modern luxury flat, the like of which I had never seen before. Their living room and bedroom were furnished in very bourgeois fashion, and the whole apartment filled me with awe, conveying as it did a sense of incredible wealth and comfort. They also had a big wireless equipped with a battery of buttons that, when pressed, miraculously tuned in to various pre-set stations!

Bo and I were now invited to dinner every Sunday. Before the meal, however, we had a hot bath in Silvie's spacious bathroom, and so our trips to the municipal baths, in which I shared the tub with Bo, uneasily confronted with her huge belly and pendulous breasts, came to an end since each of us was now able to enjoy the luxury of bathing on her own. When it was my turn, Silvie always came in because she did not want to miss seeing my thin naked body. Apparently, this sight was a very funny one, in particular because of my protruding ribs, and she invariably started to laugh, which chagrined me not a little.

She did not cook very well yet, but as I was not used to anything but Bo's tasteless meals, I did not mind. Jonas noticed that I had no table manners — no one had ever thought it necessary at home to teach me any — and he showed me how to hold my knife and fork properly, advice for which I have been grateful ever since.

At this time, I was learning to play the piano — a relative, a member of Bo's Russian family, gave me weekly lessons. I was not particularly gifted but did my best. Once a week, I went with a group of friends to late-afternoon classes in a distant school, where we were taught to read notes and to sing by them. This was a futile effort for me, because I invariably sang flat, rarely hitting a right note, and yet was painfully aware of the fact that I was managing to just miss it and was sounding awful. We walked home during the early dark evenings through brilliantly illuminated streets whose shop windows were filled with what to me was exotic food — real, not canned, pineapples and a profusion of trussed-up fowl, geese, pheasants, and turkeys, all of which were completely unknown in our Jewish shops or in the small grocer's shop on our street.

The atmosphere in Antwerp at the end of the thirties was one of peaceful prosperity, but clouds were gathering that portended no good. A ship full of German Jewish refugees, returning from a failed attempt to land in Havana, arrived in Antwerp, and the newspapers were full of photos of the passengers coming down the gangway. Antwerp was already teeming with refugees from Germany who gave disturbing reports of the anti-Semitic terror in their country and told chilling tales of "concentration camps" where Jews were systematically tormented. Wherever adults gathered, these stories were brought up and commented on. The general consensus — among Jews! — was that these reports were exaggerated to enhance the self-importance of the refugees. After all, the Germans were a nation with a great culture, and it was, therefore, highly unlikely that they should indulge in such atrocities. Maybe the potential victims were trying to reassure themselves that they were not facing a growing threat that might soon

7. SILVIE

overtake them. I, on the other hand, hovering on the fringe of these gatherings, was terrified by the sadistic details of these stories and believed it all implicitly, for in spite of the skepticism voiced by the adults, it never occurred to me to doubt the truth of what I heard.

After the annexation of Austria and the Munich debacle, followed by the occupation first of the Sudetenland and soon after of the rest of Czechoslovakia, the shadow of Hitler loomed ever larger, and discussions continually concentrated on the false — or was it wise? — policy of appeasement adopted by the British and French prime ministers Chamberlain and Daladier. A feeling of impending doom was creeping into daily life. The uneasy awareness of the possibility of our being at the mercy of dark forces in Germany was reinforced by the end of the Civil War in Spain, from which so many of Jenny's friends who had gone as volunteers to join the Republican forces never returned. It did not exactly contribute to creating confidence in the democratic countries' ability to overcome the Fascist and Nazi armies, and if we were cheered by occasional incidents such as the report that our charwoman's husband, an ordinary worker, was so incensed when he listened to one of Hitler's speeches on the wireless that he seized a kitchen chair and broke it by smashing it over the radio set, this was but scant consolation when we considered things on a larger scale.

Events abroad remained for me a distantly discerned rumbling, a muted accompaniment to daily life that I, like the adults, largely ignored. I was absorbed by my enthusiasm for the cinema — where political developments at least had the consequence that we now boycotted German and Austrian films, even to the extent of not going to see *Intermezzo*, since, on account of Ingrid Bergman's name, we mistakenly assumed that it was a Nazi production. I was also kept busy by my friends, by books, and by everything connected with school. My ravenous reading had become such an addiction that — it is with shame that I relate it — when I accompanied Bo on her outings and she took my arm to support herself, I held a book in the other hand and read while walking, for her gait was slower than mine, and I should otherwise have been bored. Reading was no longer confined to Mme. de Ségur's works. I now read *Uncle Tom's Cabin* and *Little Women*, as well as world literature, such as a children's version of *Don Quixote*, given me by Aunt Golda, and

Balzac's *Eugénie Grandet*, a birthday present from other relatives, a novel which I found very arduous, although I conscientiously plodded on to the end, vaguely aware of its quality of realism.

We were liberally supplied with homework, which often kept me busy till nine in the evening. It was in the summer of that year that Jenny and I listened together in the evenings to broadcasts of the performances given at the musical contest sponsored by Queen Elisabeth of Belgium. The candidates were required to play a piano concerto, a modern composition that at first jarred on our untrained ears, but with which we became reconciled as a result of repeated hearings. In spite of being totally naive and unschooled listeners, we recognized the outstanding quality of the best player, who was awarded the coveted first prize. The name of this Russian pianist was Emil Gilels, and for him, this was the beginning of an international career.

Bo went off to spend the summer of 1939 in Ostend, where she shared a couple of rented rooms with an aged relative, Aunt Taube. As soon as the school holidays began, I was to join them. I was eleven years old, and it was a great adventure to make the train journey — which in those days of steam engines took three hours — on my own. Jenny and Bernard brought me to the station, put me on the train, and in Ostend I was met by the two old ladies.

The summer of 1939 was a glorious one — in my memory, the sun shines perpetually, it is warm, and the beach is crowded, indeed overcrowded, with holidaymakers. Other members of the Antwerp family and a great many acquaintances congregated there daily; among them was a family called Bark (formerly Barkowski) who lived in England. Had their friendship begun in Odessa, or did it date from Bo's stay in England during the First World War? It never occurred to me to inquire.

A nephew of Bo's from Russia, a Dr. Eli Volodarsky, also put in an appearance for a couple of weeks. He had emigrated as a young boy to Norway where he became a doctor, financing the cost of his medical studies by working as a telegraph boy during the day and reading anatomical and pathological textbooks at night. He was now an established medical authority, the leading lung surgeon of the country; he was a handsome big man in his forties, and his arrival set the

7. SILVIE

assembled family in a flutter, for here was an unheard-of phenomenon in a traditional Jewish family — a bachelor! Heads were put together, and brains scoured as a great number of single young women were mentally reviewed to find one who might be eligible. When the subject was broached to Dr. Volodarsky, he proved amenable to all suggestions and averred that he was perfectly willing to get married. Nonetheless, all efforts came to naught, and he returned to Norway unwed as before. He was to play a minor but decisive role in my life later.

We spent our days on the beach, where I played in the sand with other children, building elaborate fortifications, digging trenches filled with water poured from small buckets, or burying ourselves completely in sand so that only part of our face emerged from the wet mounds that we patted into place by hand or with small spades. Among these playmates was a girl of my own age, whom I found disturbingly attractive. Her body fascinated me — she was slightly plump, and the rounded, firm sunburned flesh of her limbs mysteriously moved me.

In the intervals of playing, I also spent hours reading. One of the ladies in the circle of grown-ups on the edge of which I sat, was scandalized by the fact that I read the women's magazine *Marie Claire*, which I bought every week as soon as it made its appearance on the kiosk newsstands and read from cover to cover (fashion reports, instructions about the most effective makeup to apply, recipes, articles on how to cope with children, and, of course, romantic stories, in which a woman fell in love with her son-in-law or discovered that her husband was having an affair with her best friend); she said in a sour tone that I was much too young for this, and she wondered very much whether my mother really allowed me to indulge in this reading — I triumphantly assured her that this was the case.

We went back to the flat for dinner, and that summer a minor miracle happened. What my stay in the preventorium four years ago had failed to achieve, the bracing sea air and presumably the precursors of adolescence did: for the first time in my life I discovered the pleasures of eating. To Bo's delight, I was constantly hungry, and she no longer had to urge me to finish the meals she and Auntie Taube took turns cooking. This relative was an exceptionally meek and kind person, radiating a mildness that made me overlook (or should I say, overhear?)

her snores at night. She was very pious, wore a wig, and said her prayers every morning. I was deeply impressed by her sincerity and utter lack of fanaticism, but most of all by her sheer goodness.

In the evening, the entire family roamed along the promenade on their way to a booth where an Italian clan sold a large variety of ice cream specialities, the quality of which was extolled anew every day. To my undiscriminating taste, ice cream was ice cream, and I stuck steadfastly to vanilla or chocolate, while the grown-ups were always trying what seemed to me unnecessarily exotic flavors. We then sat down and watched the milling masses parading up and down; my relatives found the sight of some desiccated, elderly Englishwomen in evening gowns — they were promptly declared to be old maids — extraordinarily amusing.

By way of entertainment, we once went to see a German operetta, Franz Lehár's *Das Land des Lächelns* (*The Land of Smiles*), because the principal singer was Richard Tauber, a Viennese Jew living in exile. We sat in the gallery (the cheapest tickets) in a dismal, three-quarters-empty theater. The story was set in an imaginary exotic China, but to my eyes, which were accustomed to the glamour of Hollywood films, it all seemed very tame and amateurish. Richard Tauber was a rather fat man, incredibly required by the plot to be considered attractive. He obviously expected the audience to burst into enthusiastic applause after every aria, and the Jews who constituted a large proportion of this particular public complied with his expectations out of patriotic solidarity and the conviction that since he was a Jew, he was automatically magnificent. I found the whole performance dowdy and old-fashioned and the story preposterous, and the evening gave me a lasting distaste for the entire genre.

Among the relatives assembled in Ostend were a nephew of Bo's with his wife — when I watched her about to walk into the sea, in a black swimming suit, I was shocked by the sight of her flabby, wobbly, pallid thighs and wondered that her husband did not turn from her in disgust. She was to die suddenly a few months afterward, and the grown-ups in the family thought it a very tragic event, but I must own that I was secretly unable to understand this. Another great-nephew of Bo's, a son of Uncle Lezer, the very same to whom we so often went on Friday evenings, had recently become the father of a little boy, whom he

7. SILVIE

proudly sat on his shoulders. The precocious intelligence of this child, who at the age of one was able to converse in well-phrased sentences like a grown-up, was the subject of universal admiration.

Another of Uncle Lezer's children staying in Ostend was his daughter, nineteen or twenty years old, who was singularly unattractive, rather stupid, and had a pronounced limp. A young man who also seemed to have little to distinguish him, either in looks or intelligence, was courting her; and she played little games with him. She dragged me along with her (presumably as a kind of chaperone, or was it to witness the fact that she was desired?) when she ran away from him and then hid behind a cabin, waiting for him to find her in this game which I thought extraordinarily silly, while realizing that it was really pathetic. Within a year she married him, and he turned out to be a scoundrel, subsequently denouncing the Jews in Antwerp to the Germans in order to save his own life (but do we know to what the extremity of fear may drive us?). She had a baby, a daughter, who died in Auschwitz a few weeks before her mother.

But of these developments we had no inkling then. Toward the end of August, the Bark family decided to return to England a little earlier than originally planned. Although they gave recent political events as the reason for this precipitate departure, we remained blissfully unaware of what was happening in Europe, since we read no newspapers and had no wireless. A couple of days later, Jenny, who had regularly written me delightful letters during the last six weeks, phoned our landlady and said that I was to take the train the very next day and come home. Jenny and Bernard met me at the station and could not stop marveling at our utter ignorance of what was brewing in Germany and Poland and had evidently been increasingly preoccupying them. A couple of days later, the Second World War broke out.

8. FLIGHT FROM ANTWERP

The atmosphere in Belgium was very tense as people feared that the pattern of 1914 might be repeated and the country invaded. Belgium was eager to maintain strict neutrality, as evidenced by the fact that when we went to the cinema, we were presented with both the French and the German newsreels — which were surprisingly similar. We saw soldiers entering their supposedly impregnable stations on the Maginot and Siegfried lines, both French and German recruits trotting along underground corridors or alertly descending the stairs into these modern military catacombs, grinning and looking absurdly cheerful. We watched dull and boring sequences showing German and French factory workers manufacturing munitions, rows upon rows of shining bullets demonstrating the might of the respective armies that were to fire them.

All this did not affect our normal course of life, and in that autumn we gave up the flat in the Rembrandtstraat because the rent was too dear. Our finances were so straitened that we had to sell our piano to cover the costs of moving. It was bought by an old gentleman who wanted to give it to one of his grandchildren as a Christmas present.

This move was decidedly a social comedown. The Rembrandtstraat was situated in a prosperous part of Antwerp where well-to-do people lived. We moved to the Longue Rue du Vanneau or Lange Kiewitstraat in the very midst of the "ghetto," and the rooms of our new flat were not so light or pleasant. We had a very long living room, and, as we separated our household from Bo's, Jenny cooked in the darkest corner of this room, Bo being in possession of the kitchen a couple of stairs further up. I still slept with her, and she looked after me during the daytime, so I had two dinners a day, for Jenny took to cooking in the evenings.

8. FLIGHT FROM ANTWERP

On the ground floor lived a very pious Jewish family: a ritual slaughterer, his young wife, who in spite of the fact that she wore a wig was fresh and attractive, and their two little sons. The boys frequently incurred the wrath of their father, who chased them around the back garden under the windows of our living room in order to give them a good hiding. To my surprise, Jenny and the young woman took to one another, exchanging views, in particular, on the virtues and advantages of tampons that were just coming onto the market and the use of which the pious wife, who had tried them out, advocated as against the traditional sanitary towels that were then of the reusable type and had to be laboriously washed every month. (Do women realize what comfort they thoughtlessly enjoy nowadays?) Relations between these unlikely partners were not limited to social chit-chat, for Jenny regularly bought calf liver from the husband, and with my newly awakened appetite, I discovered a new dish, which I ate with great relish. One of the advantages of living in a busy central part of town was that there was a shop opposite us, where we opened an "account" which was settled at the end of the month. I was regularly sent to purchase 100 grams of smoked salmon, a delicacy that was very cheap in those days.

The upshot of this new style of living was that Jenny began to put on weight. As long as she had been contented with her staple daily diet of four bars of chocolate (which was bought in boxes containing thirty bars — a week's ration) and liberally sweetened hot lemon juice, she had been enviably slim. But when to this was added a normal amount of food, she became plump and lost some of her lithe attractiveness.

My way to school now took me a quarter of an hour instead of five minutes, and I usually walked with another girl, called Stella, who lived a few houses away. She was also eleven or twelve years old, but much taller than I and further advanced in her development. Knowing things which it was thought better not to know at our age, she had the reputation of being brazen. (It was rumoured that she consorted with boys, and that they hid behind bushes in the park to do undisclosed naughty things there.) To go to school, we had to walk through the central park, deserted on those chilly autumn and winter mornings. One day our little group of three or four girls found itself facing a sombre-looking man who stood there half-naked with his trousers lowered to his ankles. Stella took in the situation at a glance and *sotto voce* directed us to ignore the man, walk briskly past him and look steadfastly in the other direction. Regardless of her bad name, I at any rate felt very grateful for her expert handling of the situation. Being knowledgeable might not be such a bad thing after all.

Shortly afterwards, Stella had a bad accident at home. She was standing near the open door of a stove warming herself when her nightdress caught fire, and her back was badly burned. A week afterward, I went in a delegation from school to visit her in her shabby home. Lying on a couch, she dramatically described how she suddenly found herself on fire and the dreadful pain she had to endure during the following days.

Above us lived a family that had a decided resemblance to ours before Jenny's second marriage. It also consisted of a grandmother, mother, and a little girl a year or two younger than I, who took to visiting me in the late afternoons when I was doing my homework. But she did not really seek my company — what allured her was something else. In our "Petit Larousse" dictionary she had discovered some plates illustrating the anatomy of the human body. Every day she turned to the picture of the male (the female body did not interest her), in which all the muscles were depicted in shades of a reddish brown, and eagerly and gloatingly studied it. When I told Jenny this, she seemed to think that this behavior was disgusting and perverse and decreed that these visits must cease forthwith.

Despite these intrusions of sex into daily life and our assiduous visits to the cinema, where I had by now seen countless love films, I remained remarkably naive. At school, I could not help noticing — with yearning envy — that breasts were sprouting under the dresses of many fellow-pupils, a few of whom were indeed already generously endowed with a voluptuous bosom. Secretly I entertained the hope that I would someday also be able to exhibit such attractive protuberances. But when the twelve-year-old or thirteen-year-old son of one of Bo's nieces, a boy called Jacques, took to calling on me some afternoons, I could not discern in this anything but an utterly innocent and inexplicable interest in my person and was faintly irritated by the fact that Silvie was tickled to death by these visits and teased me about them.

8. FLIGHT FROM ANTWERP

One afternoon, Yeshurun unexpectedly called on us together with their Disenhaus friends Georges and Denise, who had motored to Antwerp for a business appointment. I was acutely aware of the fact that our tasteless furniture made it evident that we were the "poor relatives," and uncultured to boot, in particular since they commented on the fact that Bo's rooms seemed to be cleaner and tidier than Jenny's living room, where they found me doing my homework. Yeshurun made a great show of not understanding Bo's Yiddish, continually repeating, "What is she saying?" a behavior which, after their departure, was condemned by Jenny as indicating that he was ashamed of his Jewishness in front of his Gentile friends.

That autumn, Jenny and Bernard went to great exertions to earn additional money. After their marriage, they had bought modern bedroom furniture and were consequently burdened with the installment payments. Now, to pay it off, they acted as commercial agents for a new brand of toilet soap that was to be launched on the market, calling on small shopkeepers in the evenings, after Jenny came home from work. They were quite successful and hauled in a great many orders. Unfortunately, they had the bad luck of working on behalf of a fraudulent firm: when the ordered goods were delivered, the bars turned out to be of a coarse variety bearing no resemblance to the smoothly textured, alluringly perfumed samples they had shown to prospective customers. Not only did they earn no commissions, they were compelled to make profuse apologies to the shopkeepers and to refund advance payments out of their own pockets.

They just seemed to be dogged by bad luck, as was shown by another venture on which they embarked and in which they collected orders for coal. That year, the winter was exceptionally cold, and the price of coal soared as it was unexpectedly scarce. (It was rumored that all the Belgian coal was going to Germany, to help their war effort.) In our new flat, where we no longer had central heating but coal-fired stoves, we were also hard put to get the amount required to fuel them. Once again, Jenny and Bernard had no difficulty in procuring orders, as everyone was eager to buy as much coal as they could get. The trouble started when weeks passed by and deliveries were not made as promised, so that irate customers began to appear at the door, where they overwhelmed us with voluble complaints. I daresay it was a blessing that we had no telephone — I am sure it would not have stopped ringing all day long.

The autumn and winter of 1939–1940 were accompanied by constant rumors that the Germans were about to invade Belgium. We had read the newspaper reports and seen the newsreels of the Polish campaign, and in the spring came the invasion of Denmark and Norway. Between these events, the winter was characterized by what was called "la drôle de guerre" (the phony war) in France — a state of expectant, unreal inertia. In late autumn, the Soviet Union invaded Finland. The Belgian press roundly condemned this in much stronger terms than it used for Germany's aggressions, and money was collected at school for the Finns. This was accompanied by very emotional descriptions of the bravery of this little nation, heroically resisting the onslaught of the evil Communists.

With the approach of spring, a strange calm descended on Belgium, in spite of the fighting in Norway, and we relaxed, relegating all thoughts of an impending catastrophe to the backs of our minds, confident that everything was going to stay normal.

After Jenny had successfully organized the by now traditional party for my twelfth birthday, I went to visit the Disenhauses in Brussels during the Easter holidays. The cold weather had given way to a benign, warm spring. Our former tenant, Schlam Goldschläger, who worked as a diamond cutter in Antwerp, took me along with him on the train to Brussels, where he now lived. He had recently married a Gentile woman, and he took me to their home, where I waited for Golda to come and fetch me. His wife, a Flemish-looking blonde, resembling a somewhat sturdy Memling Madonna, was expecting their first child and well advanced in pregnancy. She sat on a chair while he lovingly combed her long hair with the look of one performing a religious ritual, and I, greatly embarrassed, watched a scene for which my visits to the cinema had not prepared me.

In the course of this visit, Isy enthusiastically told me about a film with the Marx brothers, which he had recently seen. In particular, he related a scene in which a boat cabin was packed with twenty-four people, ever more passengers being pushed into a space that was

8. FLIGHT FROM ANTWERP

already so full that it was inconceivable anybody else could still fit into it, an illustration of the saying that where there is a will there is also a way. This was not the kind of film to which we went, but I developed a taste for the zaniness of this brand of humor at a much later age, a preference that was of course powerfully aided by my adoration for my cousin. Another anecdote that impressed me was that school friends of Isy who had seen him on the street with Golda had inquired the next day as to who was the alluring young female he was taking out.

At the end of April I returned to Antwerp and school. In spite of Germany's occupation of Denmark and invasion of Norway (we were beginning to get used to such events), spring began auspiciously. Jenny was full of enthusiasm for the new fashions; after carefully choosing and purchasing flowery-patterned material for summer dresses, in which white petticoat frills were to peep below the hems, we made the usual pilgrimage to the currently patronized dressmaker. Rosy financial times were, moreover, in the offing, for in June installment payments for the bedroom furniture were due to cease. Things were looking up.

On Thursday, 9 May 1940, I sat up alone doing my homework, which I did not finish until half past ten. (I wonder retrospectively at what Belgian elementary schools expected as a matter-of-course from twelve-year-olds. If I needed so long — and I was a gifted and industrious pupil — how on earth did an average girl manage to meet these requirements?) Jenny and Bernard had gone to the pictures to see *The Rains Came* and returned as I was packing my books away for the next morning. Jenny had been very disappointed; the film fell far short of Louis Bromfield's book on which it was based.

In the middle of the night, I was roused by distant booming, but as we'd had several thunderstorms during the preceding weeks, I thought no more of it and turned over to resume my sleep. However, this thunderstorm did not gradually abate, and, re-awakened, I noticed that the sound was not a rumbling one but a regularly spaced repetition of explosions. After a while, we all got up, and it was clear that something untoward had happened. We switched the wireless on and learned that Belgium had been invaded by the Germans, and that the booming was coming from anti-aircraft guns.

Oddly enough, our first instinct was to act as if life was going to continue as usual — Jenny went to work and I to school at the normal time. However, we were sent home, for school was closed for the time being, and after half an hour, Jenny also returned to report that her employer, Mr. Strauss, had been interned with his eldest son, who was sixteen years old, on the ludicrous ground that they were German subjects, although their native country had years ago deprived them as Jews of their nationality. They were kept in an internment camp until the invaders arrived, and were then immediately turned over to the Germans for whatever kind fate these might have in store for them.

A tense waiting marked the next few days. On Saturday we went to Silvie's, where Aunt Sophie was staying on a visit from England and where Jonas and Silvie were vaguely envisioning trying to get to England with her. On the wireless, we heard the king call upon the Belgians to resist the onslaught on their country with the aid of our new allies, the French and British. Great play was made of the allegedly impregnable obstacle that the fortified Canal Albert represented. It was regarded as Belgium's Maginot Line.

Within a few days, the hope pinned on this fabulous canal collapsed as the radio announced that the Germans had crossed it in spite of the act of bravery of a single Belgian officer. Apparently, the blowing up of some rampart that was supposed to take place in just such an emergency had been "forgotten," whether by negligence or as a result of complicity with the invaders. As Belgium is such a small country, it was immediately clear to the most obtuse that with their recent record of overrunning Poland and Norway in a *Blitzkrieg*, it was only a matter of days, perhaps hours, before the Germans would enter Antwerp.

A general exodus began — on the streets, every car in sight was being packed as people prepared to leave. This urge to flee had seized not only Jews but also the non-Jewish Belgian population, and this puzzled me, for I could not understand what motive impelled the *Gentiles* to run away, leaving their homes behind. On Monday, 13 May, the whole town seemed about to be deserted. Yet Jenny was dithering and dilly-dallying about what to do. I was in the grip of hysterical panic, and a premonition of terrible dark things to come haunted me — on the landing in front of Bo's rooms, I lost all self-control and stamped

8. FLIGHT FROM ANTWERP

my feet in a frenzy, shouting "I want to go! I want to go!" In the oddly unreal atmosphere of those days, my outburst settled the issue, and all of a sudden the entire family agreed to flee.

We packed a few suitcases in a hurry as if we were going on holiday, without considering what would be most sensible to take if one were not to return, and left on foot for the railway station. The streets were thronged with people, all going in the same direction. When we got there, we ludicrously gave up some of our luggage to be forwarded to our destination. Even more ludicrously, the railway officials accepted it, giving us the usual slips with which to reclaim our suitcases in due time.

I am not sure whether we bought tickets or just boarded the train that was to bring us to De Panne / La Panne. This holiday resort is the last one of a series strung along Belgium's tiny coast, and it lies in the immediate proximity of the French border. When the war broke out in September 1939, a great many people rented villas there because La Panne had been the only locality that was not taken by the Germans during the First World War, and they blithely assumed that history was going to repeat itself.

It took several hours before the overcrowded train left Antwerp. In those days of steam engines, the journey should normally have taken three hours. But it soon became clear that such timetables did not apply in times of war. The train ran for about ten minutes before it shunted to a standstill. After a long period, it went on for a couple of miles before again stopping. And this stop-and-go set the pattern for the rest of our journey. Occasionally, the train even ran backward for a few hundred yards. At frequent intervals, trains going in the opposite direction passed us. They were transporting French soldiers to the front, wherever that might have been at the moment (at any rate still behind us!). Good-looking young men waved to us, smiling and laughing; and for a short while, we felt relief that they were coming to our aid.

Our train was packed, and here I indeed saw only Jewish people. In the nervous irritation that is normal in abnormal circumstances, a quarrel over some trivial point flared up between Jenny and some other passengers and she thought it fit to lend force to her position by shouting, "*I* am a Belgian!" implying that, since the others were not, their arguments were by definition invalid. I loved her dearly, but at that moment, I felt ashamed of my mother.

After this first night spent sitting on the hard wooden benches, Jenny, yearning for her bed, deeply regretted that we had left Antwerp, a feeling I was unable to share or understand, for I was obsessed by an urge to get as far away from the Germans as possible. On this second day, which was a Tuesday, we passed many villages and saw bombed houses for the first time; a great number had been gutted by fire and displayed their gaping windows and uncovered roofs like wounds.

Toward the end of that day, police walked through our compartment, escorting a furious-looking strapping blond woman who, upon closer inspection, turned out to be a man dressed in a dark costume, his fat legs in silk stockings full of ladders. Apparently, he was a spy who during the night had signaled with a torch to direct German bombers to their targets. Soon after this incident, Jenny fell into a heavy unnatural slumber, and she was afterward convinced that this was because of some substance this agent had released in our compartment.

On the following day we reached our destination at last and scrambled out of the train, dirty and tired. The streets of La Panne were milling with cars and refugees on foot. An hour or two later, we found, by dint of many inquiries, the villa that Uncle Lezer — Bo's nephew, at whose home we had so often spent Friday evenings in Hassidic atmosphere — had rented. It was overflowing with relatives, and we were obliged to spend the night sleeping on the floor of the living room.

The next morning, I accompanied Jenny and Bernard to the railway station, where they fondly hoped to collect the suitcases that had been sent on from Antwerp. Helpless railway clerks let us into a large storeroom where we saw thousands of suitcases, stacked in high piles, without discovering our own. Indeed, even if they had been there, it was exceedingly unlikely that we should have found them — it would have been tantamount to retrieving the proverbial needle from a haystack.

We stayed two days in La Panne, the news about the progress of the Germans becoming ever more alarming. Antwerp had fallen. The course now to be taken was heatedly discussed in family conferences — at some point, Jenny, Bernard, and Bo decided to try to flee to England, and when they announced their intention to do so, Uncle Lezer shouted that he would rather die than go again to England, where he had spent

8. FLIGHT FROM ANTWERP

the First World War and apparently suffered anti-Semitic humiliations. The hatred I witnessed on this occasion was paralleled only by an outburst of Yeshurun's at a later date, when he told me how, when he was a young man in 1919, Poles had thrown him out of a running train merely because he was a Jew. I clearly recollect how Uncle Lezer spat out his momentous words — he had his youngest grandson of one and a half years in his arms — as he angrily paced about the room. Little did he imagine that he would indeed die a few years later, and had he been aware of the terrible circumstances in which this would happen, he might have thought differently.

As rumors were spreading that the French were about to close the frontier, we took the luggage we had with us and left Uncle Lezer and his family, never to see them again.

After plodding along a road lined on both sides with cars that had been abandoned because there was no petrol to be had anywhere, our luck held, and we passed the frontier controls without any difficulty (I believe we were among the last to do so), continuing to walk along the same road with hundreds of other refugees. People were carrying bundles and suitcases, or pushing prams packed full of their belongings. Bo, a bent old woman, trudged bravely and silently along on her thick, varicose-veined legs for kilometer after kilometer. Once we went into an inn to drink tea and lemonade and witnessed a strange scene. We found there the members of a rich Jewish family from Antwerp, who, to my surprise, were not unknown to Bo and Jenny (but then the Jewish part of the town had been very much like a big village in which everybody was somehow acquainted with everybody else, at least insofar as they always knew gossip about them). A middle-aged man and a woman were struggling with their mad sister, who at home had been kept concealed behind locked doors. She was a big, handsome woman, with a mane of black unruly hair. Casting wild looks about her, she was expending furious energy on trying to free herself from the grasp of her relatives, and uttering inarticulate sounds like an animal. There was something extraordinarily painful in the distressing nakedness of this family scene. Beside the shame they obviously felt, it was moving to see how they were trying to save not only their own lives but also that of their crazed sister, whom they would not abandon in adverse circumstances.

We spent the night in a village bistro where we sat on wooden chairs, listening to the uninterrupted buzz of German airplanes flying overhead. The next morning, we tried to find ways and means of moving on. People were throwing big money about to get local car-owners to drive them a few kilometers further west. With our paltry means, we could not compete, and so we took to the road again and reached another small village late in the evening. A farmer was willing to let us sleep in his attic, where we even found beds, which he perhaps let to holiday makers in the summer. We were utterly exhausted and fell into a profound sleep. In the night, I dimly heard the roar of airplanes, and the unmistakable sound of bombs dropping (the target was an aerodrome nearby), but the tiredness that blanketed me was so absolute that even I was not able to feel the fear to which I was so prone normally, but willingly dropped into the pit of sleep again.

The next morning we heard that during the air raid, the farmer and his family had fled to a nearby shelter, without wasting a thought on our safety. However, they made up for this by giving us a breakfast, which has remained permanently inscribed in my memory as being the occasion when I ate the best soft-boiled egg of my life. Never again have I eaten an egg that had such a velvety, succulent taste. It was the only time during our flight that I ate anything with relish. Otherwise, I was so filled with the vibrations of the fear that was raging inside me that the hunger instinct was completely blocked. I was continually inwardly repeating like a mantra a prayer that ran, "Oh G'd, please, please let me stay alive and have ordinary troubles."

For a ludicrously small sum, we surprisingly found a French innkeeper willing to drive us to Dunkirk in his car. Another family already huddled inside, and as there was no room for him as well, we left Bernard behind. But soon after we reached Dunkirk, where we roamed the streets with masses of other refugees, we were reunited and heard that soon after we left, soldiers had given him a lift in a lorry. We found a baker's shop that was still open — most of the others had closed, as they had sold out following the onslaught of the Belgian crowds — and queued up for fresh baguettes before setting out to find a place to sleep. Once again, a bistro gave us shelter for the night.

8. FLIGHT FROM ANTWERP

The next morning, we went to the British Consulate, where we were given a cool reception. A young woman told us that Bo, as the holder of a British passport, could be repatriated on a ship that was due to come and collect British subjects, but that we would certainly not be allowed on board. Bo refused to be parted from us, and we decided to go on to Calais.

I cannot remember how we got there — I believe we actually went on a local train, for we arrived at the station in the late afternoon. Here too the streets were teeming with refugees, and we walked aimlessly around the town. Oddly enough, I recall seeing Rodin's great monument to the burghers of Calais outside the town hall and, despite my obsession with flight, being impressed, during a short moment's respite, by the stark simplicity of the massive sculpture.

A French family agreed to let us spend the night in their living room, where we caught fitful snatches of sleep sitting on straight-backed chairs in a gloomy room. The alarming sound of airplanes repeatedly woke us, and we heard one or two detonations from bombs dropped on the town. In the morning, we saw that a house only a hundred yards away had been demolished by a direct hit.

We again found out where the British Consulate was, and this time the staff was friendlier. Besides offering us the chance of spending the coming night in a hall where we could sleep on the straw-covered floor, they told us that a destroyer was coming to Calais that very afternoon to repatriate British citizens, and hinted that we might "try our luck" and be taken aboard as refugees.

Accordingly, we made our way to the harbor and, since an air raid warning went off when we got there, hustled into an unlit underground shelter, which resembled an elongated Anderson shelter. We were standing in this dark tunnel, listening to the bombs and the pounding of the antiaircraft guns, when somebody called out, "All those who are here for the English ship, get out immediately." Seizing our luggage, we ran out and, a few yards away, saw a gangway leading onto a destroyer. With the German planes roaring overhead, nobody bothered to ask for passports, and the crew signaled us down a stairway under the deck.

We had hardly gotten there when a tremendous thud shook the ship, and the light overhead went out, leaving us in complete darkness. It was clear that a bomb had fallen on the deck above us, and Jenny was convinced that death was imminent. But for once I did not share her fear — from the moment that we boarded the ship, a great calm descended on me and I knew we were saved. (As I have since noticed, whenever I have been in actual danger of dying, I have not felt any fear; this is not bravery, to which I am, unfortunately, not inclined, but derives from an abrupt cessation of the production of imaginative fantasies and from an inability to recognize the reality of what is happening.)

After a few minutes, the electric lights came on again; apparently the bomb had failed to explode, and the lights had only fused. Jenny found a copy of the *Daily Mirror* lying on the table, and I was much intrigued by a comic strip in which an attractive half-naked blond female called Jane played a prominent part.

The sailors looking after us were friendly and relaxed (a great contrast to the way the French had treated us; no doubt the French population was worried and frightened too, but even if one makes allowance for this, the general impression was that a majority was predominantly interested in making as much money as possible out of the refugees' plight). After a while, I imagined that I was seasick, and one of the men took me up into the fresh air on deck and showed me the white cliffs of Dover ahead. Without our being aware of it, the destroyer had left Calais just after the unexploded bomb had fallen, and it needed no more than thirty minutes to cross the Channel at this narrowest point of the straits.

PART II
ADOLESCENCE IN ENGLAND

9. THE BLITZ

The Germans enjoy a reputation as great organizers, but to my mind the British are, in an unobtrusive and unacclaimed way, the best organizers in the world. At all events, when we landed in Folkestone in the late afternoon of Tuesday, 21st May, 1940, everything was prepared for the reception of a considerable number of refugees.

We were led to a row of tables with platefuls of sandwiches and pots of hot tea, which the Women's Voluntary Service (WVS) served us, and after we had had something to eat and drink, the adults were interviewed by civil servants who inspected their passports and took down the relevant personal particulars. For some reason or other, Jenny felt that it would be too complicated to explain that I was her daughter from a former marriage (as if she were ashamed of the fact), and so I found myself saddled with a new identity — my name henceforth being Huguette Vald instead of Huberte (the name on my birth certificate which, however, had never been used, for hardly had the ink on this document dried than my family decided to call me Huguette, a circumstance for which I have ever been grateful) Silberschatz. But it is also conceivable that Jenny's decision was influenced by the German sound of the surname.

When these formalities had been completed, we were led a few yards to the back of the quay, where we got into a train and settled down to wait for its departure, for we had been told that we should be taken to London where we were to be interned. Many hours passed before all the refugees who had arrived had been registered and the train gradually filled, and it was not far short of midnight when it finally left — in complete darkness because of the blackout. We reached London in the small hours of the morning. After we had gotten out of the train, we were escorted to a double-decker bus that took us to the Crystal Palace, which had been converted to serve as an internment center. We were detained there for ten days, a remarkably short period of time in view of the fact that the British had to make sure no members of the German spying organization known in 1940 as the "Fifth Column" were able to infiltrate under cover of being refugees.

We slept on camp beds on the tiers of the big circular hall and, apart from being fed three times a day (for dinner, we were regularly served potatoes, which had an unpleasantly sweetish savor as a result of having been blighted by frost), were left largely to our own devices. I found some other girls of my age and played with them, roaming outside the building in a yard that was enclosed by a high wall. There was a kiosk where one could buy newspapers and sweets. When Belgium capitulated, an event that occurred soon after our arrival, we saw a caricature showing King Leopold, who was regarded by the British press as a traitor, in the guise of a snake wearing a little crown, and we could not help feeling ashamed that he had — in contrast to the Dutch royal family — surrendered to the enemy.

On one occasion, we were hustled into buses and conveyed to public baths so that we could all have a bath. When we returned to the buses parked outside, a crowd of onlookers had gathered to watch the curious spectacle provided by the exotic refugee creatures we apparently were. A woman came forward and gave me a box of licorice allsorts, and a journalist photographed the moving scene. (Unfortunately, I discovered that the licorice only had a remote affinity to the "zout jappekes," which Jenny and I had chewed with so much relish in Antwerp, and I never took to the British variety.)

During our internment, we found out that Silvie and her husband Jonas had managed to make their escape with Aunt Sophie, after her visit in Antwerp. They had boarded a British ship in Ostend and had landed a few days before we did.

On the tenth day, we were again packed into buses and taken to the town hall of Stoke Newington, where identity cards, ration books, and gasmasks were issued to us. During the following months, we often marveled at the rudimentary character of these identity cards. In Belgium, my mother's identity card — she was a Belgian subject, not a

9. THE BLITZ

foreigner! — had consisted of no less than three folded pages. On the cover, her photograph had occupied pride of place. Numerous personal characteristics, such as height, the color of eyes and hair, unusual distinguishing features like scars, etc., were listed. The British identity card, a document on gray cardboard paper, only stated the surname, Christian name, date of birth, address, sex, and registration number of the bearer. There was no photograph. This seems to me to corroborate my opinion of the British talent for organization. Even in times of war, this austere system of identification proved just as efficient as more elaborate and complicated bureaucratic alternatives.

After these documents had been issued to us, we were taken to private homes where we were billeted. I was separated from Jenny and Bernard, and was brought with Bo to a Jewish working-class family who lived in a house in Stamford Hill, on a street running at the back of a music hall on the main road. This theater exhibited large garish posters showing half-naked huge-bosomed blond women, and the underlying text made great play of the fact that parts of the show had been banned by the Lord Chancellor, who was responsible for theater censorship.

The family who had taken us in consisted of an older couple, their two daughters, and their respective husbands. The daughters both had dark hair with a lock over the forehead peroxided into a dramatically contrasting blond, something I had never seen before. The young men, who worked in a clothes factory, had little moustaches that made them look like spruce younger versions of the film star Don Ameche. The only books in the living room (and probably in the entire house) were photo albums of the royal family, devoted to such events as the Jubilee of King George V and Queen Mary, the coronation of the present king, the idyllic family life of King George VI, Queen Elizabeth and their daughters, or a record of the king and queen's official visit to Canada and the United States a couple of years ago, and I spent hours looking at these photographs, deeply impressed by the patriotism of our hosts.

These first lodgings were quite a long way from where Jenny and Bernard had been billeted, and a walk to them required forty-five minutes. Aunt Sophie and her husband, and Silvie and Jonas, also lived in the same part of Stoke Newington as Jenny and Bernard. During these long days, Bo and I felt cut off from all social intercourse and

Part II. ADOLESCENCE IN ENGLAND

Huguette 1940

were very bored. As Jenny discovered that there was another room vacant in the house where they were staying, she arranged to get official permission for us to move into it. I think our hosts were quite relieved to have us leave, since we found it difficult to communicate with them.

The furnished room into which we now moved was in a large semi-detached house with a neglected front garden — we were very impressed by the fact that most English houses had front gardens, and, as it was the beginning of June, marveled at the beauty of the roses that were blooming everywhere — and was owned by an elderly, aggressive, gray-haired Jewish woman, who was continually picking quarrels with one and all, so that the day was punctuated by the outbreak of loud scenes. Ironically, the wooden gate to the garden had a plate bearing the ludicrous name "Amicitia."

Nonetheless, I owe this landlady a debt of gratitude, for she signed a guarantee both for Jenny and myself, enabling us to become readers of Stoke Newington's Public Library. This opened something like a paradise to me, for there was a special children's section in a separate room. A friendly librarian was in charge, and the books on the shelves were all accessible so that one could take them down and start reading to see if one wanted to go on. No blind ordering from inscrutable

9. THE BLITZ

book lists as had been the case in Belgium. As I still knew very little English, I think I was quite cunning in my choice of the first book I borrowed. Being familiar with La Fontaine's fables, I decided to read them in translation. Jenny bought me a minuscule pocket dictionary at a Woolworth shop. It was red and had a format of roughly two and a half by three and a half inches. I assiduously looked up all the words I didn't know and in the opposite direction searched for the appropriate English expressions when talking to people. In addition, I continually pestered my mother, who was obliged to act as a living dictionary.

After the La Fontaine translation, I grew bolder — for I was learning apace — and borrowed Mark Twain's *Tom Sawyer*. I found this difficult but greatly relished the humor of the scene in which its hero transforms the punishment of having to paint his aunt's fence into a source of riches by allowing friends the privilege of standing in for him in return for generous payment. And when I read how Tom and his friends attended their own funeral and heard how they were posthumously praised and extolled as they had never been while alive, I felt a distinct twinge of envy.

I also ventured into the adult section of the public library. Presumably because a number of immigrants had in the past settled in Stoke Newington, it boasted a good foreign literature section. I borrowed some French novels, and to prevent my forgetting Flemish, I also read a few Dutch books, among them a stodgy historical novel by Henri Conscience. By chance, I hit upon a novel by a modern Dutch author, whose name I do not recall — it was the story of an upper-class family, some of whose members were diplomats. Although they were rich, they found it difficult to make ends meet, a situation with which I was familiar, in view of Jenny's chronic inability to manage her finances. But what impressed me most was that a young daughter was very neurotic and had treatment that I later identified as psychotherapy. It is a book I should like to reread today, if I knew its title or the name of its author.

We also resumed our habit of going to the pictures. As far as I can remember, the adults were given an allowance in order to relieve the billeters from having to cook for us, and we were able to spare enough to go to the movies. I recall seeing a pre-war Hollywood version of

David Copperfield. We also went to see the film of Bernard Shaw's *Major Barbara*, and Jenny and Bernard were amazed by the freedom of speech that was possible in Great Britain, for the film contained sequences in which the House of Commons was held up to ridicule, it being asserted that members of Parliament were only able to stand the stress of long sessions by having recourse to lavish draughts of alcohol.

As we had arrived in England with only two suitcases, we were short of everything and were given extra coupons so that we could buy a few clothes. We also received extra money for this from other sources — the Polish Refugee Fund, a Jewish charity that aided not only Polish refugees but also those from other countries, was one of the donors. So we went shopping. England was not a country with small dressmakers at every corner, but one in which people bought ready-made clothes in shops. We had some difficulty with the prices, which were often indicated in guineas, and to complicate the matter still further, in fractions, for instance, "3½ guineas." (A guinea was £1.1s.0d or £1.05 in decimal currency; the pound had 20 shillings.) Jenny was nonplussed by the fact that the shop assistants took no pains whatsoever to sell anything — when one tried a dress on and emerged from the cubbyhole where one had changed into it in order to view oneself in a mirror, they just stood by looking profoundly bored and saying nothing, whereas we were accustomed, from our rare shopping expeditions in Belgian department stores, to having the assistant declare that the dress looked absolutely lovely and was just the right color and design. Although we were well aware of the fact that this was a mere selling strategy, we missed it and thought the girls indolent and stupid.

A few weeks after we had moved to our lodgings in "Amicitia," a relative of Bo's called Schicke, who had a reputation for being an incorrigible liar and who worked as overseer in a textile factory in Stoke Newington, turned up. He was the son of one of Bo's nieces (said niece, owing to the quirks of a family of fourteen children, was a year older than Bo but had always called her "aunt," a circumstance that had greatly puzzled me since, to my mind, an aunt had to be visibly much older than her niece) and had been cast out of the family when he fell in love with a Gentile Englishwoman and married her. Whenever he had visited his mother in Antwerp, she had always refrained from alluding

9. THE BLITZ

to the fact that he had a wife and daughter in London. The latter, called Nora, was like me twelve years old; and Schicke suggested that I come and stay with them for a week or two. We readily agreed, and so I accompanied him to a suburb at the other end of London. After we had gotten out of the trolleybus, we walked for about ten minutes along streets lined by neat, modern, little houses. Schicke's wife was a middle-aged, dark-haired, rather ugly little woman — to my film-blurred mind, it was hard to imagine what had induced Schicke to fall in love with her. The fact that Schicke himself was also physically unattractive and that this very English woman was probably kind and pleasant to live with did not occur to me. Strangely enough, this plain couple had produced a resplendent beauty of a daughter: Nora was blond and rather athletic in build — she looked like the epitome of Scandinavian femininity, a bit like a very young Ingrid Bergman. My English was not yet exactly fluent, but I was very eager to strike up a friendship with her, and she seemed amiable and willing enough to respond. To my surprise, I discovered that she was totally unfamiliar with biblical lore, and when I mentioned this to Schicke in the evening, he said that biblical stories were fairy tales and of no consequence — obviously he did not attach any importance to the fact that Western civilization has been to a large extent influenced, if not indeed shaped, by what he, as an atheist and Communist, regarded as meaningless myths.

After I had been there three days, Schicke got in touch with Jenny and said she must come and fetch me immediately, as I was wilting with homesickness, a statement that had no foundation in fact. To this day, I wonder why they apparently wanted to get rid of me no sooner than I had settled down: was it the strain of communicating with someone who had as yet but a rudimentary knowledge of English? Or was I upsetting the delicate balance of a household of three persons? Although invited, was I after all an intruder?

Jenny came with Schicke after he had finished working, and during their walk to his house asked him whether it had central heating. True to his reputation, although he was well aware that she would be able within a few minutes to ascertain that this was by no means the case, the house being fitted with the usual English open fireplaces, he affirmed that of course it was equipped with this modern convenience.

Upon my return to my family, which represented what might be called home, I began to attend the elementary school in Stoke Newington's Church Street, a huge, forbidding red-brick Victorian building. I found myself pretty much at sea — the tuition seemed limited to English and mathematics. In English, the class was reading Stevenson's *Treasure Island* — I dimly remember unattractive, eccentric characters, one of whom kept on exclaiming "Yo ho ho and a bottle of rum." This experience put me off the book for the rest of my life. Mathematics was worse, for the class was mainly working on sums of the kind: "If a train requires 3 hours, 40 minutes, and 6 seconds to get from A to B, which are at a distance of 123 miles and 60 yards, 1 foot, 3/4 inches from each other, how long will it need to cover a distance of 74 miles, 20 yards, 2 feet, 6 1/3 inches from C to D?" Innumerable variations included sums involving gallons, pints, guineas, florins, and half-crowns. I was used to handling with some competence the splendid simplicity of the decimal system, and the required adjustment to the complexity of these medieval measures threw me completely off balance. I never recovered, and whereas in Belgium, I had been good — but not brilliant — at arithmetic, from now on it was a struggle to merely get along.

The afternoons were mainly spent doing country dancing, which I liked but which did not answer to my traditional notions of what a school was for. At regular intervals, we also practiced what to do in an air raid and rushed to the cloakroom, where we cowered under the pegs and put on our gasmasks, which in those days we always carried with us. This special part of the emergency drill was not of a nature to increase my confidence in the reliability of the gasmask, for the air inside almost instantaneously became uncomfortably humid and hot. Indeed, we never kept it on for longer than a minute or so. We also had singing sessions, in which we sang popular songs such as, "I've got sixpence, jolly, jolly sixpence, I've got sixpence to last me all my life. I've got tuppence to spend, and tuppence to lend, and tuppence to send home to my wife." This referred to the daily pay to which a soldier was entitled.

After a few weeks, I struck up a friendship with a girl called Trudi Goldblum. She was a refugee from Vienna, and her mother invited me to their home, where I was puzzled to hear her referring to her daughter

9. THE BLITZ

in German as "die Trudi" (*the* Trudi) as if she were an object, like a table or chair. I didn't then know that this is a legitimate form in South German. Trudi and I talked a lot about the cinema and books, endlessly enthusing about Louisa May Alcott's *Little Women*, which we had both just read.

The summer of 1940, which followed an exceptionally warm and dry spring, continued to bring sustained sunshine, blue skies, and very little rain. People said that even the weather was on Hitler's side. We refugees felt that we were only enjoying a respite, and when Hitler told the world that by August 1940 he would make a speech from the balcony of Buckingham Palace, we could not help fearing that this was a real possibility, although the threat left the British public quite unperturbed. At the public library, I studied articles in a weekly periodical called the "Tatler," which described the strategy and tactics used by the Germans during the invasion of France. I pored over innumerable drawings and sketches showing the massed power of the tank battalions and of the artillery that had been used in recent offensives and these brought a chill to my heart, for I could not help feeling that this formidable enemy could not be defeated.

A social life sprung up around us. The Barks, the family that had so suddenly left Ostend the year before, lived almost around the corner. We frequently dropped in to see them, and I got to know their two sons, Henry and Daniel, a year older and a year younger than I, respectively. Often, we spent the afternoons or evenings in their garden, watching the blue sky, which was full of floating barrage balloons. They looked a bit like small Zeppelins and were supposed to ward off enemy aircraft. When it came to the point, they proved to be absolutely useless, and in the course of the war they disappeared. Although we had been classified as "friendly aliens" — in contrast to the refugees from Germany and Austria, who were considered to be "enemy aliens" — we had to observe a curfew and be home by ten o'clock.

We saw a lot of Aunt Sophie and her husband and of Silvie and Jonas as well, of course. As a rule, refugees were not yet allowed to work, and Jonas was chafing at his enforced inactivity. However, the ban was lifted for him quite early, since work on diamonds was important for the war industry. As for Jenny, she went to the Belgian Embassy, which

Part II. ADOLESCENCE IN ENGLAND

Huguette feeding pigeons

offered to take her on their staff as a secretary but, as they did not have sufficient funds, said that for the time being she would have to work on an unpaid voluntary basis, and she, therefore, refused (rather foolishly, for at a later date they were able to pay a handsome remuneration).

Another Jewish English family we knew were the Schwartzes. In their living room, I discovered a *Children's Encyclopedia*, and, while the adults talked, I read many of its articles — in particular, one that described the secluded, uneventful life of an author called Jane Austen, who was the daughter of a minister, wore a funny white cap, and wrote novels sporadically, always interrupting her writing when someone happened to walk into the living room where she was sitting.

The Schwartzes had two children, a son and a daughter. The son was seventeen or eighteen years old and offered to show us London on a day's excursion. He took us to the Houses of Parliament — in front of which I fed pigeons — and Westminster Abbey, Hyde Park, Piccadilly Circus, and Leicester Square. On that day, I lost a public library book, a life of St. Joan (one of my heroines), and got quite panicky about

9. THE BLITZ

the dreadful consequences this might have on my status as a borrower. Luckily, the book was retrieved at the Lost Property Office a few days later — I had left it in a tram — and I was saved.

A few months after our arrival, this uneventful sequence of days was disturbed by the outbreak of the Blitz. The sirens started to howl at every hour of the day and night. If, upon hearing the roar of the German planes (I was very soon able to distinguish their sound from the "friendly" one of the British fighters), I was caught in the street and looked up, I could clearly see their gleaming metallic forms purposefully flying in formation overhead. At night and whenever we were at home during the daytime, we would rush to the cellar, the roof of which was propped up with wooden posts and reinforced with corrugated metal sheeting; I was very dubious as to how effective this protection might prove to be if put to a real test. As we huddled there, we could hear the bombers flying above and the increasingly frequent, long drawn-out sinister whistle of a bomb falling to explode with a tremendous thud a second later. While Jenny remained quite unconcerned, in the firm belief that it was most unlikely that we should be selected for a direct hit, I was filled with sheer terror owing to my inexplicable innate awareness of profound guilt, so that I was convinced that every single bomb dropped was seeking me out personally. I took refuge with Bo, burying my head in her lap, my body shaking like a leaf in the wind.

Two boys who lived in the neighboring house were obviously totally immune to such fears, for they incessantly played a game in the garden in which they imitated the ululations of the sirens, sounding the alarm so realistically that it would turn my stomach until I realized that it was a fake.

Our nights were increasingly interrupted by air raid warnings, and we were perpetually rushing down the stairs and wearily re-ascending them after a few hours to go back to bed. The next morning, we saw the ruins of the houses in the neighborhood that had received a direct hit. Often, a single wall supporting a fraction of a room, in which some remnants of furniture pathetically remained, was still standing beside a gap full of crumbling debris.

After a good many weeks passed in this manner, it was decided that

Jenny, Bo, and I (for I was quite hysterical as a result of the incessant alarms) should leave London. Bernard did not come with us, and I was not sorry: since he had again hit Jenny during a quarrel that broke out a few days before, I harbored a great hatred for him.

10. BEDFORD CENTRAL SCHOOL

We chose to go to Bedford, to which the Barks had moved a few weeks earlier because the school their boys attended had been evacuated there. On 11th October 1940, we accordingly went to St. Pancras station to take a train that arrived in Bedford at about half past four. The first thing we did was to ask the way to the billeting office, where they gave us an address and a notification to the landlord, a Mr. Canning, telling him that he was to put us up.

He was an old gentleman who lived with two daughters in a neat, prosperous-looking semidetached house. They greeted us with consternation, for they had just got rid of some rowdy children from the East End, and they had fondly thought they were safe from further intrusions. As it was now dark, they could not very well turn us away, and agreed to take us in for the time being, making it unmistakably clear that we should on the morrow have to make determined efforts to find other accommodations. They led us upstairs, where there was a middle-sized room under the sloping roof. It had a large bed, in which there was room for the three of us, a small table along the opposite wall, two cupboards, two chairs, and an old armchair near the window that looked out on the corner of the street. In another smaller room leading off the same landing, there was a very long table that ran alongside almost the whole length of the room, a tap with (cold) running water, and a wash basin.

During the next few days, I trotted along with Jenny as we looked for alternative lodgings — we read innumerable slips offering objects for sale, rooms to let, etc., that were tacked on boards outside shops, and followed up every clue that seemed to hold out any hope of accommodation, knocking on doors only to be turned surlily away, either because the rooms had meanwhile been let or because the landlord or landlady did not want to take in three people. After a week of fruitless hunting, we were surprised by Mr. Canning informing us that he was prepared to keep us. Apparently, he and his daughters had taken a good look at us and come to the momentous decision that we seemed to be clean, generally acceptable, and reasonably quiet. Moreover, they feared that if we were to leave, the next evacuees they could be saddled with might prove far worse than we were. We also had the impression that when we had told them we were Jewish, they had at first regarded us as specimens of an exotic species, with which they had never been confronted before, but that this had been replaced by a vague respect for Jews as the people of the Book. At all events, we were tremendously relieved that our vain search was now at an end and that we could try to settle down. Mr. Canning went out and bought a small electric heater, with two coils that could be switched on separately (two coils to be used when it was very cold) and installed it in our room. We were very grateful for this, for the weather had become uncomfortably chilly.

Mr. Canning was about seventy years old, hale and hearty with ruddy cheeks, and still worked as a commercial traveler for food suppliers. He had, therefore, been granted a permit allowing him the use of his car in wartime as he needed it for his work. On Sundays, he acted as a Methodist lay preacher. The eldest daughter was a staid old maid and a teacher in an elementary school. Her younger sister, whom we at first only fleetingly saw, had in the past been a piano teacher, but did not take in pupils anymore, ever since, as we eventually found out, she had had a nervous breakdown after her engagement to an attractive young man was broken off because her father refused to give the money for the dowry that the fiancé expected to receive. Since then, she had turned "odd" and become a total recluse. Both sisters were in their forties. Mr. Canning had other children who were married and lived elsewhere.

One night, we were awakened by hysterical screaming and the sound of agitated running on the first floor downstairs, where the family's bedrooms were. We realized that the high-pitched aggressive wailing came from the younger Miss Canning and heard father and sister scolding her as if she were a naughty child. Lying in our big bed, we were disturbed and not a little frightened, but eventually peace and quiet were restored, and when the same dramatic sounds woke us repeatedly during the coming months, we knew what to expect and accepted it as a more or less normal event. A couple of years later, this younger Miss Canning lent me an exercise book which contained a story she had artlessly written when she was still at school. The whole thing revolved around endless, vapid flirtations between boys and girls, none of whom had any characteristics besides their Christian names to distinguish them from each other.

Obviously, I had to go to school again — when we broached the subject with the older Miss Canning, she made it clear that it was inconceivable that I should attend a regular Bedford school such as the one where she worked. She accordingly directed us to an elementary school evacuated from London's East End. I found myself in a class of rough girls, in which I was the only one to show any interest whatsoever in what was being taught. When, in English lessons, the others were called upon to read a text aloud, they did so haltingly in a mechanical monotone devoid of any intonation. The result was that you could not understand anything they said unless you followed the printed text. When my turn came and I read sentences as if they really meant something, this aroused surprised hilarity among my classmates — I had the success of one doing a music hall turn, and this peculiar, unheard-of performance was put down to my being a foreigner.

This was a school in which both girls and boys were taught, but they were kept strictly segregated in separate classes. The only time they came together was for assembly every morning. After prayers had been said and hymns sung, the headmaster, Mr. Mansfield, a middle-aged, handsome fair man with a reddish complexion, meted out corporal punishment, usually to boys who had misbehaved the previous day. The names of these miscreants were called out, and they had to come up to the headmaster who publicly caned them in front of us all, a spectacle that terrified me.

However, Mr. Mansfield turned out to be a benefactor, and it happened this way: a few weeks after I had started attending the school, all the pupils were given a test that had been sent by the London Education Authority. It was in the form of a questionnaire in which you had either to reply to questions by selecting the right answer from multiple choice lists or fill in the appropriate missing words in a text. At first I thought I had failed because I did not quite manage to finish within the allotted time, but it turned out that I had produced the second best paper in the entire school (the best one being from a girl who was three years older than I), and at the age of twelve was rated as having the intelligence of a sixteen-year-old. Mr. Mansfield asked Jenny to come and see him and declared that it was a waste of talent for me to remain in his school. He thought I should go to a high school, but we found out that the Bedford High was very exclusive (or snooty) and only took in Bedford children, and so he arranged for me to go to the local Central School.

It had a somewhat higher standard than the two elementary schools I had attended hitherto and was more similar to what I had been used to in Antwerp. But the pupils were just as uninterested in what was being taught as in the London school. In English, they were reading *Macbeth* when I arrived, and the Shakespeare text met with profound indifference and total incomprehension, the girls stumbling over the lines as if they were written in Chinese, the only exception being Lady Macbeth's soliloquy "Unsex me here, And fill me from the crown to the toe top full of direst cruelty … come to my woman's breasts, And take my milk for gall," which set the whole class giggling because of its sexual connotations.

On the day I arrived, the first question put to me by one of the girls was whether I had a boyfriend. I was twelve years old, and the whole idea of flirting or "going out" was for me something that would happen in a very remote future, in four or five years' time. When I truthfully answered that I had no such relationship, my standing immediately fell to zero. As for the prestige it might be imagined I would gain by very soon becoming the best pupil in my class, this left my fellow scholars quite unimpressed. In the scholastic field, there was no emulation, and I remained an exotic outsider.

There was one girl who stood out from the rest and with whom I struck up a superficial acquaintance during country dancing classes, which here, as in London, were held in the afternoon once or twice a week. She was a thin, very pretty dark-haired girl with long, spindly legs in black woolen stockings who fascinated me as she nimbly and gracefully danced with an assurance that I totally lacked. She was unusually reserved as regards personal details and only mentioned that she was also an evacuee and that her mother lived in London. One day, without previous warning, she was gone — presumably to rejoin this mysterious mother, whom I vaguely imagined to be an actress.

The Central School's teaching included practical subjects, and, among other culinary achievements, I learned to bake an apple pie. We ate it at home, and it turned out to be surprisingly good, but, as I lacked all opportunity to practice baking (we had no oven, only an electric ring cooker), I soon forgot how to go about repeating this performance, and it remained a flash in the pan (if this inappropriate metaphor may be forgiven). Sewing lessons provided me with an effective damper to the incipient danger of becoming overly conceited. Some girls were taught to make lace — this was done by twining thread around pins stuck in a cushion, and I rather fancied learning this, but, as a way of ensuring a kind of monopoly, this skill was strictly reserved for girls born in Bedford. So I had to join the other non-locals in learning to work with a sewing machine. Here I learned something very important — what it is to feel dim and utterly stupid. I understood nothing of what I was told and shown and was not even able to produce a simple straight seam. I reluctantly realized what ungifted classmates in Belgium and England must have suffered during the lessons of composition, history, geography, etc., at which I shone and which I enjoyed so much.

Over the course of the year, I struck up a friendship with a classmate called Joan, an attractive blond girl whom I accompanied on the way home from school. I resumed my old habit of inventing stories to enliven our peregrinations, and she listened spellbound to the adventures my imagination produced. One day, Jenny came with me when I unexpectedly called on Joan; and we found her mother, in a large kitchen, surrounded by my friend and her three younger sisters, all of them blond, busy baking a cake. They were like a picture from *Little Women*, all of them with floury arms and pastry sticking to their hands; and to my surprise, Jenny found this housewifely idyll absolutely charming.

Occasionally, the routine of daily classes was interrupted by cultural events. Once the entire school filed into the gym hall, where morning assemblies were held, to see a film about Lady Jane Grey, which was presumably shown in the hope that it might encourage interest in English history. And toward Christmas, one of the higher forms gave a performance of Chekhov's *Seagull*. The amateurish acting made me think that the plot was melodramatic and sentimental. Nonetheless, once or twice a sentence or two struck a chord and gave me an inkling that there was more depth in the play than I blithely assumed. As I was a budding cultural snob, I might have looked on it with more respect had I realized that it was generally regarded as a dramatic masterpiece. Looking back on the whole thing today, I think it was quite an achievement for a provincial central school to attempt to stage it and that the girl actors were by no means as mediocre as I then judged them to be.

Jenny took me with her for lectures at the public library, and for a short while we joined a group that read plays aloud. It must have been there that we met a middle-aged, middle-class English couple who invited us to their neat house; over the course of the evening, they saw fit to regale us with accounts of their trips to Germany and Austria before the war. They also told us that they had invited an Austrian girl to visit them for a couple of months in the summer of 1938. This young woman was an enthusiastic adherent of the Nazis, and the first thing she had done upon arriving was to place a portrait of Hitler on her bedside table. It was obvious that our hosts were very sympathetic to this movement themselves, and they attempted to cheer us up by predicting that in the long run England would not be able to stand up to Hitler, who would certainly win the war in due course.

We also paid a visit to an elderly German refugee, who was living in a furnished room where she played Mozart sonatas on the piano for our enjoyment. She was deeply depressed because she too was convinced that the war was as good as lost, and she exuded such profound gloom and pessimism that it took us several days to shake off the uneasiness about our future with which she had infected us.

For a while, we also joined a circle of elderly ladies, most of them refugees, who read French plays aloud, among them Beaumarchais' *Le Barbier de Séville* and *Le Mariage de Figaro*. I took part in these readings

10. BEDFORD CENTRAL SCHOOL

with gusto and undoubtedly gave lively performances, but I was an intolerant child and chafed at the halting delivery and Germanic accents of the old ladies.

Toward Christmas we went to a concert and heard Handel's *Messiah*, and despite the fact that this was a provincial performance and the message a Christian one, I was tremendously impressed by the music, especially by the uplift conveyed by the spirited choirs.

The Battle of Britain, which had raged during the summer of 1940, was over after a few months, and, although London was still the occasional target for air raids, things generally quieted down. In Bedford we were pretty safe, though soon after our arrival, the sirens went off one night, and many hours passed before the all-clear sounded. The Cannings did not have an Anderson shelter (a small air raid shelter consisting of an arch of corrugated metal and covered with earth for protection) in their garden, and their house did not have such a thing as a cellar, either, so the six of us all huddled in the well of the staircase, as this was generally recommended as providing the best protection in case of a direct hit. There was an uninterrupted roar of airplanes flying west. Every now and then, we heard the whistle of a bomb exploding in the neighborhood. The Canning daughters were no more heroic than I was, the younger one constantly holding smelling salts to her nose, and the atmosphere during these long hours was full of tense fear. When the all-clear at last went off in the small hours of the morning, there was a general rush to the lavatory. This was the night Coventry was bombed, and Bedford lies directly on the route to it.

As restrictions on work for refugees had been lifted, Jenny decided to take a course at Pitmans in order that she might be in a position to submit an English certificate of proficiency to prospective employers, and she successfully completed this course after a couple of months. After the New Year, she therefore rejoined Bernard in London, having apparently decided to forget his assault on her, and after a couple of weeks secured a job as secretary. Oddly enough, her new employers were, like the unfortunate Strauss family that had stayed in Antwerp, pious German Jews who also traded in scrap metal. From now on, she came down for the weekend every two or three weeks, arriving by coach (the journey was considerably longer than by train and accordingly much cheaper) on Friday evening and traveling back on Sunday afternoon. On Saturdays we nearly always went to the pictures. Later, after Jenny had given notice to her first employers and had begun to work for an Englishman who ran a small business in the East End and was engagingly called Mr. Spooner, she would come on Saturday morning and take the train. She was notoriously unpunctual and frequently missed the first train, which would have brought her to Bedford at about ten, leaving us most of the day to spend together. As I always waited for her with passionate eagerness, it was a great letdown to be at the station and find that she had missed the train so that it would now take till 11:20 for her to arrive, thus depriving me of almost one and a half hours of her precious company.

My friend Trudi had remained in London, and we struck up a lively correspondence, exchanging long letters full of information about the books we were reading and the films we had seen. The Cannings had obligingly vouched for us at the public library (they themselves patronized Boots' library, which charged lending fees for books that I soon decided were far inferior to those you could get at the public library), to which I went at least once a week, returning laden with four to six books, most of them at first from the children's section. Apart from reading nonfiction books, which explained astronomy or physics in simple terms, I experimented with fiction books, and discovered that a large number of them dealt with the adventures of upper-class girls in boarding schools; after I had sampled a few of these, they struck me as pretty silly (this judgment applied both to the girls and to their adventures). One book, in particular, incensed me so much that I refused to continue reading it; it began by relating how the heroine's parents lost most of their money and had to give up their mansion to move into an ordinary middle-class house, this being described as a terrible humiliation and a major misfortune. These experiences led me increasingly to frequent the adult section where I not only inspected the fiction shelves but also roamed in the nonfiction domain, studying the titles of the sections labeled "Biography," "History," "Drama," "Film," and so on. During my years in Bedford I made wonderful discoveries in this way, hitting upon treasures such as Alexei Tolstoy's *Peter the Great*, Laurence Housman's delightful dramatic scenes in *Victoria Regina*,

10. BEDFORD CENTRAL SCHOOL

and James Agate's witty diaries, *Ego*, which were initially picked up by Jenny and which we both read, getting through four or five volumes of these aptly named reflections. We had, of course, resumed our regular visits to the pictures, and so I was never short of material for my letters to Trudi, and she responded in kind. During the next summer holidays, I spent a week or so in London with Jenny and Bernard, also staying with Trudi and her parents for a couple of days.

When the summer holidays ended, I was pleased to return to school. I was very ambitious, as a matter of fact, I was an obnoxious swot who not only did the required homework but also, out of a devouring desire to excel, voluntarily added further exercises no teacher had asked for. I also did something that certainly never occurred to any other of my classmates — I dutifully ploughed through the moralizing peregrinations of *Pilgrim's Progress*, because John Bunyan was held to be a great man in Bedford, his birthplace. The other local celebrity was John Howard, who had initiated prison reform, as I discovered when I read up on him. When the autumn term started, I found that the curriculum now included shorthand and typewriting lessons. Now, oddly enough, although Jenny had a career as secretary in mind for me, she thought it premature for me to start learning these techniques at the age of thirteen. She took a day off to come to Bedford on a weekday because she had made an appointment with the headmistress of an evacuated London high school that had only recently moved to Bedford (it had initially been evacuated to Maidstone, where, however, the air raids had been so severe that they had had to look for a safer place), and she took me to see Miss Summers, a dignified, white-haired woman, an impressively stately, yet friendly lady. She listened to Jenny giving her reasons for her wish to have me become a pupil at her school and then proceeded to interview me. It so happened that I had just read with great enthusiasm a book (from the children's section) about ancient Egypt, describing in particular Akhenaten and his town El-Amarna, and as I told her about this wonderful book, I happened to drop the word "hieroglyphs," and this did the trick — Ms. Summers was convinced that I was a suitable candidate and arranged for me to receive an "open place," which meant that we did not have to pay any fees, which would indeed have been beyond our means. To my chagrin, however, King's

Warren school required me to wear a uniform, which was unfortunately singularly unattractive, and when the girls wearing them had first made their appearance in the streets of Bedford, they had aroused much mockery. They wore a plain brown serge tunic with a beige blouse. The cut of this tunic seemed to have been cannily designed so as to conceal all characteristics typical of the nubile female. In other words, it hung from the shoulders of the wearer very much like a sack. Out of doors, one wore a brown blazer. To crown the dreariness of the overall impression, a limp panama hat was prescribed wear for the summer and a shapeless brown bonnet for the winter, the result being that all but the most attractive girls had a downright dowdy look about them.

This was the price to pay, however, if I were to attend a higher school, and at the beginning of January 1942 I reported with great trepidation to one of the mistresses in charge, who brought me to the class that I was to join.

11. KING'S WARREN SCHOOL (1)

To my great surprise, no tuition was given that morning, as on Monday mornings, the timetable began with two hours reserved for homework. On the first day after the holidays, this meant that the class did not yet have anything to do, and the girls engaged in lively chatter, telling each other what they had done in London, where they had all spent their Christmas holidays with their parents. A girl called Dorothy had read Charles Reade's *The Cloister and the Hearth*, and she illustrated a moving scene between the parting lovers by dramatically flinging her arms around her friend Cynthia. At the end of the first two hours, sports was the next subject. This was spent out of doors, where we walked to some grounds where the teacher proceeded to organize a snowball fight. My enthusiasm for this kind of activity was, to say the least, tepid.

The first morning proved, however, to be untypical. A great deal of serious tuition was provided at King's Warren School, and I settled down to learning with great gusto. The evacuated school was handicapped by not having fixed premises. In the afternoon, it used the classrooms of Bedford High School, which apparently did not provide any teaching after noon (I suppose they engaged in sports activities then). During all the years during which the King's Warren School enjoyed the hospitality of this local high school, I cannot remember that there was any contact whatsoever between the two establishments, whose pupils never even set eye on one another. It was as if the Londoners were a lower species of humanity, and it would have defiled the little Bedford snobs to even notice their existence. In the mornings, we were housed in varying localities. My first morning was spent in a room adjoining a hall, but I do not recollect that we stayed there long. For some years we had the use of the freemasons' rooms where five or six classes were simultaneously taught in a large hall. Strangely enough, this was not as disturbing as one might imagine. I was more distracted by lithographs adorning the walls than by the sound of the other classes and their teachers. One of these pictures was the Tenniel cartoon from *Punch*, in which Bismarck is depicted as an aged captain leaving his ship, while a young Kaiser leans over the railings and watches him descending with a contemptuous and triumphant smile. It bore the caption "Dropping the pilot." Another illustration showed the goddess Nicotine in the shape of a sensuous naked female emerging out of spiraling smoke. I looked at this repeatedly, for in those chaste days it had a fascination bordering on the obscene.

When I joined the class, it had just embarked in its English lessons on Jane Austen's *Pride and Prejudice*. I instantaneously fell in love with the book and read it with mounting enthusiasm. I was gratified and delighted to find that mothers whose aim in life is to get their daughters well married were not a Jewish singularity, Mrs. Bennet being a character I felt I had known intimately for years. It contributed to my feeling less ashamed of what I had thought was typically Jewish behavior. I had a similar experience later, when I discovered that greed for money or a reluctance to serve as a soldier were traits shared by the rest of mankind.

As I was bursting with enthusiasm and felt no compunction at showing off my knowledge, I very soon established myself as a star in English classes. While not quite as indifferent as the pupils at Bedford Central School had been, most girls at King's Warren did not take their lessons very seriously. Real life took place outside school. The exception was the studious Dorothy who had impressed me on my first morning. I longed to become her friend and dislodge Cynthia, a stodgy, unimaginative girl, from that position. For the time being, this remained an unfulfilled wish, and I attached myself to a very tall, good-looking girl called Lilian Crisp, who seemed much more mature than the other fourteen-year-olds and who mothered me in a casual way. When I invited her to call on us on a Saturday afternoon, Jenny was impressed by her calm and quiet assurance. This friendship was nipped in the bud when Lilian went back to London after a few months. She returned a couple of years later to visit us. She was in uniform, as she had left school to join the WAAF, and she gave us all the feeling — no doubt absolutely justified — of being part of a world dramatically different from the one in which our uneventful, staid lives took place.

Another girl who soon assumed an inordinate importance in my life was Marjorie — she was tall, dark, sturdy, and had well-developed breasts. In spite of the fact that her appearance was far removed from what I normally regarded as attractive, I fell deeply in love with her. Not a particularly good scholar, she was nonetheless self-confident to the point of appearing haughty — a character trait that I usually considered to be repulsive — but it was this very haughtiness that fascinated me. I never achieved any intimacy with her — indeed, she intimidated me so much that I was tongue-tied whenever I had the opportunity to chat with her — which meant that I was reduced to worshipping her from afar. In schoolgirl parlance, this kind of infatuation was referred to as having a "crush" on somebody. One day, it began to cool, like most loves one feels at this age, so that a year later, I was at a loss to understand why this particular young woman had exercised such power over my emotions.

The most important figures in this confined school universe were the teachers. In those days, women teachers were required to be unmarried, and so they were all spinsters (to avoid using the contemptuous term "old maids"). The English teacher, Miss Cowlin, was a plump, red-haired woman with big sagging breasts. She was good-natured and easy-going and gave us solid, if not exactly inspiring, tuition. Her colleague, Miss Hinton, a very thin, very tall, very pale woman, who taught French and whose fiancé had been killed during the First World War, was in a different league altogether. Endowed with a powerful intellect, she did not suffer fools gladly and demanded that we make an individual contribution and eschew generally accepted phrases and opinions. But this we only discovered several years later, for when I joined the school, my classmates were still busy learning the rudiments of the language, and I was of course miles ahead of them.

Miss Swales taught geography and scripture. A very tiny, elderly woman, dressed in old-fashioned clothes and wearing a narrow black velvet ribbon as a choker, she glowed with enthusiasm for both her subjects. The remarkable thing was that she managed to impart her interest in geography to all — really all — her pupils so that every one of them achieved above-average marks in general and schools certificate exams, and one or two who were particularly gifted received national prizes awarded for the best geography papers. Miss Swales was profoundly religious, and her fervor was so genuine that one could not but help feeling respect for her. In scripture, school terms were alternately set aside for the study of the Old and New Testaments and, although I could have absented myself when she dealt with the New Testament, I voluntarily attended these lessons, since her piety had nothing that was bigoted about it. I remember one occasion when she gave us her definition of hell — she closed her eyes and fervently said, "To me, hell is the complete absence of God."

History was given by Miss Tice, a white-haired lady who looked like an eighteenth-century Tory lord and had the rare gift of frequently managing to make a fascinating subject supremely boring. Miss Pinhorn taught mathematics — she was an ineffectual, feckless, well-meaning, dark-haired woman, totally lacking the art of conveying understanding to the uninitiated. As far as she was concerned, the intricacies of her subject were so transparent that she thought that merely to demonstrate a mathematical operation by chalking it up on the blackboard was self-explanatory. When I arrived, the class had during the two previous years learned the elementary principles of geometry. I never managed to reach the level of the rest of the class (although I contrived to grasp some algebraic procedures) — I understood only the logic of Pythagoras's theorem, and that was the end of it. The ultimate horror was trigonometry, which I found especially rebarbative. Today, I think it a great pity that I thus forfeited all understanding of a science which has an affinity to music, in containing its own universe. Had we been rich or had we belonged to another social class, Jenny would doubtlessly have arranged for me to have private lessons to give me a grounding in mathematics, but, as it was, not even the remote possibility of such a solution occurred to us.

The same applied to Latin. Here too the class had been learning the language for two years. When I came, we had a very pleasant teacher, and I set to work to make up for lost time with great determination. I had no particular difficulties with the vocabulary, which I memorized with ease

11. KING'S WARREN SCHOOL (1)

because I could trace French words back to their roots, and this proved a great help. The grammar of Latin, however, was a jungle in which I lost my way. I was particularly irritated by the incomprehensible distinction between gerund and gerundive, and the mere term "ablative absolute" represented an insuperable barrier to the text involved. So my initially seemingly effortless progress in the acquisition of vocabulary was set off by my inability to solve the finer points of grammar. These difficulties were aggravated by the fact that the first teacher soon became seriously ill and was replaced by a series of helpless and incapable stand-ins, and when it became clear that the regular Latin teacher was not going to recover and return, a new teacher, Miss Mansfield, was engaged. During the first lesson she gave, it was obvious that she was trembling with apprehension and patently exercising great self-control to establish her authority, but she soon showed herself more than equal to the task. She was young, intelligent, and competent, and did not tolerate stupidity. Unfortunately, in this subject, my performances were so inadequate that she might be forgiven for being impatient with me. As far as I was concerned, Latin remained a subject fraught with difficulties, and the only bearings I had were provided by my being frequently able to guess at the meanings of isolated words found in an otherwise impenetrable forest of syntactic obstacles.

Finally, there was the sports and gym teacher, Miss Baggallay, commonly known as "Bagwash." She did not take long to discover that I had no talent either for games or for what was called physical training, abbreviated as PT (i.e., gym). We played rounders in the winter and tennis in the summer. In literature, I was very quick to grasp an issue; but when I was called upon to wield a racket, I always managed to make a lunge at the tennis ball a split second after it had left the spot I aimed at. In gym, Miss Baggallay, a well-trained athletic woman, found me gawky and awkward; and as I walked with my toes pointed outward, she thought it witty to christen me "Charlie Chaplin." A year or two later we began to have swimming lessons, which became a weekly ordeal, anticipated with fear. Within a couple of minutes, the cold water gave me gooseflesh, and many were the excuses to which I made recourse — colds, periods, headaches — in order to be allowed to sit on a side-bench in my coat (for the swimming pool hall was cold enough to make an extra layer advisable). However, Miss Baggallay made generous allowances for my shortcomings, which she attributed to my being a foreigner. In one term report, she wrote "Huguette *tries* hard," which I thought was a fair and unexpectedly witty comment.

My first months at school were marred by snubs and sarcasm from the other pupils. I did not know how to cope with this harassment and at first submitted to it in silence. This was probably aggravated by my being so poor at games and by the fact that at the age of fourteen I was a specimen of a now defunct species, for which even the English language then used the German term "Backfisch." With lanky hair and ungainly movements, I was acutely conscious of my physical unattractiveness. I imagine that my eagerness to do well and my overactive participation, especially in English lessons, where I was all agog to put myself forward, did not exactly endear me to the other girls either. At any event, being dimly aware of all these disadvantages, I patiently endured these torments (which, in hindsight, were mild enough, but hurt nonetheless) for the first three or four months, until one day on the way home from the sports grounds, I lost my self-control and, half in tears, half in anger, blurted out, "You're, all of you, very mean to me! Stop bullying me!" adding that I wasn't sure that I had pronounced the word "bullying" correctly and didn't care, either. This atypical act of self-assertion had a magic effect. All baiting ceased forthwith, and in spite of my exotic character traits, I gradually became an accepted member of the class. I suspect that they had thought of me as a kind of insensible block, and my emotional outburst showed that I was a human being after all. This transition from open antagonism to unquestioning acceptance did not occur overnight but required a longer period of time, as is apparent from an event that happened soon afterward. At the beginning of the summer term, the pupils elected two form monitresses; to my utter astonishment, I was chosen as one of them. In spite of the fact that this was absolutely unexpected, I remained unsuspicious. When the class was unsupervised and the loud chattering of some thirty girls reached a deafening level, I was frequently invited to restore order, the girls calling out, "Go on, Huguette. Tell us to be quiet!" Fortunately, some blessed instinct dimly held me back, and I never complied with this exhortation or tried to impose an authority which I realized I did not possess. A few

11. KING'S WARREN SCHOOL (1)

months afterward, Lilian told me that the whole affair had — at the instigation of Marjorie, the girl I had passionately worshipped — been well-planned and engineered in order to bring about my spectacular humiliation. To say that the disclosure of this little conspiracy had a sobering effect on my vanity would be an understatement.

During my first year in Bedford, I had spontaneously approached the younger Miss Canning to ask whether she would not give me piano lessons, and had thus unwittingly set off a therapeutic process. Within a few weeks, the news that she had resumed her former teaching activity became known in the neighborhood, and quite soon other pupils (who, in contrast to me, paid for their lessons) applied to her and her afternoons gradually filled up. She lost her hunted look of a frightened bird, and the intervals between her nightly attacks of hysterical screaming became noticeably longer. When Jenny came for the weekend, she was eager to chat with her about fashions and film stars. She had a friend overseas who sent her thick glossy Hollywood magazines, and when she had finished studying them, she passed them on to us. They were full of film gossip and trivial news — but as I was still film-crazy, I too spent hours reading these ephemeral snippets informing the reader which film stars and starlets had been discovered dining or flirting together.

I had been eager to start piano lessons in the fond hope of learning to play sonatas written by classic composers. But this proved to be an illusion — Miss Canning gave me pieces by Eric Coates called "The Changing of the Guards" or "A Walk in Green Park" to play. Moreover, I was not gifted — I quite enjoyed practicing, but the span of my hands was too small for many chords, and my progress was rather slow. I never got beyond "Für Elise" (I did manage eventually to procure music from famous classics at Foyles in London) or an easy-to-play arrangement of a Mozart symphony.

Bo, Jenny, and I were very careful not to antagonize the Cannings, well aware that we were only living there on sufferance. One day, the handle of my attaché case came off as I was walking down the stairs, and the case tumbled down the steps before I realized what was happening and hit a stand in the entrance hall. The stand toppled over, shattering a plant pot to smithereens. Instantly, I was panic-stricken and felt I had committed a heinous crime. This fear of forfeiting the goodwill of our landlord and his daughters did not, however, prevent me from occasionally exhibiting a tactlessness that bordered on insolence. When the older Miss Canning told me that their family was descended from William Penn, the founder of Pennsylvania, I retorted that this was like tracing one's ancestry to monkeys with particularly silky tails (a witticism that I borrowed from *Daddy-Long-Legs*, one of my favorite books).

One afternoon, the old, white-haired father got hold of me and took me into their drawing room, where he pulled me onto his knees and proceeded to push his tongue into my mouth, a behavior that I found puzzling, as my film visits in those chaste days had not introduced me to this kind of kiss. It was not particularly pleasant, but I submitted to it passively. I had no idea what was the point of it all, and when I innocently related the incident to Jenny on her next visit, she only told me to pass it over in silence.

During the school holidays, I often went to London to spend a few days with Jenny. She took me out to plays and other cultural events. At the beginning of my time at King Warren's school, we went to see *Macbeth*, with John Gielgud in the title role and Gwen Ffrangçon-Davies as Lady Macbeth. I had "done" the play at school, but this was my first experience of what good acting can do to enhance the text, giving one a feeling of "yes, just so! This is exactly how I have visualized it in my imagination." Obviously, as I was to learn, not every rendering of a work of literature on the stage or screen succeeds in this. It must have been soon after that I saw a film version of *Pride and Prejudice* with Laurence Olivier as Darcy and Greer Garson as Elizabeth that, in spite of what would seem to have been very appropriate casting, profoundly disappointed me in falling far short of my own reading of the novel. Equally frustrating was the film of *Jane Eyre*, which was heralded with great fanfares of praise; again, the casting of Orson Welles as Rochester and Joan Fontaine as the heroine, and the fact that Aldous Huxley had written the screenplay, seemed to bode well. But it too turned out to be a great disappointment — truncated to absurd brevity, it lost all depth and even coherence so that it had all the attributes of a cheap novelette. *Macbeth*, however, did justice to Shakespeare and was an exhilarating experience. An additional treat was that Laurence Olivier and Vivien Leigh were among the audience, and we saw them coming in: her dark beauty immediately attracted all glances. She was wearing a dress and cape that in themselves singled her out from all the drably attired women around us, and a chic glamour emanated from her that we only knew from Hollywood films.

Jenny also took me to a performance given by a Polish folk ballet troupe. We were enchanted by the vitality and joy of their dancing and the gay colors of their traditional costumes. Another outing gave me my first introduction to classical and modern ballet, as performed by the Sadler's Wells company. The program included a performance of *Hamlet* set to music by Tchaikovsky with a very somber and dramatic Robert Helpmann in the title role.

In the early forties, the BBC Symphony Orchestra was evacuated to Bedford and gave concerts in the Corn Hall. We were sometimes allowed to attend their rehearsals, and, since tickets for regular concerts were not expensive, I was able to afford these as well. I became an assiduous concertgoer, religiously studying the programs and listening to the music with great concentration. Bo and I did not have a wireless set, so it was my only opportunity to hear classical music at all.

Around this time, my cousin Silvie was expecting a baby. Aunt Chiffra was living with her husband, with whom she waged continual marital warfare, in northwest London, and Silvie's husband had bought a small house not far off in Golders Green. Just before the baby was due, Silvie fell very ill indeed and had to be rushed to the hospital. She had albumen poisoning, and in spite of her having had swollen legs and other characteristic symptoms, her gynecologist had failed to diagnose it in time. She gave birth to a stillborn daughter and was very ill afterward, so that we feared for her life. Bo and I were so worried that we went to visit her in London. To our relief, she soon recovered

Silvie, Bo and Huguette in Bedford

and was discharged from the hospital. Within a couple of days, she and her mother were busy planning new clothes for her, for which Chiffra was to procure the material on the black market, for she had a talent in organizing such transactions. On the way home, Bo said that she thought this a wickedly frivolous and unfitting thing to do so soon after Silvie had been in mortal danger. On the one hand, I was surprised that Bo was capable of harboring what to me were quite unexpectedly delicate sentiments, but on the other hand, I felt that this only showed that Silvie, who had at first been very depressed over the loss of her first baby (in particular, as it was then thought that she might not have any more), was now, in what was a healthy reaction on the part of a very young woman, reverting to the interests and preoccupations of everyday life.

12. KING'S WARREN SCHOOL (2)

As for myself, I was losing at least some of my gawkiness, as a result of the normal process of adolescence, and even beginning to look moderately attractive. At last I began to take an interest in the dresses I wore. Jenny did not have the financial means to have recourse to "normal" black market channels, but nonetheless found an unusual way to circumvent rationing. Whereas one had to give up clothes coupons for conventional dressmaking material or for ready-made clothes, such restrictions did not apply to cloth for curtains, and so she bought yards of material with a pattern of big blue and white flowers from which a dressmaker concocted, in accordance with Jenny's instructions, a summer costume for me which, in spite of its slightly exotic material, I thought was quite fetching.

The improvement in my physical appearance was accompanied by an unwonted moodiness. For obscure reasons, I was frequently depressed and sulky and on several occasions quarreled with Jenny for trivial reasons. Once, carried away during a heated dispute by a hot rage, I found myself calling her a "coureuse d'hommes" (a slut who runs after men), and the moment I said it, I was horrified at using such a vile insult, which I flung at her quite involuntarily (so that it was voiced before I realized what I was saying). To this day, I do not know where I had picked up the expression, for, although it accorded exactly with the venomous abuse I had heard Bo directing at her during my early childhood, I could not have gotten it from her, since she used Yiddish and would not even have known what the French words meant. It was, moreover, strange that although we had for some time stopped conversing in French, I reverted to it for this particular insult. Even now, when I remember this, I feel deeply ashamed of my behavior, in spite of being aware that it was probably a symptom of the normal unconscious adolescent attempt to start severing the emotional ties of childhood. Perhaps Jenny was dimly aware of this, for strangely enough she did not hold this nasty outburst against me. And indeed, in a secret recess of my heart, I deeply loved her and knew very well that she also loved me.

She was enchanted to discover that I might become reasonably pretty, and when men on the street gave us admiring glances, she was delighted that she could not tell whether they were intended for her or for me. I had begun to attend a club for Jewish youngsters, to which she once accompanied me. One of its most prominent members was a boy called Ralph Ginsburg, whose keen intelligence, eloquence, and self-confidence impressed both of us. From the first letter of his surname, Jenny coined the expression a "G," which we henceforth used to refer to him in particular and by extension to any other desirable young male. The original "G" once made an attempt to approach me — he came and sat next to me, and I, like a great fool, got up and went to sit down elsewhere. In spite of my being so eager to have him as a boyfriend, a deeply ingrained inhibition and fear of men made me give an unmistakably clear signal that achieved the exact opposite of what I ostensibly wanted. To my chagrin, young Ginsburg, not surprisingly, never made me any further advances.

Another boy of my own age, a German refugee called Alfred, asked me to go out with him one Saturday afternoon. His personality was not as striking as that of the original "G," but he was a nice and intelligent boy whose inhibitions paralleled my own. Before going to the pictures, we went for a long walk along the banks of the Ouse and, in between the agonizing intervals of tongue-tied silence, tried to have a conversation that was so unspontaneous and forced that when we parted both of us silently resolved to never voluntarily repeat such an uncomfortable experience again. At a time when many girls in my class had boyfriends, I mortifyingly had to do without such a desirable accessory. I secretly envied a blond girl in my class called Betty Baker who, thanks to her exceedingly trim little figure and her pretty face, was being chased by half-a-dozen boys. True, she had not my intellectual endowments, but as I was beginning to discover, these cannot remotely compete with the fascination exerted by outright sex appeal.

12. KING'S WARREN SCHOOL (2)

Jenny certainly possessed this mysterious quality, although her personality could not be reduced — as was the case with Betty Baker — to this single aspect. She was not only sexy but also exuded a very feminine erotic attraction. And she was full of the joy of living, although life had given her little cause for happiness. Moreover, she was interested in politics and culture and was an avid reader. Besides taking me to plays and ballets, she regularly brought me books to read when she came to Bedford for the weekend. She had discovered a public library in the neighborhood of Mr. Spooner's office near Petticoat Lane which had an excellent selection of literature in foreign languages, and she arrived laden with books by Anatole France, Romain Rolland's version in several volumes of Beethoven's life, called *Jean-Christophe*, as well as the nine or ten volumes of Roger Martin du Gard's family saga *Les Thibault*, which she unpacked during her successive fortnightly visits.

In the intervening years, her relationship to Bo had undergone a radical change. Long forgotten — except by me, who had kept a vivid memory of their violence — were the venomous quarrels of my early childhood. Their exchanges of family news and gossip about acquaintances were now conducted peacefully. As of old, they also continued to share the enjoyment of our regular cinema visits.

We had news of the Disenhauses, who had fled from Brussels in 1940 and found a temporary refuge in Montpellier, in unoccupied France. My cousin Isy attended the university where he was studying, of all unlikely subjects, agriculture, the reason being that owing to his Belgian nationality he could not study music, as this would have involved attending courses in Paris. Despite the war, letters could still be sent from unoccupied France, and Isy wrote me in a delightfully humorous vein, embellishing his text with charming, neat little drawings, which I admired all the more as I was totally incapable of producing anything in that field that might even remotely reach a mediocre standard.

When the Germans occupied the rest of France in 1942, silence descended and Jenny repeatedly had troubled dreams of her sister. Finally, we received a letter from Switzerland, where they had managed to escape, only to be put into an internment camp. Later, I learned the details of their flight. After the Germans came, they remained in Montpellier, only going into hiding when the Nazis or their Vichy henchmen began to round up the Jews. Isy was away from home doing a stint of practical training on a farm. Anyway, he was not, as a Belgian national, in danger of being deported, although he shared with many Frenchmen the risk of being forcibly recruited to work in the rearmament industry in Germany. Golda and Yeshurun found refuge in a small house which they shared with nine other families, and the resulting hygienic and social conditions put a great strain on all inmates. At one point, in a reaction very similar to Jenny's wish to return home after a day spent in the overcrowded train that took us from Antwerp to La Panne in May 1940, Golda felt she could no longer stand the cramped conditions of this clandestine existence and went back to their flat, only to be promptly arrested. Alerted by a telegram, Isy got a French friend to plead with the head of the police station, who declared that he could not release her officially, but that he was prepared to leave the cell door open, thus allowing her to slip out unnoticed. Golda, however, staunchly refused to leave the prison without an official permit to do so, whereupon she was sent to the notorious camp at Gurs, where she daily saw trains packed with Jews leaving for the concentration camps in Eastern Europe. Meanwhile, Yeshurun and Isy were desperately trying all possible ways and means to get her out before it was too late. A medical certificate stating that she was pregnant saved her from being put on the next train; then a doctor examined her and found no sign of a pregnancy. In the meantime, husband and son procured forged Belgian papers. and an influential French acquaintance interceded with the commandant of Gurs, who finally agreed to release her. When Isy met his mother at the station in Montpellier, he did not recognize her until she flung her arms around him. This neat person whose hair was always demurely combed tightly back into a bun looked like a wild woman, stiff strands of hair standing out in all directions.

Now keenly alive to the dreadful dangers to which they were exposed, they decided to make an attempt to escape to Switzerland. In a village café near the border, they made the acquaintance of a Jewish couple named Rosen. Together they found a man who agreed, for a substantial remuneration, to guide them illegally across the border at night. After tramping for some time, he stopped in a village and told them they were now in Switzerland. Isy, however, noticed a monument dedicated to the soldiers fallen during the First World War and realized that they were still in France, since the Swiss had not been involved in that war. Overwhelmed by furious rage, he seized the guide and shook him until he was almost senseless and owned up to the swindle. He then led them on various tracks through thorny undergrowth. Mrs. Rosen, a very elegant woman, was wearing high-heeled shoes throughout this adventure and suddenly cried out — the heel of one shoe had come off. She lost the shoe in the darkness and could not go on walking. My young cousin carried her on his shoulders for the rest of the way, until the guide brought them to a farm where they were fed and received shelter for the rest of the night. After he had put down his living burden, Isy collapsed, sobbing from sheer exhaustion.

The next morning, they had to report at the frontier post to apply for official asylum. The officials there showed much sympathy for their plight but informed them that it was by no means certain that this asylum would be granted, since the authorities in Berne were very erratic, granting permission one day and withholding it on the next. Isy had the phone number of the father of a Swiss fellow student in Montpellier, and they rang him and explained their predicament. The father, an influential banker, immediately put a phone call through to the relevant office in Berne. This secured the permit and incidentally goes to show that the study of agriculture may prove more rewarding than one might at first expect.

They were now interned in a camp where they were put to hard physical work and were generally harshly treated. Food was of such poor quality and meted out in such parsimonious portions that a number of inmates died before the end of the war, among them a famous German singer called Joseph Schmidt. Luckily, they survived, however, and we began to receive letters from them through the Red Cross. Toward the end of the war, when its outcome was no longer in doubt, they were allowed to leave the camp and live in a furnished room in Geneva, there to await the advent of peace.

At about this time, Dorothy and I got caught in an air raid on our way to morning school, which at that time was being held in a big Victorian house on a residential street. We had gotten out of the bus at Bedford station when we noticed people staring at planes flying high overhead. There had been no alert, but as we innocently looked up like other passers-by, we saw cylindrical bombs slowly descending. (There was a munitions factory in the vicinity of the railway station, which was no doubt the target.) As we began to run toward school, we suddenly found ourselves showered by debris and rubble from houses that had been hit. We both involuntarily started to sob, and I remember that even as we ran the detonation of the bombs made me think of the siege of Atlanta about which I had just been reading in *Gone with the Wind*. Within a couple of minutes we reached the haven of our schoolrooms, disheveled and covered in dust, but otherwise unscathed. The only injury that was suffered was that I lost my panama hat, an accident that inspired Dorothy's mother to write an "Ode on the Loss of Huguette's Panama Hat." This event made me aware of the fact that, whereas I was prey to anguished pangs of fear whenever I heard planes buzzing overhead during an "official" air raid, I did not instinctively realize that peril was impending when I was actually in real danger of death, at least not until the worst was over.

Despite such events, we were on the whole living a life of uneventful normality. At the beginning of the war, when the Germans invaded one European country after another and occupied a large part of Northern Africa, we could not help feeling anxious that they would go on winning forever. The Battle of Britain had justified first timid expectations that the Germans might not be invincible after all. When they marched into Russia in June 1941, we had great hopes of the tide turning, hopes that were well expressed by a government poster depicting both Hitler and Napoleon as black shadowy figures rashly out to conquer Russia's vast expanses, the message being that Hitler would come to the same dire end as had overtaken Napoleon. But alas, during the first year, the Russian army proved unable to halt the advance of Hitler's troops and in the newspaper maps the territory still held by the Russians shrunk at an alarming rate. Toward the end of 1942, the outlook became brighter — in Africa, the British army under Montgomery was victorious at Tobruk, and the Germans suffered a spectacular defeat at Stalingrad. In newsreels we saw interminable lines of half-frozen, hollow-eyed, and pitiable German soldiers filing into Russian captivity, as well as dramatic shots of the capitulation of their general Paulus, a haggard figure with a nervous eye tic. The Allies had also begun to bomb German towns, and this gave us the feeling that our side was not only fated to accept blows forever but could also inflict them on the enemy.

In the summer of 1943, Jenny decided to take a week's holiday with me at the seaside. She agreed to take a neighbor's daughter along, a girl aged twelve, called Carolyn. Our destination was Torquay, and as the hotels were overbooked, — for like millions of other people she had selected the Bank Holiday week — she hit upon the happy expedient of phoning the hotels at the bottom of the alphabetical list on the correct assumption that most people would start at the top. Indeed, she quickly secured a reservation in a hotel called the Waldon Resort, the name of which she regarded as a happy omen, since our name was Vald.

We traveled in a particularly overcrowded train (as was to be expected, since all trains were overfilled during the war), having to stand all the way. The hotel turned out to be a very decent place, such as well-to-do middle-class people patronize — a category to which we certainly did not belong. We had a big room with three beds and large windows with a view of the sea. The weather was excellent so that Jenny could sunbathe to her heart's content. The beaches, however, were not very propitious for this; whereas our Belgian experience had made us believe that the seaside invariably consisted of sandy stretches and dunes, in Torquay and the adjacent resorts to which we went by bus in our search for a softer underlayer, the beach consisted of shingle, which hardly made it conducive to relaxing, let alone slumbering.

Nonetheless, we enjoyed ourselves on the whole, although the girl Carolyn proved to be a pain in the neck, chattering all day long in a singularly silly manner and not addicted to reading as we were, so that she was continually looking for other forms of entertainment, which she expected us to provide. Torquay was — and still is, as far as I know — a very pleasant town with roads lined by attractive villas, between which one had breathtaking glimpses of the sea, a bay full of little yachts and boats, and palm trees that we had never imagined could grow so far

Part II. ADOLESCENCE IN ENGLAND

Jenny, Carolyn and Huguette in Torquay

north, even in the mild English climate. Despite the war, the place had the atmosphere of a lively holiday resort, and we enjoyed strolling along the bustling main street with its numerous shops. Once we went to the pictures and saw *Wuthering Heights* with Merle Oberon and Laurence Olivier. In the scene in which Heathcliff and Catherine roam on the heath and the wind wafts strains of dancing music to them from the ball given by the Earnshaws, the siren went off precisely when Catherine exclaimed, "Listen! What's that?" The audience burst into laughter at this synchronicity, but my heart immediately contracted in the panic that gripped me in every air raid. I was only able to relax after the all-clear which mercifully went off soon after. Being on the coast facing France, that part of England was prone to incursions of enemy airplanes.

The week was soon over. Jenny was this time at least able to pay the hotel bill without having to depend upon a lottery win, for since

12. KING'S WARREN SCHOOL (2)

Jenny and Huguette March 1943

we had been in England, although she only had the normal income of a secretary, she had got away from the pattern of perpetual debt which had marked our life in Antwerp.

We returned to London and the following weekend made an outing to Cambridge with my friend Trudi. Her family knew a young German Jew who worked as an agricultural laborer near Cambridge, and he obligingly took us around. Siegfried, for such was his unprepossessing name, did this thoroughly and competently. He was tall, dark, and quite good-looking, undoubtedly intelligent and cultured; but he exuded so much Germanic gloom and earnestness, such a total lack of humor, that on the way home I told Jenny, "I shall never marry a German Jew!" Rash words, rashly spoken...

At the beginning of the autumn term, I returned to Bedford. I went back to school in a melancholy frame of mind because Jenny, who was trying to secure financial help for my schooling from the exiled Belgian authorities in London, was planning to have me leave school in the near future in the event of a negative reply and have me start a secretarial training course, so that I might start earning my own living. I had vigorously opposed this plan, for I had a studious disposition and wanted to continue learning subjects like English and French literature, history, and geography. All my arguments had been to no avail, and I was now beginning to feel resigned to my fate, trying to console myself by the thought that I would soon escape the irksome petty restrictions imposed by school discipline.

Nonetheless, I settled down as usual to the routine of school life as if it were not to be cut short soon. A few weeks after my return to Bedford, we were woken in the middle of the night by an air raid siren during one of the weekends when Jenny stayed with us. We no longer got up during these nightly alerts, unless we felt that the target was going to be Bedford, which was unlikely. This did not prevent me from feeling scared as was invariably the case, for I was an adept at imagining that my end might be nigh, and I cuddled up to Jenny (the three of us still sleeping in the single big bed). An odd sensation overcame me, an inexplicable awareness that this would be the last time that I would be comforted in this way by my mother. Was it a similar premonition that had prompted her in March to go with me to a photographer in Bedford to have our pictures taken, something that she had never done before? Perhaps the reason is the more innocent one that she was now able to afford the expense of such an extravagance.

For what happened on the afternoon of Friday, 19 November 1943, I propose to mainly quote from an account that I wrote down in my diary a month later.

13. JENNY

I wish to write down what happened in the last days of my mother's life in minute detail. If and whenever I write a life of her as I hope I shall, I will want to refer to this record written while the events were still fresh and clear in my mind.

[Friday, 19 November 1943]

I was expecting Mummy to come to Bedford on that Saturday. All my life now I will believe in presentiments. I felt that she wouldn't come. I was convinced that she would, at least, miss the train. I even bought a booklet giving the times of the trains and looked at

London	Bedford
10:00 a.m.	11:08 a.m.

with wistful eyes. I felt that she would ring me up to tell me she wasn't coming, or that I should come down to London.

Coupled with this, there was another feeling that seemed to deny it. I fooled myself that this was a silly feeling, and that she was coming. Every time I thought of Saturday, I felt happy. I rejoiced and looked forward to a happy weekend.

I was counting the days. By Friday morning, it was the hours ("By this time tomorrow she will be here"). I was inexplicably happy. My homework was not too far behindhand. I was at peace with the world at large.

I was having quite an enjoyable history lesson when it came: truly like a bolt from the blue. Miss Upham came in and said, "Can Huguette please come to Miss Spratt's room?" [Miss Spratt was deputizing as headmistress since Miss Summers had fallen seriously ill.] *I thought it must be some letter — Mummy had written about my leaving or some such business. As soon as we were out of the room, Miss Upham said, "Your grandmother ... it is your grandmother, isn't it?"*

Part II. ADOLESCENCE IN ENGLAND

"Yes."

"She is in Miss Spratt's room. Go right in."

I was surprised, but I thought that as a matter of course it must be good news. Some telegram from Golda, saying they were coming, some such romantic impossibility.

I entered Miss Spratt's room. Miss Spratt was bending over Grandmother. As soon as I saw her red tear-stained face, I felt that it could not be good news. She said, "You must come at once. Mummy is ill. Bernard phoned me that you should come at once."

"What's the matter with her?"

"I don't know. He didn't say."

I said to Miss Spratt [this exchange having been conducted in Yiddish], "May I go home, please, Miss Spratt? My mother isn't well. I am going to London."

"Why, of course, my dear. Go and put on your things and then come to fetch Grandma in here."

I went out and rushed upstairs. I entered the room and said, "May I take my things, Miss Tice? My mother isn't well. I'm going to London."

"Yes, of course. I'm sorry to hear about your mother. I hope she gets better."

"Thank you, Miss Tice."

I had gathered my things hurriedly, stuffed the books in with no pretence at tidiness. The attaché case wouldn't shut. I didn't care. The words were ringing in my ears: "I hope she gets better." Oh, she would, of course. Or would she?

"Good afternoon, Miss Tice. Good afternoon, Dorothy."

Dorothy looked as if she didn't quite know what to say, I noticed. I rushed down the stairs as quickly as my bad ankle [I had sprained it a few days before] would permit. As I came down, Miss Spratt came out of her room.

"My dear, Grandmother's crying. Is it because she's upset because of Mother or because she's got a bad leg?"

"Er ... both, I should think, Miss Spratt."

"Oh, I see. Well, my dear, there is a train at four o'clock. I should think you might catch that easily."

"Yes, thank you, Miss Spratt."

I put down my case outside the form room and went in. I felt strangely like a heroine in a book. If my mother were to die, it would be one of the sad bits. Very effective. Oh, I mustn't think such terrible thoughts.

"May I take my things, Miss Neaves?"

"Why yes, Huguette, of course."

I went down to the desk and put on my scarf, coat, and hat. Iris whispered, "Where are you going, Huguette?"

13. JENNY

"London. I've been called away. My mother's ill."

"Oh, I'm sorry. Hope she gets better."

"Thank you."

I ran out. "Thank you, Miss Neaves."

There lay my case. I picked it up and re-entered Miss Spratt's room. There she was, again bending sympathetically over Grandmother, very concerned.

"Oh well, thank you, Miss Spratt. I think we'd better go now."

"Oh, all right, dear. I think you can easily catch that train at four o'clock. I hope your mother will soon be better."

Oh, she will get better, of course. Or will she?

"Thank you, Miss Spratt."

"Bo, are you coming?"

She got up, and with many "Dank you"s we finally reached the door.

As soon as we were out, I asked, "What is the matter with her? When did he phone?"

"As soon as you were gone. You were hardly out of the house when it started ringing. Miss Canning, the young one, called, 'There is a gentleman for you at the phone.' A gentleman! It didn't occur to me who it might be. I went down, and then I heard it was him."

"Yes, but what did he say? What is the matter with her?"

"He said, 'Huguette must come at once. Jenny is ill. She can't come tomorrow. She wants Huguette to come at once.' So I said, 'Huguette has gone to school. She can't come today. I will send her tomorrow.' He said all right, you should come tomorrow. Afterward, I thought it over, and I thought: If she is bad enough for him to phone me, you should go today. We have already phoned twice and nobody answered."

"You probably phoned the High School. Our number is different. Well?"

"So at last I thought: 'The devil take it. I will go.' So I came. Who is the woman? Your headmistress?"

"Yes."

"She is a very dear woman. She was so concerned."

"Yes, but Mummy. How is she? What is the matter with her?"

"I don't know, he didn't say."

"Oh, God. I hope it's nothing. Still, it may be something bad. I'm very worried. Still, I hope she's just got the 'flu, and is feeling miserable and longing for company. That's quite possible. Oh God, I hope it's nothing."

We walked on.

"There is a train at five to four. I hope I shall be able to catch it."

"Yes, yes, there is plenty of time … when does it get to London?"

"Half past five, I think."

"Oh, you'll just get in about blackout time."

"I hope we can catch a bus."

"There is no such hurry."

"I don't want to miss it. I shan't know what to do, if I do."

"You'll phone me tonight. Do you hear?"

"We'll see. I may not have time."

"Not have time, what do you mean? Of course, you'll have time. You'll phone me at eight o'clock, do you hear?"

"Yes, yes, I can't promise. I'll try."

"Oh, God, now she is going to leave me without any news. Why can't you phone me?"

"I don't know. I never seem to get any time in London. Besides, everything will probably be upside-down."

"But you must phone me. I shan't sleep if you don't. I must have news. I'll burst if you don't phone at eight. You will phone?"

"All right, all right. I'll phone. At least I'll try. Don't worry yourself to death if I don't phone. I probably will. I'll do my best. But don't worry if I don't."

"What do — "

"All right, all right. I'll phone."

We walked on. J'étais atterrée. It was a nice day, though cold. We had to wait for a bus. Then after we'd at last gotten on one, and still later gotten off, we slowly walked home. As we entered, the young Miss Canning said, "I was sorry to hear about your mother, dear. Are you going tomorrow?"

"No, today."

"Today? When?"

"Now."

"Oh, what about the blackout?"

"I shall get in just about blackout time."

"Oh well, take care of yourself, won't you? Don't go rushing about with that bad ankle of yours and sprain it again."

"Thank you, I won't," I mumbled.

I walked upstairs and ran to the booklet of train schedules that I had bought that week. Yes, that's right, there was a train going to London at five to four and another one at five past four. I started undressing. Grandmother came up, panting.

"You're changing?"

"Yes, of course. Give me clean underwear."

She went to the cupboard and did so. I changed extremely quickly. I put on clean underwear, clean thick stockings, my gray dress, my green cardigan, my blue scarf, hat, and coat. I seized the orange suitcase.

13. JENNY

"What are you taking?"

I rushed into the other room and returned with my gray costume. I took out two blouses.

"Give me some clean underwear to change into."

"What do you need it for? You'll be back on Sunday evening."

"How do I know?"

"But you must come back Sunday. You can't leave me here alone."

"And I can't leave Mummy if she's ill. She may be very ill, you know. Besides, what does it matter if I take some extra clean underwear?"

"What do you need to drag it all that way with you? It'll only be an extra weight."

"Damn the extra weight. Besides, I've told you I may not come back on Sunday. I very probably won't. So put it in. Have you given me some handkerchiefs? Lots?"

"Yes. I've put some in."

I seized my school case and emptied it. I could see myself sitting near Mummy's bedside, with her asleep, and I thought that I might profitably study my Latin then. You see, I only passed in Latin in July, and Miss Spratt thought I had better take it again. I felt that I could do a lot of studying. So I filled my case with books. Grandmother asked me why I need bother to take them, and we had an argument again. Then she put in some food. And at last:

"I think I'm ready."

"Yes, you've got everything. Well?"

We kissed, and she called down, "Don't forget. Phone me at eight o'clock."

"All right, I will. But don't get worried if I don't."

I rushed down the stairs and outside walked quickly away. I arrived at the bus stop. I put down my suitcase. There was a woman there who insisted on talking trivial tattle about buses not running to time, her children waiting for her at home, etc. At last, the bus arrived. I got on. When I came to the station, I sat down and waited for the train. I had to wait quite a long time — half an hour, at least. It was bitterly cold. I bought an Evening News.

The train came in, and I got in and sat down. There was a Bedford High School girl opposite who wanted to know when the train arrived in London. I told her. The train pulled out. It was bitterly cold, and my feet were frozen. I felt again as if I were two persons. One of them knew that when I would come back to Bedford, Mummy would be dead. The other one was observant and believed that nothing was serious.

I read the film criticisms — it was a Friday — in the Evening News. There was a nice new film at the Odeon. I felt I'd like to see it. It was The Demi-Paradise with Laurence Olivier and a girl called Penelope Ward. There was also a new film I felt must be awful. It was about an Australian boxer (played by Charles Laughton) and was called The Man from Down Under. The time passed slowly. I felt as if I were living a book. It was cold — the kind of fog that permeates every fiber of your being.

The train at last came in at St. Pancras. As I came out of the tube station at Manor House, I began to smell a queer smell. That smell did not leave me until the day of Mummy's funeral. Later, I remembered that in For Whom the Bell Tolls, Pilar tells Roberto about a certain smell that comes into her nostrils if persons she knew well were going to die. The smell she described was awful — but my smell was just annoying. It was an indefinite kind of smell; the nearest to it is the smell of burning wet leaves.

I got onto a bus. It was getting dark; every minute, the darkness seemed more intense. I paid my fare and when I got out hurried as quickly as I could. I was frightened I might be attacked by some drunken American. I visualized getting into the house. I mentally saw Mummy lying in bed, and I propped up her cushions and combed her hair. Then she went to sleep, and I took out my Latin books and started memorizing declensions and conjugations. I also cleaned the kitchen and put a fresh white tablecloth on the table, and then after the illness I became a heroine and was praised by everybody.

At last I got to 112 Bethune Road. The house looked dismal. I knocked twice. I heard somebody running down the stairs. Bernard opened the door and said in a tone of happiness, "Ah, Igett!" and kissed me.

I said, "How's Mummy? What's the matter with her?"

"Oh nothing. She's got a bit of grippe."

I heard somebody pull the lavatory chain and go to the bathroom door. I was explaining to Bernard the events of the afternoon as I went upstairs. Mummy came out of the bathroom and entered the living room with me. She looked ill. Her hair was black and greasy and hanging loose. Her face was feverish. Her voice was hoarse.

She lay down on the sofa, then went and sat down on one of the armchairs, and Mitzi sprang onto her lap. Then she looked up and said she felt too weak to stay up and that she was going back to bed. When she was gone, I told Bernard that I thought she looked very ill. He told me the doctor had come on Thursday morning and said it was a bit of flu. There was some bright red medicine on the table and a sticky spoon.

I made some tea and went down to Mummy. I sat down on her bed. I tried to talk about interesting subjects. She asked me about a few things I had written about in my last letter and was worried about my ankle. I felt ill at ease. She looked very feverish. I decided it was best to leave her and let her go to sleep. All my life, if anything had ever gone at all wrong with my mother, I had always seen her better after a good sleep.

I went upstairs, and Bernard and I had a miserable supper, a mocking

13. JENNY

semblance of all the other Friday evening dinners we had had. Then a horrible Jew came up to visit, and while I listened to the wireless and tried to read a book Mummy had given me, I heard their conversation. Bernard was telling the man about some well in Palestine that had been sealed up for many hundreds of years. The man kept on asking stupidly naive questions.

I tried to read Pepita *by Victoria Sackville-West. I looked at the pictures and was cross that the one of Pepita herself should be missing. I thought of Saturday and the following days. I had an idea I would still be in London on Monday, but that I would go back to Bedford on Tuesday. Mummy and I would go to the pictures on Sunday or Monday —* Holy Matrimony *was playing. Mummy had told me that on Saturday evening they were going to broadcast* The Barretts of Wimpole Street. *I thought Mummy might be well enough to listen to it tomorrow, that she would lie down on the sofa, and we would listen together.*

At last, at about half past nine, Mummy came up once more, and the question of where I would sleep came up. I thought of how uncomfortable I had always been on the sofa and chose to sleep in the bed with Mummy. She was coughing by now. She said she wanted the sheets to be changed. We went downstairs, and she told Bernard and me what to do. She looked and was very tired and could hardly wait to get back into bed. At last she did. We made her a hot-water bottle. She urged me to undress as quickly as possible and complained about the light and buried her head in the cushion. She said she could not help herself, but she was letting water in the bed. That coming from Jenny — Jenny who always kept herself so clean — frightened me.

I got into bed after having put on my nice new pink pajamas and turned off the light. It was then that I heard a queer noise. It sounded as if someone were blowing into a rubber hot-water bottle and then pressing the air out just afterward. It came from where Mummy was lying, on my right side. I listened to it for a few minutes. Surely it couldn't be her breath. It was such a terrible noise to issue from a human being, especially my mother. I was frightened of disturbing her, but at last I couldn't stand it any longer and I said, "I'm very, very sorry to disturb you, but what is that noise?"

"It's a rattle in my throat."

A rattle, a rattle, a rattle. Un râle, un râle, un râle, un râle.

It was unbelievable. They are things you read about in books. You don't hear them, *except when you go to the pictures. I had heard one on Tuesday when I saw* Back Street. *But one never read of a rattle in anybody's throat unless that person was dying. Mummy was dying. Of course, she wasn't.*

I fell asleep, but many times she woke me up and asked me to switch the light on. She wanted to spit mucous stuff out. The last time she woke up, it was roundabout two o'clock. She couldn't sleep.

It was the last time I was ever to sleep in the same bed as my mother. It is with shame that I remember how I took care not to touch her body. I was frightened of falling ill myself and also of touching the wet patches on the sheet. I feel now as I felt then — a traitor to the love we bore each other. My little mother.

[Saturday, 20 November 1943]

I woke up toward eight o'clock to hear Bernard stirring upstairs. He didn't come down. I asked Mummy whether she felt better. She did not and hadn't slept enough.

I got up toward nine o'clock. I didn't wash very thoroughly. I felt very miserable. Then the doctor came. His name is Dr. Brown. He is a tall cold man. He is friendly in an obviously artificial way. He looked at Mummy and exclaimed in answer to our anxious queries, "Of course, she isn't ill. Nothing wrong with her. A spot of 'flu. I'll prescribe her some medicine and a syrup for going to sleep. You make her believe she's ill by making a fuss of her. There's nothing the matter with her. She shouldn't really be in bed, but let that pass. I'll come again tomorrow morning."

He enjoined her to collect the phlegm that she was constantly coughing up in a glass jar. That was all. That doctor is really a murderer. And I am a fool. I believed it was nothing serious because I wanted to believe it. Whereas if I had used my intelligence, I would have understood that the continual labored breathing and extremely loud rattle that had not stopped during the night could not result from "a spot of 'flu." But no, we allow ourselves to be impressed so very easily by people we believe know better than we ... but let that pass. I feel too guilty.

I felt as though I had been in the house for an eternity. The air seemed to be stifling and permeated with germs. Surely it wasn't yesterday that I had come. It seemed such a long time ago. I felt I must have some fresh air at all costs.

So I left all quite selfishly and went out for a short walk (ten minutes). I went and bought a Radio Times *for the next week. There was a picture of Elsie and Doris Waters, two popular comediennes, on the cover. It was raining, and the wet seemed to permeate me through and through. I walked along and felt acutely unhappy. It was impossible to believe in anything bright and happy. When I got home, I felt I was struggling against an insurmountable mass of ... I can't think of the right word. I longed for Grandmother. I hated Bernard for his unconcern and his utter inability. I hated him for everything he personally was, and also I hated all men through him. Men seemed to me the most abominable and selfish and repellent of beings. I took out this diary and wrote for a bit.*

13. JENNY

I began to cry. I felt so unhappy and oh, so helpless. I felt that I should have been helpful and efficient. I was so ignorant of what was to be done.

Mummy came up. I couldn't hide my tears. Bernard tried to console me, and I hated him for it. Mummy was concerned and begged me not to cry and said that everything would be all right, and her words cut me to the heart and numbed me at the same time. She went down again.

I followed a few minutes later. I was extremely thankful when she said she thought I'd better phone Grandmother in the afternoon and ask her to come. (I'd phoned her at eight the previous evening, by the way, and had tried to make her believe it was nothing.) I readily concurred. But where was she to sleep? Mummy told me to go and ask Mrs. Schwarz. [A friendly acquaintance living a few doors away.]

So I went out and saw Mrs. Schwarz. She proved to be far less sympathetic than I had expected. She wasn't very concerned and said the 'flu was nothing, and Dr. Brown was a good doctor. She didn't have room for Grandmother.

I came back home, where Mummy put forward the suggestion I should go and ask Mrs. Cutner. Mrs. Cutner used to live in Bedford and used to be friendly with Grandmother. Mummy gave me the address, and I went.

She was frigid. I felt like a beggar dressed in filthy clothes. She coolly, cruelly cross-examined me. At last she agreed — with what reluctance! — to let Grandmother have a room.

Back home, I told Mummy (what a coward I was to complain) that Mrs. Cutner had been extremely nasty. Jenny told me to bring down a pail for her to let water into and to go and buy her a proper commode. Also, she agreed that I might just as well see whether Trudi might not perhaps accommodate Grandmother for the night.

I went out of that squalid house once more and tried to forget all the troubles I might have tried to remedy. I tried to forget that every time the bedroom door was opened, a draught fell on my mother.

I caught a bus and hoped Trudi would be at home. She was. I told her family everything there was to tell, and they said they didn't mind putting Grandmother and me up for the night. I thanked them and waited while Trudi made ready to come with me.

We went to a Boots chemist, and I got a commode specially made for ill people. I had to pay 15 shillings or more. Then Trudi wouldn't take a bus because it was Saturday. We walked, talking about all sorts of things. Trudi told me something about a book by Vicky Baum.

Back home, I told Mummy the good news, and she murmured feebly, "You see, you can rely on a good friend." That was the last time we ever spoke about Trudi, and now I like to think it was a denial of all her previous injunctions to drop her.

I went up and put some water to boil to make tea. Then I went down and phoned Grandmother and told her everything she was to do to get here. Then back upstairs, I made some tea for Mummy. Bernard went away to give some lessons or something.

I took the tea down to Mummy and asked her whether she'd rather remain alone, or whether she wanted me to come and sit downstairs. She preferred to remain alone. I wanted to plump up her cushions because Mrs. Samet [the landlady] had told me that it was good for her, but she refused and insisted on keeping the cushions as low as possible and burrowing her face into them.

I went back upstairs, and Trudi and I went on talking and gossiping. We even laughed. I don't understand it, now, in the light of after events. My mother was lying downstairs, her throat still rattling (though less than in the night. I never heard the rattle as loud as during that night, not even on Tuesday), the sheet dirty from urine and pellets of ... and upstairs I was laughing. Laughing hysterically, nervously, guiltily, and telling with relish the story of The Man in Grey to Trudi. At half past four, I dressed and asked Mummy whether she'd be all right. She said yes. She had slept a little that evening. Trudi and I walked to Manor House Tube, met Bernard who was going home, and parted ways once I arrived at the tube station.

I met a tearful and worried Grandmother at the station. I tried to reassure her. I didn't believe anything serious had happened. It was an attack of 'flu, a particularly bad attack, true, but nobody ever died of 'flu. Besides, it was inconceivable that Jenny, my mother, should die so young. That is what I believed, or at least part of me. The other part, of which I was not taking notice, believed that my mother would die no matter what anybody might do to try and prevent it.

Grandmother and I at last got home. Grandmother saw Bernard for the first time since 1940, and they talked to each other as if they had left on the best of terms. Then Grandmother went in and kissed Mummy on the forehead. Grandmother asked Mummy what was the matter with her. Mummy said that she's just gone up to the lavatory and that she didn't know how she was still alive, and she could not control herself anymore. I was relieved when Grandmother set to work; she changed the sheets and Mummy's nightgown and washed the dirty ones. We came in at about six o'clock. We had supper at about half past seven.

At half past eight or thereabouts, there was a warning, and we went down to Mummy's room. I was as frightened as usual but felt oppressed as well by a sense of doom. We heard some very distant gunfire. Mummy was restless and wanted us to leave her alone. Grandmother was worried about going to Trudi's house. What would happen to Mummy in the night? To me, and this is true, the only thing that seemed at all sensible was to go and have a proper night's

13. JENNY

sleep at Trudi's house, come back early in the morning, and take good care of Mummy then. It really and truly seemed the most sensible as well as the most selfish thing to do.

The all-clear went. Mummy was complaining about the light and wanting to go to sleep. I urged Grandmother to hurry, or we wouldn't be able to catch a bus to go to Trudi. Grandmother was still worried and reluctant to go and was wailing, "What should we do? What shall I do? I can't leave her alone like that." And all the time, Mummy's voice was weakly complaining.

At last we quickly gathered our things and went away. There was a dense fog outside, and the wet atmosphere was wetly, coldly, clinging. Our torch made a despondently bright circle as we walked. Grandmother kept on uttering her thoughts aloud. I was hurrying her as much as I could. We got to the bus stop. We were told by somebody that this stop had been canceled, and so we walked on to the next stop, where some other people were waiting. We waited some time. No bus. And yet longer. At last somebody suggested that perhaps some buses weren't running because of a threatened strike of the transport people or something. So everybody began to walk. We tried to keep up with the party, but it was no use: we soon got left behind. We felt very much abandoned and alone in the world, and as we walked, I think both of us had a vision of my mother in her bed. There seemed an awful load of responsibility on us.

When we arrived at Trudi's house, we were given something to eat and drink. Grandmother dissolved in tears, and for once I did not feel like reproving her. If only I could have cried myself.

I remember Trudi wanted me to go to bed with her, but I believe her mother insisted on Trudi coming to bed with her and Grandmother having Trudi's divan while I went to sleep on the settee near the window. They made me a hot-water bottle, and I went to bed. My feet felt like wet pieces of ice. I fell asleep quite quickly.

[Sunday, 21 November 1943]

I was woken up by Grandmother at about eight or half past. It was still dark and very, very cold. I dressed as quickly as I could but didn't warm up much, nevertheless. I don't remember having a breakfast, but we may have had one, I don't know. We went out to catch the first bus (Sunday morning: nine o'clock). There was a Jew with a beard and side curls and gaberdine waiting as well. We waited for about quarter of an hour.

When we got to Mummy, Bernard said she was better and had slept. But it wasn't true. The sheets and nightdress were soiled again. Grandmother clamored that we should do something. Call the doctor, quick. Bernard was reluctantly persuaded to go out and ask Dr. Brown to come as soon as possible.

"Perhaps Dr. Volodarsky could be sent for," Grandmother said. Dr. Volodarsky is some family from Grandmother — her nephew by marriage, I believe, or perhaps a still more distant relation [and had joined the family when we were staying at the seaside in Ostend in the summer of 1939]. He's lived in Norway since the last war. He is supposed to be a very good doctor.

Bernard came back and said that Dr. Brown would come as soon as his surgery was finished. Grandmother changed the sheets and spread out the one she had washed and dried yesterday. Then she took the nightdress off, and just as she was going to put on a clean one, the doctor walked in. Every time the bedroom door was opened, there was a draught on Mummy. He began to examine her. "Don't leave her quite naked, poor thing," he said. He examined her thoroughly. He had also done so the previous day and had commented (the last time anybody ever did so) on how young she looked to be the mother of so grown up a daughter. I had felt the habitual glow of pride, pride of my mother's youthfulness, rush into me, for the last time. There is something so irrevocably heartbreaking about those words, "the last time," that it tears my heart every time I write them.

This time, he did not seem so sure of himself, even though he was quite sanguine. At the end of his examination of Mummy, he turned to Bernard and asked him whether he had another room, and could they talk there. On receiving an affirmative reply, he went out. Bernard showed him the way up and I trooped on after the doctor.

When we got into the other room, Bernard asked how he had found Mummy. The doctor answered, "Well, she's not so good. We'll have to send her to hospital."

"Is she dangerously ill?"

"Oh no! But the atmosphere here is not good. It depresses her. Besides, she will be looked after better in a hospital. You understand?"

"Yes ... yes, of course."

There followed some technical details. Mummy was to be sent to the hospital in Hackney. I think I had a feeling of relief at the responsibility being taken off our shoulders, but still I had that awful sense of doom.

I went downstairs to open the door for the doctor, that man whom I feel was guilty in part of my mother's death. Grandmother came out crying and wanted to ask questions, but the doctor pushed her away as if he were frightened of her and ran out of the house.

Grandmother was very upset when she heard that Mummy was to be sent away to a hospital. Bernard and I tried to comfort her but in vain. Then Grandmother told me to go and phone Aunt Sophie. I went into Mummy's bedroom and asked her for the telephone number. She remembered it by heart and gave it to me.

13. JENNY

I went and phoned. Silvie answered the phone, and I told her everything. She said she'd send Aunty over as soon as possible. When I entered Mummy's bedroom, Bernard was sitting on the bed and holding her hand. I was terribly jealous of him. He was a monster and partly responsible for her illness. I hated, loathed, detested him.

He had to get up for something or go upstairs, I've forgotten which, and I took his place. Mummy's hand was hot and seemed lifeless. It was very soft and white. I stroked it, gently. Grandmother was sitting down, downcast and abject. From time to time, Mummy said, "I can't control myself." It was terrible.

Now and then, she would look up and smile at me. That was worse than anything else. It seemed to make my heart tight and fit to burst, and something hurt deep down in my throat. I sat there a long time, stroking Mummy's hand and thinking, though I tried to chase the thought away, that there was an awful sense of finality about it.

At last Aunty came, and we went out to speak to her. She looked upset and asked why we hadn't phoned her before; she would have come to look after Mummy.

I forgot to say that on Saturday afternoon a letter came for Mummy. It was from the Belgian [exile] government, and I guessed that it must be about my grant. I therefore opened it and found that they refused to pay me anything. I was somewhat disappointed. It meant I was definitely leaving school at Christmas. But I wasn't very upset, and the other trouble was so immense in comparison that nobody took any notice of the letter, and I relayed the thought to a faraway corner of my mind. Mummy took no notice and showed no sign of interest whatsoever, and that shows how very weak she must have been.

Also later, Bernard told us this: at Friday dinnertime, Mummy was sitting upstairs in the kitchen wondering whether she'd be well enough to come to Bedford on the next day. Apparently, she thought it quite probable that she would still come. And she was also debating whether she ought to phone me.

The ambulance came somewhere round half past eleven. Two men came in carrying a stretcher with a few thin, dirty-looking blankets and hoisted Mummy on it. She moaned and asked for one of the cushions on the bed. She was carried out, and Grandmother and I stood at the door. Grandmother was weeping. I thought, "She must believe that if somebody goes to hospital, it means that they will die." Then quickly to show myself that I wasn't frightened, I said, "What a stupid old-fashioned idea! Of course, Mummy will come out nice and strong."

Bernard and Aunty also went in the ambulance.

After that, Grandmother and I stood about disconsolately and talked to Mrs. Samet. After a bit of time, we tried to tidy up and I had some food. Mrs. Schwartz came around to see us.

Aunty returned, and after taking stock of the situation she decided that the best thing to do was for us to come over to Silvie's house and stay there. Aunty told me, but not Grandmother, that Mummy was very seriously ill and had been put on the danger list. I was very surprised and upset. I tried to realize how terrible that was, but the idea was so appalling that my mind would not grasp it.

Aunty and Grandmother went to Finsbury Park Station, where they were to wait for me. I had to go to Trudi because we had told them we were coming back the same night, and I had left my things there.

I got there, told Trudi that my mother had been taken to hospital and was on the danger list, collected my things, and went off. When we got to Golders Green, Aunty left us. It was a bitterly cold day, and I remember waiting for the bus and shivering. When we got to 18 Templars Avenue, Silvie made us nice and comfortable.

Later, Aunty and Silvie got to talking, and then — I'm very confused about this — somehow Dr. Volodarsky had contacted us, and they decided to try and move Mummy. I believe it was Bernard who got into touch with Dr. Volodarsky, and that they went to the hospital together, and from there (Aunty had gone again), Dr. Volodarsky asked Silvie to come over and help them to try and do something.

Blackout was falling, and we were frightened for Silvie's safety. We tried to get a taxi but couldn't, so Silvie went out without one. Dr. Volodarsky phoned after she had left, and I had some difficulty explaining that Silvie had already left.

The time passed slowly. Jonas came in. Then Aunty also came. She was cross she hadn't been at home, for in that case she would have gone instead of Silvie. Everybody was sorry they hadn't known before how seriously ill Mummy was. If they had, they said they would have seen to it that she was taken to a better hospital.

At last Silvie returned. She had seen Mummy, and that seemed to make Silvie a heroine. Grandmother, Aunty, and I all forgot that we had seen Mummy a few hours ago and looked on Silvie as we might look at a person who had just come from the North Pole. Apparently, Mummy had recognized both Silvie and Dr. Volodarsky and had said that she felt better than at home, that the nurses were all very good to her, and that she felt comfortable. Oxygen was being given to her. When Silvie described the apparatus, I naively imagined that the hospital looked like one of those beautiful white buildings one sees in Hollywood-produced films. Mummy was neither better nor worse. Dr. Volodarsky could do nothing. Doctors who did not belong to the hospital were not allowed to attend patients. He couldn't move her either, and if he had been able to do so, it would have been too dangerous. He was wild that he had not been told before. He would have had Mummy taken to a special chest

13. JENNY

hospital. Mummy had pneumonia. The illness didn't strike me as particularly dangerous. Some people died of it, but surely not strong, healthy, young people like my mother. Silvie had been able to get a taxi and had had to pay a lot for it — a few pounds, I believe. That somehow brought it all home to me, and a few painful tears trickled slowly, funereally down my cheeks. Silvie comforted me. She was very, very kind indeed all through those days.

I had dinner. I had a huge appetite and was intensely ashamed of it, even though everybody told me to eat and said it was silly not to.

A mattress was spread upstairs, and Grandmother and I shared it. I went to sleep with a heavy heart, but nevertheless, I fell asleep quite quickly.

[Monday, 22 November 1943]

I can't remember the next morning's happenings, except that we phoned the hospital, and we were told there was no change in Mummy's condition.

In the afternoon, Aunty and I set out for the hospital. People who are on the danger list are allowed two visitors at the bedside every day. Grandmother had wanted to come, but everybody had agreed that she mustn't. She would be able to go when Mummy was better. Grandmother had also decided that when Mummy would be convalescent, we would take her to Bedford. I had happy visions of my going to school and coming home to find Mummy in bed. Of our going to the pictures together. Of my sitting on the edge of her bed and talking to her about film actors and actresses, books and school ...

And the previous evening, Dr. Volodarsky had told Silvie that Mummy would probably not survive the night.

It was a long journey to the hospital and took about an hour and a half to two hours. We met Bernard outside the hospital. Silvie had been there in the dark and so hadn't seen it. It was an ugly, dirty, huge Victorian, decrepit, depressing, militaristic, hopeless building, the exact negation of my vision of a lovely, white, clean, ultra-modern hospital. When I saw the place, my heart sank. [Here, my mother, whom I could not remember ever having been ill except for a single day in Antwerp, lay in a huge ward lined with twenty to thirty beds on each side.] *Mummy appeared to me to be far better than she had been since I had come to London. She was very feverish, but she spoke as a healthy person might. She asked after Grandmother, how we had slept, and how Mitzi was. I answered and reassured her many times that she was going to get better.*

[Tuesday, 23 November 1943]

It was a long journey to East Hackney from Golders Green, and on the way there the next day, I was rereading H. Ryder Haggard's novel She, about a mysterious, powerful white woman ruling a tribe in the depths of Africa in the nineteenth century. She, who was referred to as "She who must be obeyed," had discovered the secret of eternal youth, was extraordinarily beautiful, and fell in love with the hero. The book ends dramatically with her demonstrating to her beloved how she renews her youth — she leads him to a spot where a fire eternally burns. Entering the flames and bathing in the fire, she enjoins him to follow her example; however, something goes wrong, and she emerges as the old woman of four thousand years she really is, — a wizened gruesome something looking like a shriveled monkey — and dies within a few minutes. I found it absolutely fascinating.

When we came to the hospital, *we found Jenny extremely weak, with tubes for oxygen stuck in her nostrils. She took off her watch and begged me to put the time right and wind it up, which I did. I felt that this was a good sign, implying that she wanted to go on living. I had sat down on a crease in my coat, and this made me uncomfortable, and I felt what a trivial thing this was to worry me at a final meeting as this was — for I knew it to be final even then. I held her hand, which was very soft, very white, and stroked it gently. She stopped talking and every now and then smiled tenderly at me. My heart seemed to sever every time I smiled back at her. The ache in me was well-nigh intolerable. Aunty could not bear to remain at the bedside because of Mummy's labored breathing, but the latter seemed much better to me, and I found it in me to look at the walls, the other patients, and a woman cleaning the ward. Then a nurse came and told me to go, and go I went — leaving my mother conscious for the last time.*

In the evening, the hospital phoned us and said that we were to come immediately. There was an air raid on, and we managed to find a taxi to take us to East Hackney — it was a long drive in the blackout and took over an hour. I realized my mother was now dying and sat in the car tense as a wound-up spring, silently and incessantly imploring Jenny in my thoughts not to die, telling her she *must* stay alive. When we arrived and stood waiting in the vestibule, my tension snapped like an elastic band, and a few seconds later, Bernard stumbled out of the ward, crying, and said, "Jenny's dead." It was between ten and eleven o'clock of the evening of Tuesday, 23 November 1943.

14. THE SUMMER CAMP

It is customary for Jews to bury their dead very quickly, and the funeral took place on Thursday. I refused to go to the mortuary where I could have taken a last look at my mother, saying that I wanted to retain an unsullied memory of Jenny as the vibrant, joyful woman she had been, but I have a nagging suspicion that this was a welcome pretext for a cowardly reluctance to look at her dead face. For some reason, the women of the family only went to the mortuary and did not follow the funeral procession to the cemetery and participate in the burial ritual.

We stayed at Silvie's in London for the customary week when Jewish mourners "sit Shiva" for the dead, and relatives and friends call to show their concern and sympathy. Custom prescribes that the mourners rend their clothes as a sign of their distress; to conform to this rule, Aunt Sophie took a pair of scissors and cut a small, a very small, triangle from a pocket in the front of my green woolen dress — this was easy to mend afterwards, and during the war, clothes were rationed, although I must confess I cannot remember ever wearing this dress afterward. My mother had left the princely sum of £5 on her postal savings book, and so Aunt Sophie decided to sell her clothes to get some additional money. As a result of a notice pinned on a board in a shop, several women called who were told that the clothes for sale had belonged to a relative who had emigrated to the States, it being considered unwise to mention that they had been worn by a woman now dead. To my chagrin, the summer costume that Jenny had had made for me out of unrationed curtain material and that I thought had unusual chic was also sold.

Quite a large number of relatives — mainly Jonas's sisters and family — and friends from Aunty's and Silvie's circle of acquaintances called on us. We also saw a lot of Eli Volodarsky, who once caught hold of me when I happened to be alone in the sitting room, drew me onto his knees, and proceeded to give me what I later learned were "French kisses." It left me utterly unmoved and a bit puzzled at the peculiar tastes of elderly men, since it was a repetition of my experience with Mr. Canning.

The question of my future was now raised and discussed at length. Aunty and indeed the rest of the family, except for Bo, thought I should leave school immediately and take a course in shorthand/typing. Eli Volodarsky protested vigorously when he heard about this plan. He thought an intelligent girl like me should go on to university. "Who is to pay for her upkeep?" Aunty asked. To our surprise, he spontaneously offered to do so — he proposed to send Bo £8 per month for me. The generosity of this unexpected solution silenced everybody, and it was settled that I should not cut short my education after all. Thus, Jenny's death paradoxically saved me from leaving school prematurely to become a shorthand typist.

At the end of the mourning week, we accordingly returned to Bedford, and I went back to school. On my first day there, conscious that I was being watched as an interesting object of compassion, I was repeatedly seized by uncontrollable fits of giggling. But after a few days, life resumed its normal course as if nothing untoward had happened. And indeed I often felt as if nothing had changed — Jenny had come to visit us every second or third weekend, and apart from the fact that I often imagined I saw her on the street until I realized that I was looking at a totally strange woman, it now seemed as if she were always going to come the next weekend.

Bo was much more deeply affected. She lost weight dramatically and was visibly downcast. She kept on repeating, "It's not right for a mother to lose her child; it should be the other way round." In my naivety, I was surprised at this — the terrible scenes of my childhood, when she had cursed Jenny for her loose behavior with men, were still fresh in my memory (one of the curses had been "May you come under the earth!"), and I had rashly concluded that this meant she had not loved Jenny, whereas the opposite was the case. Bo was uncontrolled in anger, but undemonstrative if moved by positive emotions. She was naturally

14. THE SUMMER CAMP

reticent as far as both verbal endearments and physical expressions of affection were concerned.

I used to buy an evening paper (*The Evening News* or *Star*) from a street vendor every day and translate the main news to her in Yiddish, since we had no wireless and this was our only means of finding out how the war was progressing. This gave me the idea of whiling away the time during the Christmas holidays that followed soon after Jenny's death and distracting Bo from her gloomy thoughts by reading the whole of Margaret Mitchell's *Gone With the Wind* to her. I of course had to translate it into Yiddish, which was something of a tour de force. I must admit, however, that the translation was of a rough and ready nature, my knowledge of Yiddish deriving solely from the spoken idiom. Since I was unable to read it on account of its being written in Hebrew characters, I could not have recourse to a fund of literary vocabulary. I accordingly condensed descriptive passages into a nutshell, and the details of landscape, in particular, were summarily waved aside by my saying, for instance, "The garden is in bloom and smells good." All the same, I succeeded in whiling away the dark winter days and brightening Bo's thoughts to a slight extent.

Eli Volodarsky at first sent the promised money punctually, and once in the spring, he turned up in Bedford to pay us a visit. He was wearing the uniform of a Norwegian colonel (he was in the medical corps of the exile army) and brought an elderly male friend along. But after about six months, the payments petered out — oddly enough, the question of my upkeep and of my staying on at school was not raised again, I suspect because Bo kept quiet about it, as she wanted me to stay with her in Bedford. She somehow managed to pull us through. I cannot remember that we ever had any quarrels about money — true, there was not much that one could buy during the war. The money Bo received from the Assistance Board sufficed to pay for our clothing and food — most of which was rationed anyway, although one could get as much bread and potatoes as one wanted — and nearly all the books I read I borrowed free of charge from the public library. We were able to go to the pictures as often as we wished, and I did not consider queuing up for the cheapest seats a great hardship. It was even possible to buy a book as a modest present for Dorothy's birthday.

In the spring, I fell ill with chicken-pox. As I was sixteen years old and from the medical point of view an adult, I was severely stricken. I ran a high temperature and was covered all over with innumerable itching pustules. It was hard to withstand the urge to scratch. Only the vision of being permanently disfigured restrained my hands, but that did not prevent me from involuntarily scratching myself when asleep. The fact that our elderly doctor was not sure until the fourth day that I did not have smallpox alarmed Bo, so she phoned Silvie. She came down for the day to see me and comfort Bo, one of the many kindnesses she showed me in the course of my life. She brought the news that she had become acquainted with a wealthy Belgian Jewish lady who had known my father's family in Brussels and who sat on the board of the Zionist youth organization "Habonim." She had taken the opportunity to arrange for me to spend part of the summer holidays in a summer camp.

The school year was drawing to an end; I had spent it in the Lower Sixth Arts, which consisted solely of Dorothy and myself. Some of the pupils had gone back to London, the school having split up into two sections, one located in the old school building in Plumstead, and the other, evacuated part in Bedford, which explains why there were only two of us in this form. We had passed general schools certificate during the previous summer, having taken nine subjects, in two of which I failed: art (I was incapable of producing even a mediocre drawing) and maths. Art was not important for my future, and it was held that I was such a hopeless case in maths that it was pointless for me to sit for it again; the headmistress decided that I should take Latin again instead and convert the pass I had got to a credit, in which undertaking I succeeded. For higher schools, we were taking English, French, History, and Latin, the latter being required for most subjects we might decide to study at university. We were to take all four as main subjects, thus outdoing the London boys' school attended by the Bark boys since they took only two main subjects and the other two as subsidiary ones. It meant a lot of work, which on the whole we did willingly enough. Indeed, I was so eager to learn that I even volunteered to have extra lessons in German for a couple of months. There being only two of us had obvious advantages as we had to all intents and purposes private lessons. But it also involved disadvantages: thus, in English, we once had to read Chaucer's *The Miller's Tale* as part of our homework. There is a passage in it in which an obscene incident is described — or at least Dorothy and I felt it to be not only very funny but also (to our unspoiled minds) unprecedentedly obscene. During the next English lesson, Miss Cowlin demanded that I give a rendering in my own words of the action of the tale. She had obviously forgotten the details of the story. I began to relate the tale fluently enough, but when I got to the crucial scene, my words petered out and I could not go on. Miss Cowlin, who was ordinarily an equable, good-humored woman, got into a temper and scolded us for not having done our homework, for Dorothy did not fall into the breach, being as embarrassed and crimson-faced as I was. We were not even able to indicate in a roundabout way what it was that prevented us from giving an account of the story.

We were a docile pair, Dorothy and I, but sometimes in a quiet manner we got our way. Miss Cowlin had chosen Walter Scott's *Old Mortality* as one of our set books for English. Although we were both avid readers, we found this so unutterably boring that we put up a stubborn resistance, reacting in such a limp and pointedly unenthusiastic manner during lessons that our disheartened teacher capitulated and substituted Thackeray's *Henry Esmond*. We did not like this much either, but anything was better than *Old Mortality*, and we felt we could cope with it.

We had become inseparable. Dorothy's friend Cynthia was gone (whether she went to the London part of the school or left it altogether I cannot remember; she eventually became a missionary), thus removing a much resented rival from the scene. The fact that we were always doing everything together provoked Miss Cowlin to once sarcastically remark, "You are not Siamese twins, you know!" This continual companionship had the result that people even thought that we increasingly resembled each other physically. During that school term, we were seized by the spirit of insubordination. Whereas in the past we had been obedient and willing to a really unnatural degree, we now felt impelled to rebel against what we felt were petty school rules and discipline. Our infractions were mild ones, but we thought them to be nothing short of revolutionary. The odd thing is that whereas other girls who broke the rules in a much bolder way got away with it, we were invariably found out. For instance, one afternoon, we sat unsupervised in the library of Bedford High School, where we were supposed to be reading literature about Napoleon III's reign (this being our special period in history), when we decided on the spur of the moment to depart; it was the last lesson of the day anyway, and we felt we'd had enough. We packed our stuff and went off, but as we strolled along the streets of Bedford we were observed, and the next day we were summoned to the headmistress to give an account of ourselves.

Although we were more or less constantly in disgrace at the end of that school year, the powers that be reacted very wisely. When we reassembled for the autumn term, we were informed that we had been appointed school prefects, and regrettably this meant that sedition came to an end. However, I had learned my lesson, for I realized that in life if one does not have an inborn skill for a certain type of behavior, it is best to refrain from it — one just doesn't get away with it.

The summer holidays came, and the date arrived for me to leave for the summer camp. I was very excited when I got on the train from Bedford to London, where I was to meet a group of youngsters boarding a train that was to take us to Swindon in Wiltshire. In the compartment on the way up, I made the acquaintance of two girls with whom I was to share a tent for the next fortnight. Helen Posner, nineteen years old, worked as an assistant for a Harley Street ear specialist — she was a tiny trim person, five feet tall, a very pretty, self-possessed young woman with a warm, slightly reddish, shade of blond hair, neat features, and a clear complexion. I thought her lovely, and the fact that a few days later she confided to me that she was having a love affair with a Polish officer enhanced her attractiveness in my eyes. The other girl was Sonia Lepinski — she was studying German at Oxford, was tall and black-haired, with the kind of looks Moroccan women have.

Six of us shared a tent, and with my fifteen years I was the youngest, so that according to the rules that were imposed I was not allowed to stay up after ten o'clock. We had to do agricultural work for neighboring farmers for five hours every day — and for somebody as unused to physical work as I was, this was very hard. Most of the time, we had to lift sheaves from the ground in order to prop them up into haystacks, locally called "stooks." Within ten minutes, all energy seemed to have seeped out of my body, and with a tremendous effort I dragged myself through the remaining hours, longingly awaiting the short break allowed for sandwiches and tea, and after that even more fervently looking forward to the end of the seemingly interminable five hours. One day, I worked alone with a young man who acted as a monitor. He was a particularly virtuous Zionist who looked upon our work as serious preparation for later membership in a kibbutz, and during the lunch break he mercifully fell asleep. We were sitting in the shade, as it was very hot — the weather was uniformly glorious during the entire fortnight — and I was overjoyed as the time allotted for the break came to an end, and he went on undisturbedly sleeping the sleep of the just. Every minute that elapsed without physical exertion was precious. However, after a respite of a blessed twenty minutes, he woke up and was terribly stricken that he had unwittingly shirked his duty, so that he vehemently reproached me for not having woken him up.

Besides this agricultural work, a full program was provided for leisure hours — we sang Hebrew songs, danced "horahs," attended lectures, staged sketches. One evening, we were given a report of the uprising of the Warsaw ghetto — although I conscientiously read the evening paper I regularly bought from beginning to end, this was the first time I had heard of it and the first intimation I had that Jews were able to fight to defend themselves. It was only much later that I realized that before they were driven into exile and became a permanent minority, the Jews had been a very belligerent nation. But in this case, it was a minority group who in despair, and fully aware that they could never win the battle, had decided to fight and to sell their lives dearly. It was a somber and tragic story, but it also showed that Jews could put an end to the meek submission they had shown for centuries and assert their dignity.

We also heard a lot of classical music from records. Those who were interested gathered in a barn and sat or lay down in the hay while dreamily listening to Beethoven's "Sixth Symphony" or Dvorak's "New World Symphony."

Needless to say, a lot of flirting went on. Moreover, we all became involuntary witnesses to a passionate love affair. There was an eighteen-year-old boy from Derbyshire called Derek with whom I was a bit in love myself. He was small of stature, dark, and intelligent, with looks and demeanor that reminded me of Lord Byron, of whom I had just read two biographies. Derek and Sonia fell violently in love with each other and were so oblivious to the rest of the world that they lay together tightly clasping and embracing each other on the ground in the center of the open space around which our tents were pitched, for one and all to see. I was embarrassed and disturbed by this sight, and indeed to this day I think that physically passionate acts should take place in seclusion and privacy.

The coming of the Sabbath on Friday evening was celebrated by a so-called Oneg Shabbat, in which sketches, songs, and the reading of biblical texts put us in a festive mood. On one Sunday (mercifully the weekends were free from agricultural work), we went on a ramble, tramping through the countryside and singing Hebrew songs. We covered a distance of seventeen miles, which meant that upon our return to camp, long queues formed outside the first aid tent in order to have our oversized blisters lanced and plastered. In the evenings we sat around an open-air fire, again singing Hebrew songs and Negro spirituals.

There was an eighteen-year-old boy called Johann, who came from Germany. As a matter of fact, he looked like the stereotype of a young Nazi — clean-cut features, blond hair and blue eyes, and an athletic body. I found him very attractive, and he liked me too and tramped alongside of me. One evening toward the end of the fortnight, some of the inmates of my tent were invited to a "kummsitz" (come and sit) in the tent where Johann slept. I was even allowed to stay up after my normal curfew. We huddled together in the dark, chatting and drinking the excellent local cider, and Johann and I had a shy cuddle.

Soon after my return to Bedford, my cousin Silvie, her husband Jonas, and Aunt Sophie rented a small flat in Bedford to get away from the threat of the V-bombs. Silvie was again expecting a baby. They were by no means the only Jewish families to make this trip, and on his daily train journey to London, Jonas sat in a compartment with other businessmen, who whiled away the hour and a half trip playing cards.

14. THE SUMMER CAMP

The Jewish population in Bedford had grown so much that a house was rented to establish a Jewish center for adults and youngsters. I began to attend it regularly — it provided a longed-for opportunity to meet boys. After spending a couple of hours talking or making gawky attempts to dance, we walked home discussing all sorts of topics. The young lads were in many respects better-informed than we girls. From a boy called Leslie Brod I first heard about James Joyce and his revolutionary way of writing, whereby he remarked that since I was such a lover of literature I might well be better able than many others to understand the puns and allusions so abundant in Joyce's writings. They were also enthusiastic about jazz, a taste which I did not share. I was a firm advocate of classical music, and the center provided us with an opportunity to learn more about it. Mr. Freyhan, an Austrian refugee music teacher, invited us to come to his home, where he played records to us and commented on musical points of interest.

We had the privilege of being able to attend the regular concerts given by the London Symphony Orchestra, which had been evacuated to Bedford toward the end of the war: there were special youth programs, in which the conductor, Sir Adrian Boult, gave an introduction to each item designed to further appreciation. It must be admitted that these chats were of a very elementary, popular nature. We were also allowed to attend the rehearsals free of charge, and from these I got an inkling of the meticulous attention that has to be bestowed on musical details.

At school, Dorothy and I founded a music club that consisted of the president (Dorothy) and secretary (myself), there being no further members. This gave us access to the school's gramophone and to its collection of records. We took to coming half an hour early in the afternoon in order to listen to the records of a *History of Music* album. These improvised lunch-hour concerts took place in a cubbyhole of a room in which there was just space for the small table on which stood the gramophone and two stools for us to sit on. The present generation does not know how short the records of those days were: they ran for scarcely longer than five minutes. Before putting on each record, we had to change the needle; the gramophone arm had to be gingerly lowered and gently applied to the record. No doubt the quality of the sound would be regarded as inadequate nowadays. We were unaware of this, however, and delighted in repeatedly listening to Gluck's aria *Che faro* from *Orfeo ed Euridice*, various Schubert songs, movements from Beethoven's Fifth, Schubert's Ninth, and Dvorak's New World symphonies. Our activities were not restricted to passive listening; after school, we met and gave each other lectures. For instance, after reading a book about Schubert, I gave an outline of his — tragic! — life and works, illustrated by records, to Dorothy, who was the entire audience.

At the Jewish center, sex reared its serpent head among the young. Conversations seethed with sensual images and allusions, and all the boys became obsessed with the subject. This did not apply to most girls — for them, it was principally a matter of prestige to have a boyfriend and to be sexually desirable, since this was a sure way of acquiring admirers. On the whole, however, the sexual urge of the girls was remarkably quiescent. As for myself, I had some years earlier realized from remarks made by my schoolmates that here was an uncharted territory that I ought to know about. On one of her weekend visits, I had challenged Jenny to enlighten me, and with evident — and to me rather surprising — embarrassment, she had proceeded to do so. A few months afterward, her period was late, and she was worried that she might be pregnant. The realization that she and my stepfather had carnal intercourse gave me a profound shock of disgust. Meanwhile, a book that had been unobtrusively lurking among other books of the school library and which chastely explained what was known as "the facts of life" had been discovered by my schoolmates, and it promptly made the rounds of the class. It began with an account of the reproduction of plants, went on to bees and insects, then to mammals, and finally at long last reached man and woman. The description of what they actually did (and this was the only form of intercourse in which we were really interested and the sole reason why we read the book at all) was disappointingly brief and did not fill more than a single page. Soon after, a "dirty" joke in the guise of a military report of a wedding night, in which the bridegroom was the attacker and the bride the fortress to be taken and penetrated,

14. THE SUMMER CAMP

circulated clandestinely during a lesson from one pupil to the next. We thought this witty and boldly salacious.

I was eager to be physically attractive, and I became very figure-conscious. Upon my return from summer camp, I had developed an enormous appetite, eating four slices of a dark, almost black, rich "Youma" bread liberally spread with margarine when I came home from school at five o'clock and having a proper supper only two hours afterward, and as a result I put on a lot of puppy fat. Horrified at this, I resolutely cut down on my portions, omitting the "Youma" bread altogether, and was rewarded by losing sixteen pounds within a surprisingly short time. I was not very good at doing my hair up in curlers or skillfully combing it, so I somehow managed to find the money to have a perm at regular intervals. Like all the women of our family, I considered clothes to be very important. In contrast to Jenny, who had loved frills and flounces, I inclined to simplicity. The result of all these efforts was not altogether unpleasing — and the boys at the center were not uninterested.

I received my first kiss from Henry Bark — boys of that age were usually inexperienced, and he was no exception. It was a very innocuous kiss and aroused no particular sensations — I thought of it rather as a kind of trophy, proving that I was attractive, in spite of the fact that deep down I did not believe that this was the case. A few weeks afterward, a boy called Joel Levine took me from the center to Silvie's flat, where I often spent the evenings. On the way there, the conversation veered to the ineluctable and ubiquitous subject of sex, and he told me that he had had intercourse with a girl in London — her parents had conveniently been away for the weekend, and they had been able to spend a whole night together. He enthused about what a wonderful experience this had been, describing in rhapsodic terms the softness and warmth of his partner's flesh. Before we parted, he kissed me in the doorway — he was very good at it, and at the touch of his lips, sensual waves that arose from unsuspected depths inside me swept over my entire body.

The experience with Joel frightened me, and I was quite relieved that there were no further opportunities to repeat it or to explore this strange territory any further. Instead, another person appeared on the scene.

15. ABE

It must have been some time in 1944 that American airmen arrived in Bedfordshire — there was an aerodrome at Cardington, where they were stationed. During their time off, they descended in droves on the nearest town, which was Bedford. It was rumored that the saying was current among them that they had never before seen a cemetery with traffic lights in it, for they regarded Bedford as the nadir of provincial dullness. On the other hand, the British comment on the presence of the GIs was that they were overpaid, oversexed, and over here.

Most of them were good-looking with a clean, almost hygienic appearance, enhanced by the fact that their uniforms were made of much better material and had a smarter cut than those of the British soldiers, who looked downright shabby in comparison. Unabashed, they leaned against buildings and let out a lustful whistle whenever a remotely attractive female approached. and when I ran the gauntlet of such impertinent admirers, I became very confused and, at a loss as how to react in a dignified manner, hurried past them, blushing with my face averted as if I were running away, which of course I was.

The Jewish community had grown so much that a synagogue had been installed in Bedford, and some of the Jewish Americans attended the religious services. The Barks invited one of them to spend his free afternoons and evenings in their home. His name was Abe Landauer, and when we met he fell in love with me, a circumstance of which I remained utterly unaware for quite some time, until I accidentally heard of it from a girl in the Jewish center to whom he had confessed his interest. The reason why I did not realize this to start with was that whereas I had gained a precarious confidence in dealing with boys of my own age, I was very shy with grown-up men, and Abe was twenty-four

15. ABE

years old, which to a sixteen-year-old seemed very grown-up indeed. He found my shyness attractive because he was himself extremely shy, and although he had been to college and was quite good-looking in a hale, slightly chubby way, he had never had a girlfriend, as he was — that rare specimen — a virtuous fellow and considered flirting frivolous (rightly; that's what makes it so charming).

As the months went by, he became bold enough to actively seek my company and began calling on me at home. Perhaps because even she sensed that he was fundamentally a "good boy" and therefore safe as far as these approaches to me were concerned, Bo accepted him with indifferent tolerance. I had reached a state of truce with her — I lived with her without confiding anything to her that I considered important. Our exchanges were confined to the trivialities of daily life. We often went to the pictures together, and I had taken over Jenny's role of translating the essentials of film dialogues for her. However, she viewed my excursions to the Jewish Youth Center with profound suspicion, and once, during one of those quarrels that occasionally flared up between us, she maintained that I was ready to lie down like an animal to have intercourse with, of all unlikely people, Henry Bark. This showed how atrophied her instinct for sexual attraction was. She was of course in a state of latent alarm because I had reached an age when erotic entanglements were not unlikely and she was haunted by the memory of Sarah's and Jenny's escapades. On two occasions, when I was sitting cross-legged on our bed and reading, I burst into tears because I was so affected, once by the sad fate of Jean Valjean, left alone by the young lovers at the end of Victor Hugo's *Les Misérables*, and the other time by the tragic ending of Thomas Hardy's *Jude the Obscure*. In both cases, Bo adamantly refused to believe that I could be moved to such passionate sobbing because of what happened to people in a book and was convinced that I was — in the tradition created by Jenny — concealing a love affair that was not going the way I wanted.

She had, I now wonder where and how, made the acquaintance of several Jewish people. First, there was a family — father, mother. and daughter. The parents were professional musicians; their daughter Frances an ungainly, gawky, fat girl, who was the apple of her parents' eyes. They were very eager for me to become friends with their adored

Frances. However, I instantly took a strong dislike to the entire family — I was convinced that they were mediocre musicians and deeply irritated by their calling violins "fiddles," which seemed to me to confirm that they were essentially vulgar. Probably because of my obvious repugnance, this relationship petered out within a few weeks.

Bo's other cronies were an old Russian Jewish couple who aroused my hostility by being violent anti-Communists. I was in many respects a rude, intolerant, and snobbish girl. The trivial fact that they constantly pronounced the word "revolution" as "revelation" was further proof to me that they were not to be trusted, for I blithely ignored the fact that they could draw on experience to back their views. I was an enthusiastic advocate of Russian Communism and believed that I was better informed on the subject than these eyewitnesses. At school, we had all been invited to a lecture given in the assembly hall by a young woman journalist, who gave us a glowing account of her stay in Russia and the state of education there. I listened with breathless enthusiasm to her remarks, and her testimony carried greater weight than that of Bo's new friends, with the result that in the course of the heated arguments that sprang up between us I felt no compunction in rudely contradicting them.

The war was progressing well. In the summer of 1944, I was at the hairdresser having a perm when the news came over the radio that a German officer had planted a bomb in Hitler's headquarters, which, however, had failed to achieve its objective of killing the Führer — a surprising inefficiency, considering that the man had a high position in the army's hierarchy. Had he and the conspiracy to overthrow the regime been successful, much bloodshed and suffering might well have been avoided. On the other hand, this would no doubt have had the consequence of reviving in Germany the First World War legend of treason on the home front being responsible for defeat; moreover, the government that would have been installed would have been ultraconservative and even reactionary. These are of course idle speculations, like those indulged in by unhappily married people on the theme of "if I had not married so-and-so, I might have led a happier life" (but possibly an even unhappier one).

Belgium was liberated, and I received a telegram reading "Congratulations to you and Belgium!" from a girl who had left school

15. ABE

the year before. Air raids were now a memory, and our nights were untroubled by alarms or by tense listening to the throbbing of aircraft engines to determine whether they were caused by V-bombs or by Allied airplanes, an art in which we had become surprisingly skilled.

One day in May our lessons were interrupted by a teacher coming into the classroom to tell us that the war in Europe was over, and we could go home for the rest of the day. As one of my ears was clogged, I at first went to the out-patient department of the local hospital, where the doctor in charge inserted a sharp instrument to remove the wax so deeply that a sharp pain pierced me and blackness overwhelmed me. Terrified by the thought that I was about to faint, I managed to avoid doing so by an immense effort of will. During my early childhood I had been scared of falling asleep, and now I panicked at the idea of fainting and of being hauled back to consciousness from a deep well of helplessness. After this minor medical operation, I went home. In the afternoon and early evening, I went with Abe to the green, which was situated two minutes from where we lived — a great crowd had gathered, a band was playing, and people started to dance. It was the first time I saw jitterbugging, and I watched the twitching and contortions of the performers, the come-hither gestures of the women, the apparent abandon and wildness of the men (many of them American soldiers) and women with amazed fascination, aware that I was not only reluctant but also utterly incapable of joining in. Fortunately, there was no danger of this happening, since the virtuous Abe was averse to such lascivious pleasures, and, in this respect at least, we shared the same inhibitions.

School resumed the next day, and in June 1945, Dorothy and I sat for higher schools examinations. We took four main subjects: English, French, history, and Latin. The first three did not present any particular difficulties for me, and I managed to pass Latin by having recourse to various devious devices. I learned the English translation of the set book, which was the fourth book of Virgil's *Aeneas*, by heart and was able to instantly tell at which point the translation tallied with the Latin original. I somehow managed the unseen translation, which, if I remember rightly, was a passage from Caesar, whom I always found to be fairly accessible in contrast to, say, Tacitus, whose vaunted terse

Abe

and compressed style in *Germania* was a cryptic code to me, or Cicero, whose convoluted, legally intricate, and interminable sentences made me despair. The paper on Latin history was as easy to master as those on English or French history. I therefore contrived to get a pass. In French and English, I was "very good," and I got a credit in history. But of course we did not receive the results until months later.

Silvie, Jonas, and Aunt Sophie returned to London after the war in Europe had come to an end. Some time before, we had celebrated the two "Seder" evenings of Passover in Silvie's flat in Bedford. As I was the youngest member present, it fell to my lot — as a seventeen-year-old! — to ask the prescribed *Ma Nishtana* questions, which are normally put by a very young child. I also hid the *Afikoman*, the *matza* required for the after-dinner blessing, and was able to demand a price for revealing its hiding place. I asked for two tickets for Bo and myself

15. ABE

for the cinema in the West End where *Gone with the Wind* had been running exclusively for the past year or two.

Very soon after Germany's capitulation, the Cannings told us that we should vacate our rooms as soon as possible, and we agreed that we would return to London when the summer term and school year came to an end. Meanwhile, Silvie's confinement was drawing near, and one day I came home from school to find Bo leaning out of the window, beamingly eager to tell me that she had just received a phone call: Silvie had delivered a girl to be called Susan. This time, there had been no complications.

A month afterward, in July, a general election was held. Bo as a British citizen was entitled to vote, and I accompanied her to the polling booth, where she authorized me to cast the vote on her behalf and I dutifully put a cross beside the name of the Labour candidate, Skeffington-Lodge, who, to our great surprise, was elected for the normally Conservative town of Bedford, — part of the landslide that swept Labour into office. On this particular political issue Bo was, incidentally, in agreement with me.

Soon after, we moved back to London, into a large furnished room which Aunt Sophie had found for us. It was on the first floor in 64 Lordship Park in Stoke Newington and had two beds, a wardrobe, an easy chair, a small table, a couple of chairs, and a gas ring with two jets. Water had to be fetched from a tap out on the landing. There was a public telephone in the hall downstairs, serving the needs of the various tenants. This meant we could now be reached by phone. For heating we had an electric heater, as in Bedford. A couple of stairs up was a bathroom with a geyser which, like the telephone, was fed with pennies. Three pence provided a good hot bath. The windows gave on the street and Bo took to sitting in the easy chair at the window to watch what went on in the street below, all the while assiduously knitting. She had already done this window watching in Bedford, but here the outlook was much more rewarding. There was a bus stop for the No. 73 immediately in front of the house. At first, the noise of the bus arriving and departing at twenty-minute intervals from 5:20 a.m. regularly woke us up, but after a while, I got so used to it that I slept happily on until it was time to get up.

Soon after we had moved in, we made an incredibly luxurious purchase: we bought a small radio. Ever since our arrival in England, we had not owned one, and at school I felt the lack of it acutely when schoolmates quoted the catchphrases from a show called *ITMA* (*It's that Man Again*), and I had no idea what they were referring to or why these remarks were supposed to be funny. At the end of the war, a more intellectual program called *The Brains Trust* became very popular, and I only realized who Julian Huxley or Professor Joad were from reviews of their performances in the newspapers I read. Occasionally, I caught snippets from the Cannings' wireless — I remember a few momentous phrases from one of Churchill's famous addresses, and on a couple of occasions I was infuriated hearing bits of classical music tantalizingly wafted upward but invariably turned off within a few minutes. We bought a little, modern set, and I took to listening to the wireless with avidity, in particular to the Third Programme, which had begun to broadcast a cultural program of exceptional quality.

Abe came up to London regularly to see me — during the last months, his courtship had become free of all shyness, and we had reached the stage of kissing and fondling. Soon after our move to London, he proposed to me. I asked for a couple of days to think it over. At home, I sat at the small table and drew up a balance sheet with two columns, one listing the factors that spoke in favor of a marriage while the other one enumerated the points militating against it. I steadfastly ignored a sneaking feeling that the very fact I was basing such a momentous decision on arithmetical considerations was proof that I should not marry him, and I came to the conclusion that there were a few (a very few!) slightly more positive than negative factors. My decision was strongly influenced by the fact that during the past year I had felt a very great longing for what I called "putting down roots" and yearned to live a calm, peaceful, domestic, uneventful life — a bit after the pattern of my cousin Silvie's life.

Various applications had to be made. Abe's commanding officer had to issue a certificate stating that he raised no objections to the proposed marriage, and I had to go for a medical check in which I was tested for venereal disease. Had the result been positive, it would have been impossible for me to enter the United States. Aunt Sarah over in

15. ABE

Huguette 1945

New York State was overjoyed at the prospect of my coming to live in Connecticut. She immediately went to visit Abe's parents and sent me a postcard on which Abe's mother added the words "Abe, here am I." This cast a chill on me, as I was so obviously excluded. From a materialistic point of view, I was making a very good match — Abe's parents owned four general stores, rather like Woolworth shops, in various villages. Abe's announcement that his mother would begin her relationship with me by setting me to scrub floors was not exactly reassuring either, and when I voiced my wish to partake of cultural life and he told me that the supplement to the Sunday issue of the *New York Times* was so voluminous that it would supply all my needs during the coming week, I felt that this was not really what I had had in mind.

    Since, at the age of seventeen, I was a minor, and since I was also an orphan, — after my mother's death, no guardian had been appointed for me — I had to get a judge's permission to get married. At the court proceedings, the judge remarked that as far as he knew it was customary for Jewish brides to have a dowry and he pointed out to Abe that I was penniless, to which he gallantly replied, "I'll take her as she is." This settled the issue, and the judge gave his consent, asking me, however, to send him a postcard from the United States to tell him how I was faring. There was a report on the session in the local paper under the heading "BRIDE PROMISES TO SEND POSTCARD!"

No sooner had the formal obstacles been cleared and a date fixed for the wedding than dejection befell both Abe and me. He was obviously scared of how his dominating mother, whom a photograph showed to be a big hefty woman, would react. As for myself, the thought kept nagging at me that I was taking the wrong road and ruining my future. Abe was very religious and did not believe in divorce under any circumstances, and this also worried me. The fact that when we went for walks, we did not hold hands but left a big gap between us and let our heads hang, eloquently showed that we felt that something was wrong.

The day before the appointed date, Silvie's husband, Jonas, took matters in hand and called us together in the living room to discuss the proposed marriage. Jonas was a rough diamond, a self-made successful businessman with no great schooling, but fundamentally very kind. Aunt Sophie, Silvie, Bo, and I sat with him around the table — Abe was not present. Jonas put it that we were obviously, both of us, unhappy, and that the wedding should therefore be called off. Bo strongly supported this proposition, for she did not relish the idea of my disappearing to a village in the backwoods of New England (the United States were a long way off in the forties — normal people rarely made such a trip, and when they did they traveled by ship, which was very expensive). Aunt Sophie, however, raised an objection: "Who will take her if she doesn't marry him?" — as if this, at the age of seventeen, was my last chance to avoid becoming an old maid! Jonas reacted to this remark with great vehemence — I learned that in Antwerp our family had been notorious for fearing that its daughters might not find husbands and thus marrying them off with unseemly haste. Bo joined in by saying that if fate had decreed that this be so, I would undoubtedly find a husband later. Aunt Sophie sarcastically retorted, "And no doubt you think that he will come and knock on her door!" "Yes," said Bo, "if it is decreed on high that this should happen, he will do so." (Incidentally,

15. ABE

this is, strangely enough, just what did happen a few years later.)

The upshot of this conference was that the wedding was canceled, to the immense relief of both parties. A few days afterward Abe boarded a ship for the United States. During the next few months, we exchanged a few lukewarm letters, and he sent me a very pretty blouse, but at the end of the year the whole thing petered out, and I never heard from him again. I had had what schoolbooks refer to as "a narrow escape" and felt that an enormous load had been lifted from my heart. A personal catastrophe had been averted.

Since I had successfully passed my exams and the results were very good, I was considered as having attained the level of an intermediate BA so that I need only study for three years to get a BA honors degree. I was accepted by Queen Mary College in London, where I would read French. My real preference would have been English, but as I believed that this meant that I could only become a teacher, I chose French. Thanks to Isabella Blum, a Belgian politician who was a friend of Aunt Golda and Uncle Yeshurun and who intervened in my favor with the Belgian educational authorities, I was to receive a grant of £180 per annum, which enabled me to begin my studies on a sound financial footing.

Once more, I felt that I had been reprieved and granted a fresh lease of life, as had been the case upon my landing in Folkestone in May 1940. Who knew what possibilities the future held in store? I could hardly wait to find out.

And there is the end of this story. Perhaps, however, I may be permitted to give a small hint to those who have been waiting to read of my own happily-ever-after. I did, in fact, marry a German Jew; and in the end Bo turned out to have been quite a prophet. The man I married at last did not actually knock on the door, but two years after the end of the war he rang the doorbell. The rest of that story, however, can fill a book of its own, and lies outside the purpose of this volume. My war experiences end here, and I hope they succeed in describing a personal history that is as yet underrepresented in the literature of the era.

AFTERWORD

I first met Huguette Herrmann in February 1977, in the German Literature Archive in Marbach, near Stuttgart, where she held a post as librarian; I was a 'user,' newly arrived that day, exhausted after a grueling overnight boat and train journey from my home in England. A lecturer in German at a university in the south of England, I'd come to Marbach to research the history of comedy, supported by a generous grant from the West German government. The occasion—it was Shrove Tuesday— was strangely appropriate to my sense of disorientation: carnival revelry ruled in the streets outside, library tranquility inside. I seriously wondered if my commitment to spend my six-week sabbatical in the archive had been a wise decision. Should I cut my losses, I wondered, and abandon the research plan? Huguette saved the situation: she introduced me to her library colleagues and very kindly invited me to her house, where I met her children. The family immediately made me feel at home. Half a lifetime later, our friendship is still going strong; my wife and I have followed the events in Huguette's extended family— the happy times and the sad, but mainly the day-to-day concerns— ever since. Given all of that, I trust I shall be forgiven for referring to Huguette by her first name.

I knew Huguette was writing her autobiography; indeed, I'd encouraged her to do so when she first mooted the idea and had read an early draft, but I was surprised and honored when she asked me if I would consider writing an afterword. This, then, is my response, a personal response to what Huguette has written.

Dates matter. Huguette and I arrived in England in May 1940, within twenty-four hours of one another. On Tuesday, 21 May, Huguette dramatically crossed the Channel from Calais to Folkestone on board a

AFTERWORD

British Navy destroyer, accompanied by her mother and grandmother. I arrived a day later by a more conventional route, making my appearance in a Liverpool maternity clinic. There's a bizarre causal link between the two events, but that's another story. This coincidence of events is not simply a curiosity: it has deeply influenced my appreciation of and reaction to what Huguette has written. In the course of reading her account I have repeatedly been struck by the interplay of personal perspectives. To a large extent this is intrinsic to the autobiographical form: we have here the perspective of an 80-year-old who looks back on her life more than 70 years earlier, assembling memories of a world originally experienced from the perspective of a growing child. Now, this is no place to pursue the intricacies of reception theory—heaven forbid—but I would like to mention a further perspective: the reader's. The reader's own story inevitably colors his/her response to the written account. And this has been my own experience with Huguette's book, more so than with any other biographical account I have read. Time and again the people and incidents inhabiting her account have reminded me of my own past: my childhood world, all but forgotten, now unexpectedly brought back to life.

If the past is a foreign country where things are done differently, for me the past as depicted by Huguette is close to home. *Mutatis mutandis*, aspects of her childhood in Antwerp in the 1930s uncannily resemble mine in Liverpool 60 years ago. The locations are similar in that both were major international ports—Antwerp still is—and immigrant cities, due to their transatlantic connections. Antwerp and Liverpool were important embarkation ports for mass migration to the United States long before Huguette and I were inhabiting them, Antwerp for the Jews fleeing pogroms in Russia and for other citizens of central and eastern Europe, the economically deprived seeking a new life, and Liverpool for economic migrants from throughout Britain, and above all for Irish emigrants during and after the Great Famine. Many of those who made their way to the two ports decided to end their journey before crossing the sea. Huguette's grandparents came to Antwerp from Lodz and Odessa, planning to emigrate to the USA. Failing to find a foothold in New York, they soon returned to Antwerp. As far as I have been able to piece the evidence together, my Irish great-grandparents who

─────────── AFTERWORD ───────────

left Kilkenny in the 1870s planned to join relations who had already established themselves in Brooklyn—where one went on to found and run an orphanage—but, for whatever reason, they remained in Liverpool; the McKenzies, of Catholic Scottish stock, arrived at roughly the same period, in search of employment.

Anyone who lived through this turbulent period will recognize the long shadow cast by Adolf Nazi (to borrow the disparaging epithet coined by the former West German chancellor Helmut Schmidt) and his henchmen. If the Second World War was a cataclysmic event for everyone in Europe and further afield, for the Jewish people it was a catastrophe without parallel. The historical watershed of 1939-45 has become a mental watershed for those of us of a certain age: it's second nature for us to think in terms of pre-war and post-war. In both senses, Huguette's absorbing and often amazing account of her young life falls into two distinct halves: May 1940 clearly marks the half-way point between her childhood in Antwerp and her teenager years in London and Bedford in the south of England; it is also the turning point in her fortunes.

What are the deepest impressions Huguette's book made on me? One, certainly, is her vivid portraiture: you come away from it with the sense that you know her grandmother, Bo, and her mother, Jenny, as old family friends. They would make fascinating characters in any novel, but here they are, drawn from real life: Bo, whose "most striking contribution to [her daughters'] welfare was to create an atmosphere compounded of screaming and cursing", and Jenny, with her irrepressible flirtatiousness: "With a thick crop of straight black hair, bobbed in the fashion of the twenties, almond-shaped eyes, high cheekbones, pouting lips, and a slim figure, she could not fail to arouse attention. She relished this admiration so much that all else faded into insignificance." But, above all, it's the author you come to know through the events narrated, the ironic asides, and the distinct authorial voice.

Similar expert depictions appear of the minor characters, those with walk-on parts, bringing them vividly to life. Here Huguette's eye for the significant detail and her ironic, not to say waspish, tone come into their own. Three examples well illustrate this skill of characterization: the complex, contradictory figure Yeshurun Disenhaus, "the erstwhile

AFTERWORD

firebrand taking out his phylacteries and prayer mantle in order to duly recite his morning prayers in deference to his parents"; Simon Silberschatz, Huguette's absentee father, "a dreamer, a gentle young man of twenty-five, characterized by a striking lack of willpower"; and the miserly Sakoschansky—tellingly, his first name remains unknown—urging Bo, his estranged wife, to join him in Romania, "[praising] the country in the highest terms, in particular mentioning that potatoes were much cheaper there than in Belgium."

Two sections in the book call for special mention because of their particular impact. First, I must speak of Huguette's diary entries of the days leading up to her mother's death, which are heart-rending. I first read this with a sense of mounting anguish, so poignant and direct is her account. I must confess that rereading it has proved almost unbearable—nevertheless, or possibly proven by this, it ranks as a truly remarkable piece of narration.

The second section that demands special mention is Huguette's detailed account of the family's escape from Antwerp to Britain over thirteen days, between 9 and 21 May 1940. She first sketches the events that led up to the outbreak of war in 1939, effectively capturing the sense of impending doom that accompanied the appeasement of Nazi Germany by the British and French premiers, Chamberlain and Deladier: their supine acceptance of the Anschluss, Germany's annexation of Austria, the occupation of first the Sudetenland and, shortly afterwards, the rest of Czechoslovakia. (From the reader's distance, it is possible to wonder whether the French and British policies were realistic in view of the military unpreparedness of both countries? Were both buying time to rearm?) Her depiction of the period between the outbreak of war in September 1939, when Germany invaded Poland, and the German invasion of Belgium in May 1940—the so-called phoney war—is particularly effective in the way reports of cataclysmic world events are interweaved with references to the happenings of everyday life, producing a grotesque contrast. The story of the family's escape, in the nick of time, makes powerful reading: the journey by train from Antwerp to the French frontier on the Channel coast, the lift they hitched to Dunkirk, and the onward train journey to Calais. Then by a quirk of fate, they were taken on board a British ship

AFTERWORD

bound for Folkestone, thanks to Bo's British passport and the confusion of mass evacuation: if all this featured in a film you could be forgiven for dismissing it as improbable and over-dramatic. For me, at the heart of this episode is the courage of a twelve-year-old who grasps the urgency of the situation and convinces her mother and grandmother of the need to act at once. This isn't a starry-eyed interpretation of events. What I sense here is the single-mindedness of youth, uninhibited by habit and experience, which in this case took the right decision, the only sane decision. Of course, it could all have gone horribly wrong, but fortunately it did not. Had the family remained in Antwerp…

There is a further dimension to the story: the narrative intensity that characterizes the family's escape to Britain is underscored by the subsequent account of the exodus of the Disenhaus family from France to Switzerland, a hair-raising parallel. There is indeed no end to man's inhumanity to man.

Dunkirk, of course, occupies a central place in Britain's mythology: it is the scene of the calamitous encirclement of British forces in May 1940, but also of the heroic rescue of over 300,000 allied troops by sea, and so the term "Dunkirk spirit" has come to mean snatching something positive from the jaws of defeat. After I'd first read Huguette's draft of this dramatic episode, Dunkirk spirit took on a new meaning for me. Over the years I have driven along the coast between Dunkirk and Calais dozens of times—30 miles of dreary road lined by sand dunes, derelict industrial premises, and down-at-heel housing, which skirts the outer rim of one of France's most economically depressed areas, the pancake-flat, featureless landscape of Flanders. Historical awareness is one thing, but with Huguette's harrowing experience in mind, I now travel this road with a different perspective, conscious of the huge human sacrifice it has witnessed.

The parallels between Huguette's early years growing in Antwerp and mine in Liverpool are uncanny—though maybe the uncanniness has less to do with the parallels themselves (after all, they reflect common childhood experiences) than with the spark of recognition they generate in the reader. One searing childhood memory we share is the trauma of having one's tonsils and adenoids removed—one of the medical fads of the 1930s and 1940s—and the subsequent vomiting

AFTERWORD

on ice-cream, a treat held out beforehand as an inducement to submit to the torture. In an age which was medically far less advanced and which for many was characterized by substandard housing and poor food, recurrent bouts of ill-health were the norm for many children. "I rarely enjoyed reasonable health for more than three or four weeks running": I could have written this sentence myself, growing up as I did in a tobacco-fired kipper factory (appropriate, doubtless, for the son of a fishmonger)—my father was a sixty-a-day man. And then there are the small but telling observations of everyday life: for example the sense of shock Jenny felt when, newly arrived in England, she encountered for the first time the routine, casual indifference of English shop assistants—I can confirm that the breed is even now by no means an endangered species. Other parallels may perhaps be accounted for as being part of the ambiance of big-city life. For instance, Bo, and several female relations of mine, found their natural habitats in the cafés of big department stores, where they were liberally fed and watered with cakes and tea. (The attachment to the city-centre café went deep: my grandmother's will left fifty pounds, a sizeable sum in 1956, to Peggy, her favorite waitress in the café of Liverpool's leading department store; to her own sister she bequeathed exactly the same amount. It's not difficult to imagine the uproar that caused.) Is there something more profound operating here than simply the lure of cream cakes? For people living in dreary, substandard accommodations and leading less than fulfilled lives, such cafés offered the illusion of a well-to-do world, a glimpse of life as it might be.

Huguette's account of life in war-time Britain similarly triggers a multitude of memories in me, some half-forgotten, some ever-present. The sound of a factory siren—used back then to warn people of an imminent bombing raid—still grips me with irrational fear. A feature of everyday life in wartime Britain was the Anderson shelter, which Huguette mentions several times. These were made of galvanized corrugated steel panels; normally half buried in back yards, they offered considerable protection during air-raids. My parents and I shared one with my grandparents, who lived next-door (my grandmother, as defiant as she was claustrophobic, refused to enter it). Huguette's account of the air-raid in Bedford that she and her friend Dorothy were caught up

AFTERWORD

in on their way to school is a striking reminder of how defenseless and exposed the civilian population was. Huguette mentions the intense fear she experienced sitting in shelters during air-raids, the sense that each bomb dropped was seeking her out personally. The fear was well-founded, for air-raid shelters, especially if brick-built, could themselves be death-traps: my cousin Eva's parents were killed when their brick shelter was hit in one of the most intense raids on Liverpool, the May blitz of 1941.

Other shared memories include barrage balloons tethered high in the sky over open ground, which were used as anti-aircraft devices. As Huguette comments, they proved to be militarily useless; as a very young child, though, I found them attractive and somehow reassuring: they resembled inflated elephants. And then there was the arrival of GIs. As Huguette comments, they looked amazingly well-nourished in comparison with British people (for the obvious reason: they were better fed). No youngster of the 1940s can fail to remember the presence of GIs: they were extremely kind to children, offering them sweets like chocolate and some new-fangled stuff called chewing-gum (the weekly ration for sweets and chocolate then stood at three ounces). The GIs also came armed with nylons and perfume—intended for very different recipients.

To misquote William Wordsworth, the child is mother of the woman. It goes without saying that in an autobiography the sections that deal with the writer's childhood are crucial: they establish certain attitudes and themes that are to recur in later years. And so it is with Huguette's account: here we meet the highly articulate child, fluent in a trio of languages, biddable and determined at one and the same time, observant and insightful. We learn in particular of her love of film, and her weekly habit in those days of "going to the pictures" irrespective of what film was being shown. In Huguette's case, only the venue has now changed: latterly, TV, video tapes, and DVDs have taken over from the cinema. A second recurrent theme is her passion for literature—indeed, it would be true to say, for the written word. This is perhaps especially characteristic of only children who grow up surrounded by adults and who, inevitably, are often left to their own devices. This may also account for Huguette's characteristic style in English, a style that shows the mark of one who has read widely and acquired a sovereign command of idiom and structure. At all events, the child's linguistic skills and love of books were to inform the teenager's choice of university course and lead to career opportunities for the grown woman, as a trilingual translator and a librarian in the German Literature Archive, with responsibility for exchanging books with other institutions at home and abroad, and for translating speeches and letters for the Archive's academic staff.

I'm conscious that what I've written does not do justice to, for want of a better expression, "the Jewish context." I'd better come clean: my hesitation here is informed by my experience of growing up in a multi-ethnic city which was host to numerous religious communities. All too easily, remarks by an outsider can descend into stereotype, however well-intentioned a comment may be. So I'll simply say how much I have much appreciated Huguette's references to her Jewish heritage—indeed, I would have welcomed more.

Huguette's account takes us up to 1945, when, having narrowly escaped an unsuitable marriage, she is about to embark on a BA course in French at Queen Mary College, London. In her final paragraph here are the words: "The man I married at last did not actually knock on the door, but two years after the war ended he rang the doorbell. The rest of that story, however, can fill a book of its own, and lies outside the purpose of this volume." Well, Huguette, you've more than whetted our appetite; we're waiting impatiently for the sequel. So, how about it?

John McKenzie

ALSO PUBLISHED BY ACADEMIC STUDIES PRESS

GRANDDAUGHTERS OF THE HOLOCAUST
Never Forgetting What They Didn't Experience
Nirit GRADWOHL
Cloth 978-1-936235-88-9
Electronic 978-1-61811-105-0

Granddaughters of the Holocaust: Never Forgetting What They Didn't Experience delves into the intergenerational transmission of trauma to the granddaughters of Holocaust survivors. Although members of this generation did not endure the horrors of the Holocaust directly, they did absorb the experiences of both their parents and grandparents. Ten women participated in psychodynamic interviews about their inheritance of Holocaust knowledge and memory, and their responses to this legacy. These women provided startling evidence for the embodiment of Holocaust residue in the ways they approached daily tasks of living and being. The resulting narratives revealed that unfathomable events are inevitably transmitted to, and imprinted upon, succeeding generations. The implications for healing processes through the emotional work of resilience are explored.

Nirit Gradwohl (PhD Adelphi University) is an Israeli-born, American-raised member of the third generation of the Holocaust.

S e r i e s : Psychoanalysis and Jewish Life

SURVIVAL AND TRIALS OF REVIVAL
Psychodynamic Studies of Holocaust Survivors and Their Families in Israel and the Diaspora

Hillel KLEIN
Edited by Alex HOLDER
Cloth 978-1-936235-89-6
Electronic 978-1-61811-107-4

This book offers psychodynamic studies of Holocaust survivors and their families in Israel and the Diaspora. It is a most moving account of the desperate struggles of these survivors to overcome the horrendous experiences in the ghettos and concentration camps and their subsequent attempts at the revival of their lives after the Second World War. Hillel Klein, the author, was himself one of these Holocaust survivors. Later, as a psychoanalyst, Klein interviewed survivors in Israel and the United States of America and evaluated the consequences of the Holocaust and its aftermath from a psychoanalytic point of view which, together with his own memories contained in the book, gives it a special depth and contributes to making it a most moving account.

Hillel Klein was born in Krakow on 20 March 1923. He was 16 years old when the Germans marched into Poland. After a few months he joined the resistance and went underground. In 1942 he was captured by the Germans and locked up. He survived the horrors of several camps and ended up in Theresienstadt where he was liberated by the Red Army at the age of 22. He subsequently studied medicine and became a psychiatrist and psychoanalyst, practicing in Jerusalem. He died at the end of 1985.

S e r i e s : Psychoanalysis and Jewish Life

www.ingramcontent.com/pod-product-compliance
Lightning Source LLC
Chambersburg PA
CBHW050107170426
43198CB00014B/2494